Liberalism against Liberalism

Defence of the market and economic freedom has been one of the main objectives of liberal thinkers. Economists of the stature of Milton Friedman and Gary Becker from the Chicago School of Economics and F. A. Hayek and Ludwig von Mises from the Austrian School of Economics are united in this standpoint.

Ideas from both of these traditions are often used interchangeably but *Liberalism against Liberalism* refutes the tendency. With special emphasis on the work of von Mises and Becker, Javier Aranzadi illuminates the theoretical and methodological differences between the two schools. The book will have wide appeal to all students and researchers of the methodology of economics, economic philosophy and scholars interested in the social sciences in general.

Javier Aranzadi is Associate Professor of Economics at Universidad Autónoma de Madrid, Spain.

Foundations of the market economy
Edited by Mario J. Rizzo, New York University and Lawrence H. White, University of Missouri at St. Louis

A central theme in this series is the importance of understanding and assessing the market economy from a perspective broader than the static economics of perfect competition and Pareto optimality. Such a perspective sees markets as causal processes generated by the preferences, expectations and beliefs of economic agents. The creative acts of entrepreneurship that uncover new information about preferences, prices and technology are central to these processes with respect to their ability to promote the discovery and use of knowledge in society.

The market economy consists of a set of institutions that facilitate voluntary cooperation and exchange among individuals. These institutions include the legal and ethical framework as well as more narrowly 'economic' patterns of social interaction. Thus the law, legal institutions and cultural and ethical norms, as well as ordinary business practices and monetary phenomena, fall within the analytical domain of the economist.

Other titles in the series:

Liberalism against Liberalism

Theoretical analysis of the works of
Ludwig von Mises and Gary Becker

Javier Aranzadi

Routledge
Taylor & Francis Group

LONDON AND NEW YORK

First published 2006 by Routledge

Published 2017 by Routledge
2 Park Square, Milton Park, Abingdon, Oxon OX14 4RN
605 Third Avenue, New York, NY 10017

Routledge is an imprint of the Taylor & Francis Group, an informa business

British Library Cataloguing in Publication Data
A catalogue record for this book is available from the British Library

Library of Congress Cataloging in Publication Data
Aranzadi del Cerro, Javier.
Liberalism against liberalism / Javier Aranzadi.
    p. cm.
'Simultaneously published in the USA and Canada.'
Includes bibliographical references and index.
1. Free enterprise. 2. Liberalism. 3. Austrian school of economics.
4. Chicago school of economics. 5. Economics. I. Title.
HB95.A75 2006
330.15'53—dc22   2005022725

ISBN13: 978-0-415-36543-7 (hbk)
ISBN13: 978-0-415-49357-4 (pbk)

To Amelia

Contents

List of illustrations

Figures

Tables

Preface and acknowledgements

Discussing liberalism raises heated passions: people argue for or against it, but they seldom clarify what they mean by it. They proclaim that it is the system that guarantees freedom, but will it suffer the fate that befell Socialism, which claimed to be the defender of society, but ended up by destroying it in the communist countries? Will liberalism finally eliminate freedom, on the altar of economic efficiency? These questions are important now that communism has proved to be a failure, because liberalism is being recommended as the only solution to economic and social problems. It is offered not as one of the solutions but as the only viable one. Its supporters recommend market liberalization and the elimination of trade barriers, while the scope of monetary calculation is being extended to phenomena which have never belonged to economics. Thus the economics of law and the family are appearing, and people speak of an 'economic imperialism' that is invading the social sciences.

But there is one fundamental question that must be explained. If we acknowledge that it was Eugen Böhm-Bawerk, L. von Mises and F. Hayek who offered the best arguments in favour of the market in the debate on economic calculation in a communist society, why have their ideas been marginalized when it comes to offering a view of society? Why is pre-eminence given to the liberalism of the Chicago School and their *homo economicus*? It is generally argued that the contributions of the Austrian School have been absorbed into the present liberal neoclassical paradigm. I consider this argument to be false and the object of this book is to refute it. The theoretical positions of the Austrian School and Chicago School do not converge. The former is characterized by its construction of a theory of action, whose core is the creative capacity of people in their social and cultural environment. The latter reduces all human behaviour to a mere optimization of functions with restrictions. And here arises the radical question in the present debate on the social sciences: does the overcoming of socialism imply reducing man to the neoclassical *homo economicus*? In the following pages, you will find the arguments in favour of a humanistic economics based on the contributions of the Austrian School in order to transcend the so-called scientist reductionism of the Chicago School.

Finally, I would like to thank Mr Richard Garsed for his help in translating the original from Spanish into English, Professor D. Rafael Rubio de Urquía for his example of scientific dedication and tenacity in pursuit of the truth and Professor D. Jesús Huerta de Soto for his untiring teaching and support in the study of the Austrian School of Economics.

Note

For convenience, the male pronoun 'he' is used in a collective sense in this book, and human beings are spoken of collectively as 'man'. No sex or gender discrimination is intended.

1 Two economic approaches to human behaviour in liberalism

The object of economic study

There exists a general idea as to what phenomena are the proper object of economic science. Many people agree that the aim of this branch of knowledge is to investigate market phenomena, that is, to enquire into the nature of the types of exchange that exist between the various goods and services. The difficulties of economic analysis do not come from any uncertainty over precisely what the object of the study is: the problems arise when we try to explain what constitutes the economic behaviour which causes these market phenomena. On the other hand, the explanation of economic behaviour allows us to delimit the area in which the economic phenomena originate.

Although it is true that economics began with the study of market phenomena, it was necessary to go beyond the sphere of the market itself and of mercantile transactions in order to explain these phenomena. The marginal revolution supposed a generalization of the field of economics as a result of an enlargement of the anthropological basis which supports the explanation of economic behaviour. The most important and radical advance has been to confirm that all economic behaviour is based on the same elements that conform any action. The explanation that we give of economic behaviour will allow us to include within the scope of economics many types of behaviour that are not market exchanges, since when we talk about economic behaviour we are dealing with concepts of preference, valuation, choice, ends and means. These are all concepts that are present in the explanation of any human behaviour. This coincidence, which seems to be obvious but is often overlooked, determines the scope and potency of economic science, depending on the response that is given to the following three questions:

1 If, in order to explain the phenomena of the market, it is necessary to go beyond market transactions, what is the scope of economics? Does economics include mercantile and non-mercantile transactions?
2 If, as we have said, the basic elements of economic behaviour are to be found in every action, is it permissible to ask ourselves what the difference is between market phenomena and non-mercantile phenomena?
3 Very closely linked to the second question, we can ask, can all human behaviour be reduced to market transactions?

The scope of economics

In this book we are going to analyse the work of two authors, Ludwig von Mises and Gary Becker, because, from their different schools, they give consistent answers to these three questions. We shall choose the theories that are based on the study of the market. These schools are often called 'liberal' for their defence of the rule of law and market economics. In this book we are going to focus on the study of the second defining characteristic of liberalism – market economics. The best-known school for the defence of the market is the Chicago School, as it is this university which has created a group of researchers dedicated to the study and diffusion of the theories for the defence of the market. There exists another school research group, the Austrian School, which offers alternative theories. Generally, the ideas of the two schools are often interchanged, so that they can be grouped together under the name of market defenders, without taking into account the theoretical and methodological differences between them.

This confusion increases when we observe that leading members of both schools belong to the same societies and foundations which promote the ideas of market economics. Thus the economic policy objectives of these societies penetrate into the world of economics and into public opinion in general, so that the theoretical differences of the members of these organizations do not matter. Authors like M. Friedman, G. Becker, R. Coase and F. Knight belong to the Chicago School and mix with L. Mises, F. Hayek and I. Kirzner, who belong to the Austrian School. People tend to consider that the arguments of Friedman or Becker are compatible with those of Hayek and Mises, but this idea is entirely false and causes much confusion. To demonstrate this, we must analyse the works of the two authors of these schools who have contributed the most important theoretical and methodological work to resolve the three questions we have already posed. The economist from the Austrian School is Ludwig von Mises, the one selected from the Chicago School is Gary S. Becker.

Both Mises and Becker consider that the scope of economics includes the whole of human behaviour, although the characteristics of economic behaviour which support this statement are different in the two authors. We must distinguish two subjects in their work which are very closely related to the three questions presented previously: (1) the justification of the end pursued together with the enlargement of the scope of economics; and (2) the theory provided for such an end that is the characterization of economic behaviour. The theoretical doctrine which each author offers determines a different method of economic analysis. In this section, we shall see how Mises and Becker respond to the first question; in the next section, we will analyse their theoretical responses to the two remaining questions.

Mises' and Becker's motive for enlarging the scope of economics is their dissatisfaction with the current theories. Mises (1981a) deals with the criticism of the principle of economic rationality of the classical school of economics because it does not take into account those motives that cannot be expressed in money terms. He argues that economic theory has become an objective science by enlarging the subjective base of economic behaviour. The characteristic that defines economic behaviour is the unchangeable reality of having to make choices between scarce means and alternative ends. Therefore, for Mises the scope of economics includes every action where the human agent chooses between different alternatives in order to change his current situation. Mises establishes the fact that the end pursued does not characterize the economic principle or the means that are used (Mises 1996). The essence of economic behaviour is the unchangeable choice between different alternatives created in the action. He rejects the following lines of research:

1   It is a vain effort if we start from the study of market phenomena, and if we try to delimit its scope by appealing to the motives which impel men to act, or to the nature of the objectives which the action may pursue in each case. In Mises' words: 'the classification of actions according to their various motives may be momentous for psychology and may provide a yardstick for a moral evaluation; for economics it is inconsequential' (Mises 1996: 233).
2   Another line of research that is destined to fail is that of limiting the field of economics to those human actions whose objective is to provide people with tangible, material goods from the external world. Mises argues:

> the advice of a doctor, the instruction of a teacher, the recital of an artist, and other personal services are no less an object of economic studies than the architect's plans for the construction of a building, the scientist's formula for the production of a chemical compound, and the author's contribution to the publishing of a book.
>
> (Mises 1996: 233)

These two lines of research do not allow us a better understanding of market phenomena because the essence of economic behaviour is neither the nature of the end pursued, nor the nature of the means used. The economist's only responsibility is to confirm the existence of a dissatisfaction which motivates the person to act, and that the agent perceives or realizes that certain goods, be they material or immaterial, may serve him as a means.

These considerations that Mises makes about the theoretical paths that must be abandoned, are also present in the work of Becker: (1) economic access to reality, according to Becker, normally finishes when it bumps up against tastes. So, 'in the traditional vision, an explanation of economic phenomena reaches its limit when it meets the difference in people's tastes' (Stigler and Becker 1977: 76). In the face of this traditional vision, Becker offers an alternative vision, in which 'the economist continues the search for differences in prices or income, in order to explain any difference or change in behaviour' (Stigler and Becker 1977: 76). The essence of economic behaviour is not based on the motives or tastes which define the end that is pursued, (2) neither is economics restricted to the study of material goods. The economic means may be both material and immaterial. The following paragraph by Becker is explanatory:

> The definition of economics in terms of material goods is the narrowest and the least satisfactory. It does not describe adequately either the market sector or what economists 'do'. The production of tangible goods now provides less than half of the market employment in the United States, and the intangible outputs of the service sector are now larger in value than the outputs of the goods sector. Moreover, economists are as successful in understanding the production and demand for retail trade, films or education as they are for autos or meat.
>
> (Becker 1976: 4)

For both authors economic behaviour is based neither on the ends nor on the means. The definition of economics in terms of scarce means and alternative ends presents the following problem, which has been posed accurately by Becker:

> This definition of economics is so broad, that it is often a source of embarrassment rather than a source of pride to many economists, and usually, it is immediately qualified to exclude the greater part of non-market behaviour. [This definition] simply defines the scope [and does not tell us] one iota about what the 'economic' approach is.
>
> (Becker 1976: 4)

Where must we look for the essence of economic behaviour? The nature of the economic problem cannot be resolved by studying the ends and means that are used in the market. The area in which actions are produced, based on the scarcity of means and the need to make choices, exceeds the area of market phenomena. Both Mises and Becker are fully aware that in all human behaviour there is a choice between different courses of action. In other words, every choice supposes a benefit and implies a cost: therefore the scope of economics includes for both authors many more phenomena than those of the market. Becker has pointed out different phenomena which do not relate to the market but in which a choice is produced:

> Scarcity and choice characterize all resources allocated by the political process (including which industries to tax, how fast to increase the money supply, and whether to go to war); by the family (including decisions about a marriage mate, family size, the frequency of church attendance, and the allocation of time between sleeping and waking hours); by scientists (including decisions about allocating their thinking time, and mental energy to different research problems); and so on in endless variety.
>
> (Becker 1976: 4)

It is clear that enlarging the scope of economics poses the second and third questions asked at the beginning of this chapter. It is necessary to determine exactly what is understood by economic behaviour because the two problems, already mentioned, are presented here:

1   If economics includes and goes beyond market phenomena, what distinguishes the monetizable problems from the non-monetizable problems? In other words, what distinguishes market phenomena from the rest of human phenomena?

2   Based on whatever the definition of economic behaviour may be, is it possible to reduce all human phenomena to market phenomena?

The characterization of economic behaviour

The objective of this book

Depending on how we treat the constitution of the means, the generation of ends and the evaluating system, we are offered two alternatives for distinguishing between monetizable and non-monetizable phenomena.

The first line of theoretical development is based on explaining the elements that constitute any human action. The starting point is an analysis of the categories implicit in any action; from there we proceed to explain the economic behaviour which gives rise to market phenomena as a particular case. In this approach, the enlargement of the anthropological basis of economic behaviour converts economics into a general theory of action. This line of development was explored and established by Ludwig von Mises, whose mature work is *Human Action: A Treatise on Economics* (Mises 1996), which starts with the study of the elements that constitute any action and ends as a study of market phenomena as a particular case. In the first part of the book, called *Human Action*, he establishes the categories necessary for the study of any human action. He goes on to analyse the elements which characterize market phenomena as a special area within the general theory of action: action in the social framework, which allows him to analyse the theory of the market in the fourth part of the book.

The work of Mises offers clear answers to the second and third questions. The second question is answered by saying that economics is converted into a general theory of action in such a way that the principle of economic behaviour is converted into a principle of action. This conversion allows him to distinguish within the general theory of action between economic actions and non-economic actions, the former being understood as constituted by market phenomena and the latter as being constituted by social interactions. If we use Mises' terminology, the first actions are called catallactic market actions and the second praxeological or social interactions.[1] The response to the third question is negative. It is impossible to reduce all human behaviour to economic behaviour, if we understand economic behaviour as what can be expressed in monetary terms. As Mises enjoyed mentioning, praxeology or general theory of action includes the catallactics or theory of the market.

Gary Becker, a winner of the Nobel Prize for economics, offers another theoretical proposition. In the book written in his maturity, *The Economic Approach to Human Behavior* (Becker 1976), he establishes the assumptions which define economic behaviour. In his own words, 'the combined assumptions of maximizing behavior, market equilibrium, and stable preferences, used relentlessly and unflinchingly, form the heart of the economic approach' (Becker 1976: 5). These three assumptions, which define economic behaviour, are enough to reduce all human behaviour to economic behaviour. There are no doubts as to the object that Becker is proposing:

> I do not want to soften the impact of what I am saying in the interest of increasing its acceptability in the short run. I am saying that the economic approach provides a valuable unified framework for understanding *all* human behavior.
>
> (Becker 1976: 14)

Becker contributes a specific determinant of economic behaviour, called *homo economicus*, which allows him to respond affirmatively to the third question, about it being possible to reduce all human behaviour to *homo economicus*.[2]

With their growing interest in non-market phenomena, economists are often accused of 'economic imperialism' for trying to include areas traditionally reserved for other social disciplines. This accusation can be understood in two ways as referring to the enlargement of economics or to the definition of economic behaviour.

If we are referring to the scope of economics, the accusation of economic imperialism has no basis. The confirmation that the categories that we deal with in economics, the ends, the means, value, preference, choice, are present in all human behaviour, offers a reasonable argument to seek a common basis for all the sciences which study human behaviour.[3] On this point both Mises and Becker agree in pointing out the unchangeable reality of choice, which exists in all human behaviour. But the enlargement of economics raises the second and third questions. The two characterizations of economic behaviour which we have presented as possibilities of theoretical development are completely different. If we adopt Becker's characterization of economic behaviour, then we may declare the reduction of all human behaviour to maximizing utility behaviour in a context of market equilibrium. In this case the accusation of economic imperialism is appropriate, in that the theoretical mean for the enlargement of the scope of economics is based on the application of the neoclassical paradigm, and all human aspects are reduced to prices.[4]

If we bear in mind that both authors are attempting to study every aspect of human behaviour, the problem that we face is not a simple choice between two technical models. We are not dealing with a choice based on the inclinations of the researcher. Our critical analysis and therefore our choice must be based on seeking the most suitable and appropriate model for the study of human behaviour. The comparison of the praxeology of Mises and the *homo economicus* of Becker makes it clear that they are not two alternative models, but perfectly valid models. In other words, the characterization of economic behaviour made by Becker implies such severe restrictions that the theoretical validity of its application is restricted to phenomena that are limited and of little analytical importance. This does not mean that the neoclassical model is totally unimportant. As I. Kirzner recognizes, phenomena of practical importance, such as the effects of price controls and minimum wage laws, can be explained with simple neoclassical models (Kirzner 1997: 62).

However, the characterization of *homo economicus* cannot include any element that define the man of flesh and blood: his historicity, his project and his futurity. In short, the person's own dynamic is excluded from *homo economicus* because these characteristics are displayed in all human behaviour. And if we take into account that a market phenomenon is the result of human action, then it is not necessary to go beyond the sphere of the market to demonstrate the radical insufficiency of neoclassical proposals. It is important therefore to emphasize that it is incorrect to consider praxeology as a valid model to explain non-monetizable phenomena and at the same time to use the neoclassical model to explain market phenomena.

In our demonstration it is necessary to distinguish three elements:

1   The theoretical doctrine of each author. The enlargement of the scope of economics to all human action is the outcome of the theoretical characterization that is offered of economic behaviour. Economic behaviour is not characterized by the means or the ends pursued. Economics includes non-market phenomena. The theoretical differences between the two characterizations of economic behaviour are based on the following:

    a   The Misian conception defines the economic agent as an active and creative human person. The theoretical analysis of the division between alternative ends and scarce means is focused on determining the analytical elements necessary to explain the economization as the process of perception and the constitution of a system of ends and means. The economic phenomenon is studied as the outcome of a dynamic process.
    b   Becker's conception of the economic agent defines the economic agent as a passive, robotic and mechanical maker of choices. The theoretical analysis must focus on the mechanical computation of the solution of maximization, implicit in the configuration of a system of given ends and means. The difference is radical on a theoretical level. The Misian version considers that the essence of economization is a process of the constitution of the system of ends and means: his economization has a procedural character. For Becker, the essence of economization is to calculate the maximums of the ends and means that are already given. Becker's economization is about taking decisions.[5]

2   These two theoretical conceptions determine the two distinct methods of economic study:

    a   The Misian method is based on methodological subjectivism. His method, as a propedeutic principle of theoretical advance, rests on the analysis and study of the actions of man.

  b Becker's method is based on the application of the maximizing principle, stable preferences and market equilibrium. His method is to reduce all action to *homo economicus*.

3 If we consider that the method gives us access to the reality of things, it is appropriate to ask ourselves: what real phenomena are susceptible to explanation using both methods of economic approach to human behaviour? Taking into account that both authors defend the maximum area for the application of their method, the point that this book has to demonstrate is this: the reduction of economization to simple decision-taking leaves no room for human reality. The movement from a situation of equilibrium to another mechanical and passive situation prevents us from recognizing the importance of man's activity as a source of the phenomena which are the object of study. Becker's method, which attempts to explain all human behaviour, constructs a fictitious world where the real man has no place. On the other hand, the methodological subjectivism of Mises offers a way for us to approach all human action based on the theory of human action.

The structure of the book

In Chapter two we will demonstrate the theoretical structure of Misian praxeology; in Chapter three we will demonstrate the dynamic structure implicit in Mises' theory of action. This object is laborious because of the flat rejection of Mises' work which often occurs among economists. We will use four chapters to explain the necessity of basing economics on human action. In Chapter four, we will analyse the discovery of means and the creation of possibilities. Chapter five will examine the system for evaluating ends and means, and in Chapter six we will focus on causality as a praxeological category. Finally, in Chapter seven, we will analyse the dynamic structure of the action projects.

   With respect to Becker's work, in Chapter eight we show that the conception of the economic agent as *homo economicus*, based on the assumptions of maximizing behaviour, the stability of tastes and market equilibrium, implies as a condition of equilibrium the law of equality of marginal utilities weighted by price. In other words, Becker's economic behaviour is based on the consideration that the person always acts 'as if' to maximize a function of utility. We will make a critical analysis of the stability of preferences hypothesis in Chapter nine. In Chapter ten, we will analyse critically the maximizing behaviour hypothesis and market equilibrium. In the last part of that chapter we will demonstrate that: (1) Mises' theory offers a genetic–causal explanation of price formation. Prices are explained as the outcome of a process of discovery and information exchange between persons of flesh and blood. (2) Becker's theory offers a functional explanation of price variation. Starting from given prices, he explains their variations by the law of equality of marginal utilities weighted by prices. He does not offer any explanation of price formation because in his model human reality, which originates the prices, is reduced to the minimum. The problem of the functional theory of prices is that it excludes the explanatory framework of human reality, which generates market phenomena. The object-led and creative reality of man is reduced to a simple choice between predetermined situations.

Chapter 11 recapitulates the fundamental differences between the two conceptions of human behaviour. The main difference between the two approaches is that praxeological-based economics is converted into a theory of action which can be used to explain any human phenomenon. In other words, praxeological economics is a part of philosophical anthropology. In addition, the enlargement of subjectivity that permits this transformation of economics in praxeology does not imply that all phenomena pertaining to the field of philosophical anthropology are considered as economic phenomena. These phenomena constitute a partial field of human phenomena. The economic approach to all human behaviour is possible because economics is converted into a general theory of action.

Part I

The economic approach of Mises

Praxeology

2 The definition of economic behaviour in the work of Mises

The structure of the work of Mises

The works of Mises dedicated to establishing the foundations of economics are, in chronological order: *Epistemological Problems of Economics* (1981a), *Human Action* (1996), *Theory and History* (1966) and *The Ultimate Foundation of Economic Science* (1978a). This last book Mises published at the age of 81. Mises himself considered that his most important works were *Human Action* and *Theory and History*, while in his opinion *The Ultimate Foundation of Economic Science* was 'a supplement to and a commentary on [the two previous works]' (Mises 1978a: xvii). *Human Action* is a book clearly divided into two parts: the first develops the basic categories of all human action: it is a treatise on praxeology, a word coined by Mises from the Greek root *prâxis* or action. The second part is a theory of the market and of economic calculation, catallactics in the Misian terminology – a word from the Greek original *katallattein*, whose translation is exchange or swap.

It is important to emphasize this structure in the work of Mises, in order to correct a fairly common error that is made when approaching Mises' work. Economic science for Mises is the catallactics, the direct exchange of goods, commodity–commodity, or an indirect exchange of goods, commodity–money–commodity, subject to economic calculation. Praxeology is the theory of the prerequisites, requisites and categories in all human action. As market actions are a particular case within the possible actions, praxeology includes catallactics. Mises expresses this relation between both fields of action in the following phrase: the theory of action or praxeology and its most developed branch, economics or the catallactics. Mises never wrote that praxeology was economics. The explanation why Mises considers that it is correct to include the catallactics in praxeology is given in *Epistemological Problems of Economics*, where he enlarges the scope of the subjective theory of value to criticize the differentiation between economic behaviour and non-economic behaviour of the classical school.

In *Human Action*, Mises' principal work, he bases the whole of his theoretical system on the conclusions arrived at in his previous work. His second great book, *Theory and History*, is directed towards the use of the already developed analytical model to make a study of society, taking individual action as a starting point. A large part of this book is dedicated to a refutation of materialism, historicism and positivism. It is the refutation of positivism that led Mises to write *The Ultimate Foundation of Economic Science*, in which he attacks the pretensions of panfiscalism to apply the method of the natural sciences to every study that is thought of as scientific. In Mises' opinion, there are events in which the methods of the natural sciences are useless: such as those produced by 'human action' (Mises 1978a: xi).

For these reasons we consider that the fundamental book for understanding Mises' work is *Epistemological Problems of Economics*. In this book, he proposes the limitations that the characterization of the classical economic agent implies for the explanation of economic phenomena. Mises expounds the lines of theoretical development which, following the steps of Carl Menger and Böhm-Bawerk, extend the subjectivism of the theory of value, including economic actions in a general theory of human action.

Development of the subjective theory of value

To overcome the distinction made by the classical economists between rationality or economic behaviour and irrationality or non-economic behaviour, Mises begins *Epistemological Problems of Economics* with a study of the objective and field of the science of human action. He begins by establishing the logical character of 'the universally valid science of human action' (Mises 1981a: 13), that is, the basic concept of action and its requirements. For the first time, he defines human action or, 'as it is tautologically called, rational action' (1981a: 23). The prerequisite for the action is a state of dissatisfaction and the possibility of changing this situation. The end which motivates us to act is external to the action. It is a feeling, a subjective perception that the situation can be improved by means of the action. In short, it is a value judgement. Science or rational explanation has nothing to say about what we must or must not desire: this is the responsibility of rules of ethics. The economist must only register the existence of a state of dissatisfaction that triggers the action. The choice of the means is based on the individual appreciation of their suitability for obtaining the desired end. An individual may be mistaken and not use the means adequately. He is not irrational but has simply made an error. If a person frequently changes the desired ends he is not being irrational, he is simply being inconstant. If he does not use the means adequately, he fails to achieve the desired end.

Mises argues that the division of the 'economic' and the 'non-economic' based on the ends or the suitability of the means for the achievements of these ends is false. Our objective is not to judge the ends or the means, but to study the process by which the human agent creates the structure of means and ends. The economic principle cannot be based on the ends, since these are outside the scope of economics, and for their part, the means do not allow us to obtain an economic principle, since the choice of the means is the result of a person's subjective appreciation. On the basis of these considerations, Mises discards the idea of obtaining an economic principle through the classification of ends and means. The search for such a principle leads Mises to wonder about the essence of economic behaviour. If economics studies the use of the means for the attainment of the ends, the economic principle has to be something more radical than the choice of the ends and the means, independently of whatever these ends and means may be. This principle is the reality of having to discover a structure of means and ends, of having to choose between different ends and opt for one of them, while renouncing the others. The economic principle is 'the conflict of *several* ends and therefore the necessity of *choosing* among them' (1981a: 79).

If every action implies choosing among different possibilities, every action is economical with the means available for the attainment of the achievable ends. Therefore, the fundamental law of action is the economic principle – every action comes under its dominion. Whoever wants to deny the possibility of economic science has to begin by questioning the universal validity of the economic principle, which is the need for economizing as a characteristic of every action because of its own intrinsic nature (Mises 1981a: 80). This definition of economics poses some immediate problems and Mises was aware of them. On the one hand, they allow him to attack the classical *homo economicus*. This classical abstraction only includes one side of man, 'the economic, materialistic side. It only considers him as a man engaged in business, not as a consumer of economic goods' (Mises 1981a: 180). But on the other hand, had he not said that every action by its own intrinsic nature is economic? Why criticize the classical *homo economicus* for only being concerned with economics, if economics includes everything?

To explain this situation it is necessary here to introduce two concepts used by Mises: 'economics in the broad sense' and 'economics in the narrow sense'. The first term refers to the general scope of the action that fulfils the economic principle. The second term refers to those actions that are subject to monetary cost–benefit considerations. Mises says:

> The special characteristic of economic calculation is that the sphere of its use seems to be a special province within the broadest dominion of every action. In daily use, the sphere of economics extends to where it is possible to make a monetary calculation. Everything that goes beyond this point is considered the non-economic sphere. . . . Considering the economic calculation in monetary terms, the most important and basic mental tool indispensable for long term production, it is expedient to make a terminological separation between these two spheres.
>
> (Mises 1981a: 157)

Mises admits the division of the scope of economics into two spheres because of the resulting greater clarity of explanation; moreover, he affirms: '[if] all conscious conduct is an act of rational economizing, then one must be able to exhibit the fundamental economic categories involved in every action, even if this action is called "non-economic" in popular usage' (Mises 1981a: 148).

Mises introduces these fundamental categories in order to explain price formation. If we accept the neoclassical definition of economic behaviour, many of the prices that are paid would have non-economic behaviour as a cause. This is because according to the classical theory every person acts economically only if he buys in the cheapest place and sells in the most expensive place. This supposed economic rationality is easily refuted. Let us consider the following example: a person who lives in a politically disputed territory, let us say Czechoslovakia, is a German nationalist and wants to buy all the military paraphernalia to join an athletic-military organization. If he is able to make his purchases more cheaply in a Czech than in a German shop and decides to buy in the latter, we should conclude that he is acting anti-economically. Is that right? No, since the classical theory was only capable of explaining the action of the businessman and was incapable of explaining everything that goes beyond this situation, 'its thinking was orientated toward bookkeeping, the supreme expression of the rationality of the businessman' (Mises 1981a: 175). Against this vision, Mises declares: 'the fact is that modern economic theory begins with the subjective valuations of the human agent and the action governed by such valuations' (Mises 1981a: 10).

It is clear that for Mises, every explanation of prices must enlarge its scope to consider as an economic cause any state of dissatisfaction perceived by the human agent, who also consciously perceives the existence of the means to make this state disappear. In the example of the German nationalist and the dissatisfaction with the political situation of the German minority in the Sudetenland, the means to resolve the dissatisfaction is to help a fellow German by buying in his establishment. These characteristics, which explain the formation of any price, are the requisites of every human action. Thus the scope of the economic aspect encompasses every human action.

> By means of its subjectivity, the modern theory becomes an objective science. It does not make value judgments about the actions; and explains market phenomena, not on the basis of correct actions, but on the basis of actions that are given.
>
> (Mises 1981a: 180)

With this explanation it is pertinent to wonder if Mises considered the possibility of extending the economic calculation to every field of human action. Or in his words, is it possible that 'economics in the narrow sense' can include 'economics in the broad sense'? The answer is clear:

> It is absurd to want to apply the elements of this calculation (cost–benefit) to different problems, other than those confronting the individual person. One may not extend them to *res extra commercium*. One may not attempt by means of them to include more than the sphere of the economic in its narrower sense. However, this is precisely what is attempted by those who undertake to ascertain the monetary value of human life, social institutions, national wealth, cultural ideals, or the like, or who enter upon highly sophisticated investigations to determine how exchange ratios of the relatively recent, not to mention the remote, past could be expressed in terms of *our money*.
>
> (Mises 1981a: 159)

The impression is that Mises is quite clear about the separation between those actions subject to economic calculation and the rest. The former were productive or instrumental actions in their market of catallactic scope. These actions participate in the axiom of human action and its categories, studied by the general theory of human action or praxeology: the general theory of actions includes and goes beyond economics.

Mises did not delimit in any of his works the frontier between the two spheres. He never specified which human actions are not, nor will be, subject to economic calculation. What is certain, in our opinion, is that in this work Mises was not convinced of its classification and restricts economics as a science to the sphere of the 'economics in the narrow sense'. This conclusion is clear from the following text: 'the research into the determining factors (the values) is the task of other sciences, not economics. Economics is the science of the catallactics' (Mises 1981a: 168). This is certain, but it is also certain that, if we want to explain economics as part of the theory of action, it is necessary to distinguish between the two fields.

The Misian theoretical system

The relation between 'economics in the broad sense' and 'economics in the narrow sense'

The non-existence of a criterion of demarcation between the two spheres of economics is a subject that Mises deals with again in *Human Action*. The difficulties we come up against when dealing with the scope of economics do not arise from the fact that there is uncertainty over which are the phenomena that must be examined. Economics is a science; in the words of Mises, 'all that can be contended is this: economics is mainly concerned with the analysis of the determination of money prices of goods and services exchanged on the market' (Mises 1996: 234). The scope of economics is confined to the exchange of the goods and services used in monetary calculations. In his terminology, this is strictly economics in its 'narrow sense'. The problems arise in the analysis of market phenomena where it is necessary to go beyond the strict sphere of the market. In a market transaction, non-material elements are introduced which are essential for the analysis of the market phenomena: knowledge, the way the human agent deals with the things, and the persons themselves are constituent and determining elements of the exchange, but they are not reducible to the good or service that is exchanged. Mises concludes:

> But then it is no longer possible to define neatly the boundaries between the kind of action which is the proper field of economic science in the narrower sense, and other action. Economics widens its horizon and turns into a general science of all and every human action, into praxeology. The question emerges of how to distinguish precisely, within the broader field of general praxeology, a narrower orbit of specifically economic problems.

(Mises 1996: 232)

This last text suggests that Mises conceived economics as 'not about things and tangible material objects; it is about men, their meanings and actions' (Mises 1996: 92). This definition implies that in order to study market phenomena it is necessary to move beyond the strict framework of such phenomena and to analyse them from the point of view of the persons who make them. Each step in the understanding of the reality of the person has supposed an advance in economics. However, the fact that the advance in economics is produced by an ordering of economic phenomena, within a general theory of action, does not imply that every human action is reducible to monetary terms. To separate both fields precisely, see Figure 2.1.

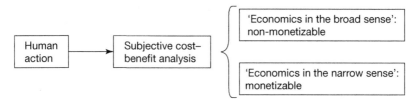

Figure 2.1 Fields within human action

The structure of the Misian theory of action

For the explanation of market phenomena it is necessary to construct a general theory of action, and the first two parts of *Human Action* are dedicated to this task. The remaining five parts are deductions of economic laws. As Mises says himself, any extension of his theoretical system of action is the basis for improving the economic theory and its methodology. The first part of the book is an analysis of action: the starting point of praxeology 'is not a choice of axioms and a decision about methods of procedure, but reflection about the essence of action' (Mises 1996: 39). His method is to reflect on the components which are present in every action, so that the said action arises. What then is the irreducible cause by which the action is produced? It is the category of action itself. If a person wants to deny this principle he is making a conscious volition and by definition all conscious conduct is an action. Mises therefore concludes that this person has acted in denying the category of action. The action is an axiom; it is irreducible to other causes and a necessary condition of our knowledge. Mises' theory of human action is constructed on the assumption that human action is an irreducible presupposition and his entire theoretical edifice starts from this assumption. It is a self-founding principle.

Although the action cannot be reduced to another cause, man has to perceive a situation of dissatisfaction before acting. Mises writes: 'Acting man is eager to substitute a more satisfactory state of affairs for a less satisfactory' (Mises 1996: 13). He has always to prefer one state to another. Indifference is only produced in a being who is 'perfectly content with the state of his affairs [and] would have no incentive to change things' (Mises 1996: 13). Even perceiving this unsatisfactory state, the man cannot act. When does this happen? In Mises' words:

[when the man does not have] the expectation that purposeful behaviour has the power to remove or at least to alleviate the felt uneasiness. In the absence of this condition no action is feasible. Man must yield to the inevitable.

(Mises 1996: 14)

Therefore, with regard to the axiom of human action, Mises considers as an exterior requirement, or rather as a prerequisite, these two conditions, the subjective perception of dissatisfaction and the consideration of certain things as resources for the attainment of an end.

The axiom of action has a well-defined meaning. In order to surpass the classical vision of the *homo economicus*, Mises seeks an economic principle which is rooted neither in the choice of the means, nor in the choice of the ends. Establishing the new economic principle in the unchanging reality of every action, man must choose among the different alternatives of action. The economic principle is the prime reality of every action – in order to act it is necessary to choose between distinct possibilities. This supposes that: (1) every action fulfils the economic principle, and that (2) if the economic principle is not a criterion of the allocation of means to ends, the choice of the means depends on the person's subjective appreciation of his suitability for the attainment of the end. Therefore every action is rational.

Here, then, we have the individual with dissatisfaction who wants a change in his situation and considers that the means exist for changing it. What things can he use as resources? If an individual does not know how to relate to the elements in his environment, he does not know what to expect: he does not have a *ratio*, a measure among things. He does not have any reason to act and will have to discover the causal relations that provoke changes. Mises affirms: 'Acting requires and presupposes the category of causality' (Mises 1996: 22). The category of means and ends presupposes the cause–effect relation. This relation responds to the question, 'where and how must I interfere in order to divert the course of events from the way it would flow in the absence of my interference in a direction which better suits my wishes?' (Mises 1996: 22). Man has to know the causal relation for every action, but this does not imply that he knows exactly the cause of every phenomenon. The principle of causality has been proposed in the search for the regularity of the phenomena, in the search for laws: if A then B. However, given that our knowledge is partial, we will have to establish the law in statistical terms. We will say, if A then B in 70 per cent of the cases, C in the remaining 30 per cent. The philosophical, epistemological and metaphysical problems of causality and imperfect induction are outside the scope of praxeology. Mises concludes: 'we must simply establish the fact that in order to act man must know the causal relationship between the different events, processes and situations' (Mises 1996: 23).

Starting from the axiom of action, its prerequisite was the existence of dissatisfaction and the desire to change that situation. Whoever acts distinguishes between the past, the present and the future. This difference is not adequate in philosophical terms. Every present moment is sunk in the past. There is no more than a tenuous line between the future and the past. Whoever acts distinguishes between a time antecedent to the action, the past, a time of action, and a time consequent to the action, the future, in such a way that the person perceives the causal relation in this antecedent–consequent sequence. If on the one hand the action implies the desire for change, causality is necessary to interrelate with the recourses which can produce this change. The action and causality are intimately linked. On the other hand, the causal antecedent–consequent relation is presented in a procedural temporality. Causality and temporality are inseparable. Mises concludes: 'The concepts of change and of time are inseparably linked together' (Mises 1996: 23).

The fundamental structure of the Misian system is almost finished with respect to the first part: his theory of action. The basic element is the irreducible axiom of human action. The second step has been to clarify the prerequisites of the action, preference. The third step was to analyse how this prerequisite implies the causal category in order to know how to distinguish the means–ends relation. The fourth and last step is to explain the sequential character of the causal relation. The conclusion that Mises reaches is that the action is a perceived temporal preference like a means–end relation.

To respond to possible misunderstandings, Mises enlarges on the epistemological considerations of the praxeology. He asks a question about the origin of these categories: Are they the consequence of an empirical study or are they the result of a conceptual analysis of reality? They cannot be the result of any experiment because the experiment presumes the category of action. In fact, an experiment is a conscious action. Therefore the study of reality has to come from the study of that thing that allows us to have knowledge of the world, the human mind. In his opinion the subject that occupies us alludes to the constitutive and obligatory character of the structure of the human mind. These categories, principally the axiom of action, are a priori. Mises understands by a priori, prior to all experience: prior to all experience in the sense that it is not the result of an external stimulus. He subscribes clearly to the line of thought of Leibniz and Kant and against that of Locke and Hume. To clarify what he understood by prior to all experience, he always cited the following example: 'Locke said "there is nothing in the intellect which has not previously been in the senses", to which Leibniz replied "except the intellect itself"' (Mises 1978a: 12). Thus the fundamental logical relations cannot be the object of demonstration nor of refutation. Trying to demonstrate its certainty obliges us to presuppose its validity.

Mises' theory of action is now complete. We have all the basic assumptions that shape the hypothetical–deductive model of economic theory. These elements are: the category of action, the category of causality and the praxeological character of time. All of them constitute the pillars of economic theory and they can be compared, if one admits such a comparison, to sulphur, hydrogen and oxygen, themselves independent elements which react together give rise to a substance, sulphuric acid. In our study, this sulphuric acid would be economic theory. Just as the sulphuric acid has emerged thanks to the physical–chemical properties of the elements, the economic theory is the result of making explicit all the implications of the praxeological categories.

Our next step is to explain from praxeology how money has arisen in order to unite praxeology with the theory of the market. The second part of *Human Action* is the study of action in the social framework. In this section, the phenomenon of the division of labour and the evolutionary origin of money are explained. Mises approaches the study of society with the evolutionary vision expounded by Carl Menger (1985). Menger analyses the emergence of social institutions as the result of the interaction of individuals. This is a spontaneous interaction in which each individual seeks to attain his ends through cooperation. Mises uses this same concept in his section 'Action within the famework of society' to explain how exchange is produced in society (Mises 1996, Chapter x). With the appearance of money the process of the division of labour is accelerated. With the economic concepts already defined and with the explanation of the emergence of money, Mises proceeds to the explanation of economic calculation and the theory of the market. The last sections of *Human Action* are an exposition of the results of the different legislations and the effects that they have on the functioning of the market.

In *Epistemological Problems of Economics* he has enlarged the scope of human subjectivity in order to base economic theory on broader ground, on the theory of human action. To lay the foundations for the new base, he defines the building blocks of this new structure, which are the praxeological categories, and, in the first part of *Human Action*, explains the relations between the building blocks. In the second part, he applies his technique and constructs his theoretical edifice.

The Misian methodology

We now have the theoretical edifice. The next question is, can we live in this edifice? Is it finished? Without the use of this simile of construction, we are asking ourselves if we need another block to apply this theory. Do we need more theoretical blocks to be able to apply this system and begin to 'do' economics? The different economic theorems have their application in those situations in which the conditions that characterize the problem are present. So, the problems of indirect exchange do not have any importance in barter economies. Another example would be for us to propose a situation in which work had no disutility. Does this situation exist in reality? Could we, without any problem, imagine different hypothetical examples in which to apply the praxeological categories and to analyse how this hypothetical world would function? It would be a good exercise. However, as economists, our objective is the explanation of real phenomena to which we have to give adequate treatment. Experience and the historical situation show us what these problems are.

The study of history has a different method from that of praxeology. Praxeology is analysis a priori of the categories derived from the axiom of human action. This a priori implies two things: first, the perception of this axiom is not hypothetical and it is not an arbitrarily chosen assumption, whose validity is corroborated by empirical verification. In other words, the axiom of human action is 'true knowledge of the meaning of action and its categories deduced by means of formal logic' (Hoppe 1993: 230). The second characteristic is the universal character of this assumption. Every individual human action is explained with the categories of the action. History, on the other hand, is a study of the individual and of the unrepeatable. Every past action is a fact – as Mises writes, 'is an ultimate datum' (Mises 1996: 49). The natural sciences interrelate the irreducible data in a functional manner and, if it is possible, they quantify these relations. The historian, on the other hand, tries to understand them. For him, the information that is given by the natural and a priori sciences is not enough. He needs to assess the relative importance of the value judgements of the human agent in order to interpret the events as they happened. The historian may manage to understand these motives 'because he is himself a human being' (Mises 1996: 49).

This vision of history is a direct consequence of methodological subjectivism. If it is the person who acts, there is no hypostatic concept of society. The science that most closely approaches the reality of the individual is history. This precision in detail is, however, offset by its lack of generality. The act is unrepeatable. This original understanding is what is known in German methodology as *das spezifische Verstehen der Geistewissenschaften* (the specific understanding of the social sciences) or simply *Verstehen* (understanding). Mises continues: 'historians and all other people always apply [*Verstehen*] in commenting upon human events of the past and in forecasting future events' (Mises 1996: 50). Comprehension as a method is used when one wants to consider to a greater or lesser degree the effects that an act has had in a process. It is the interpretation of those phenomena 'which cannot be totally elucidated by logic, mathematics, praxeology, and the natural sciences to the extent that they cannot be cleared up by all these sciences' (Mises 1996: 50). The Misian division of the sciences is clear: there are the a priori sciences, mathematics, logic and praxeology,[1] and in second place the experimental sciences, physics, chemistry etc. In third place lie the comprehensive sciences, principally history.

Economics as a branch of praxeology is a science with an a priori method. Every human action is explained with the axiom of action. Every economist is a person and as such can understand the relative importance of the value judgements in an action. In this regard the method of history is the understanding of the particularities which constitute each individual action as a differentiated and unitary whole. These particularities are what are abstracted in order to seek the causes of every action, which is why they remain outside the study of praxeology. The method of praxeological economics has two fronts integrated by two episte-mologically different methods (Mises 1996: 66). Economics does not only use logical reasoning, it also proposes *assumptions* that experience tells you what must be studied. Therefore there is no sharp distinction between pure science and the practical applications of the theorems to historical and political situations. The Misian system is fully explained. Mises' way of working is a clear example of rigorous method. First, we analyse the subject that we are going to discuss: this establishes the fundamentals of the subject. Second, we establish the theoretical structure suitable for the subject of the investigation. In the third stage the theory is put into practice: the method. This is the triad of fundamentals–theory–method.

We will close this chapter with some consideration of *Theory and History* and *The Ultimate Foundation of Economic Science*. *Human Action* was a book that took a long time to come to fruition. After the publication of the first German edition, it was the object of two profound revisions and the translation into English by Mises himself. In spite of the revisions, the basic structure of the book was maintained, and, more importantly, the theoretical structure did not undergo any variation. Neither the praxeological categories nor the economic theorems vary. With the theory developed and the method defined, Mises produced a social study, *Theory and History*, which he described as an interpretation of social and economic evolution. As the subtitle of the book – *An interpretation of social and economic evolution* – declares, this study has two clear ideas that structure the work:

1   The analysis will be made using methodological dualism. As we have already explained, this method makes economics a science which has to use both a priori reasoning and comprehension or *Verstehen*. Thus the sciences are classified in three groups: a priori, natural and history. The danger in this situation is clear. Each science may try to occupy terrain in which it does not belong. One must not forget the Viennese origins of Mises. The Vienna of his youth was the place where M. Schlick and R. Carnap developed positivism with the founding of the Vienna Circle, whose scientific vision of the world was defined essentially by two characteristics. The first is empirical and positivist, that is to say, knowledge only exists from experience, which is based on immediately acquired experience. The second, the scientific conception of the world, is marked by the application of logical analysis. The object of scientific endeavour is to reach the unified science through the application of logical analysis to empirical material (Neurath 1939).

Another danger arises precisely from the study of history. The German-speaking countries were immersed in historicism; the social sciences could only aspire to the study of the characteristics themselves of each fact. They denied the possibility of abstracting the particularities for the generation of explanatory structures applicable to every human action. Positivism tried to reduce all reality to its quantifiable positive aspects in order to be considered an object of scientific study. It considered that the application of the physical model of the nineteenth century was the only path of scientific progress. It was the search for functional relations. Man was reduced to stimulus–response. This situation has created a curious chaos. Positivism considered that every statement that is not analytical or experimental is a mere expression of emotions, without any meaning. All value judgements are absolutely relative. It is in this situation that Mises wrote *Theory and History*. The book is structured in chapters according to the subjects that he is trying to refute: positivism, materialism, determinism, dialectical materialism, historicism, positivism that in its support of the sole science has come to be known as 'scientism'. The whole book is an argument in favour of methodological dualism, refuting the different reductions of history that have been made.

2   In *Human Action* Mises considers that 'human action and its vicissitudes are tremendously real. Action is the essence of man's nature and existence, his means of preserving his life and raising himself above the level of animals and plants' (Mises 1996: 18). The only way that man can defend himself both in nature and from nature is action. It is the application of the praxeological categories to the division of labour which allows Mises to conclude that this evolutionary process has made possible the greatest generation of wealth in history. He considers that the study of economics, as part of praxeology, has been fundamental for the development of the West during the last two hundred years:

> This civilization was able to spring into existence because the peoples were dominated by ideas that were the application of the teachings of economics to the problems of economic policy. It will and must perish if the nations continue to pursue the course that they entered upon under the spell of doctrines rejecting economic thinking.
>
> (Mises 1996: 10)

This thought is a constant in Mises' work. Progress is the result of a better understanding of the role of the individual in society, and while this process has occurred, it could go into decline. There is no reason to trust in the constant progress of society. History is not only important as a science that allows us to understand individual actions and to know how to take measures of economic policy; it is fundamental because it transmits the ideas and values which make it possible to understand man: 'it opens the mind toward an understanding of human nature and destiny. It increases wisdom. It is the very essence of that much-misinterpreted concept, a liberal education. It is the foremost approach to humanism' (Mises 1966: 293). Culture is not reduced to knowledge of the state of science, of technology. This knowledge is important but it is not fundamental. The fundamental thing about culture:

> is the assimilation of the ideas that aroused mankind from the inert routine of a merely animal existence to a life of reasoning and speculating. *It is the individual's effort to humanize himself by partaking in the tradition of all the best that earlier generations have bequeathed.*
>
> (Mises 1966: 294, my italics)

These are the reasons why the defence of methodological dualism must be radical: radical in the sense of risking the possibility of future progress if any of the conceptions of history which Mises attacks manages to triumph.

Regarding *The Ultimate Foundation of Economic Science*, there is little to add to what Mises himself has said and to what has already been mentioned in the first note of this chapter. This book is an appendix to *Theory and History*. It is an analysis of what he considers to be the most pernicious aspects of positivism. This honour for positivism to be deserving of a monograph is explained in the last paragraph of the book.

> As far as the empiricist principle of logical positivism refers to the experimental methods of the natural sciences, it merely asserts what is not questioned by anybody. As far as it rejects the epistemological principles of the sciences of human action, it is not only entirely wrong. It is also knowingly and intentionally undermining the intellectual foundations of Western civilization.
>
> (Mises 1978a: 133)

3 The structure of the general theory of action of Mises

Economic act and economic action

Economic phenomenon as action

The observed economic phenomenon, that is, a market transaction, is an assignable act for each one of its participants. Each person has decided on the end to be achieved and has evaluated the adequacy of the means for the attainment of the end.[1] Each agent, using the prices, values the means and decides which is the advantageous exchange for him. The observed fact is the exchange of goods for money. This interpretation considers the economic phenomenon as an assignable act, as a historical act in which a quantity of goods has been exchanged for money. In this context, the definition of economics given by L. Robbins is important: 'it is the science which studies human behaviour as a relationship between ends and scarce means which have alternative uses' (Robbins 1969: 16). This is certain and it allows us to affirm that in every economic phenomenon, considered as an historic fact, there exists a relation between the sums of money and the quantities of goods. The economic phenomenon is, however, somewhat more complex and radical than the mere exchange of goods for money. This historic exchange is the concrete representation of a set of elements which have intervened in its constitution or in its execution. In order for the exchange to be produced, each person has to *perceive* a situation of dissatisfaction and the possibility of changing it by making an exchange.

For the exchange to be carried out, all the elements indicated by Mises participate. If we only consider the exchange itself, the reality that originated it is not reflected in this exchange. The explanation of a price starts by considering that the people who intervene in the exchange pursue ends: ends which are things, either material or immaterial, which are desired and whose possession supposes a change in the state of dissatisfaction prior to the exchange. On its own, the dissatisfaction does not trigger the exchange. Each person has to perceive the possibility of making the exchange. However unsatisfactory the situation may be, if we do not know how to change it, there is very little we can do. Every action is rational because in order to change the situation, it is necessary to know the way to alter it. The original dissatisfaction has its concrete representation in the attainment of an end, which supposes a change in the situation. The knowledge that every person has not only activates the possibility of the exchange but also makes it possible, through the calculation of the monetary cost–benefit, to evaluate whether the means that each person has at his disposal are adequate for the attainment of the end. The fact of observing the exchange does not explain the circumstances involved in its origin and development. If we say that the price of a kilo of potatoes is 1 euro we are not mentioning the causes that have originated this price.[2] The exchange as an observed act must be explained using the praxeological categories.

The dynamic character of the economic act

The evaluation of the means makes it possible to assign them to the attainment of the end. Mises considers that it is not for economics to catalogue the ends which are pursued when exchanging goods: economics is there to explain how the means are adapted to the ends. It appears that the only problem is to seek the most suitable means to achieve the end. Mises says: 'the mental acts that determine the content of a choice refer either to ultimate ends or to the means to attain ultimate ends. The former are called judgments of value. The latter are technical decisions derived from factual propositions' (Mises 1966: 12). However, the evaluation acts not only on the means, but also on the ends. Mises is aware that the ends that are pursued may vary:

> As soon as people venture to question and to examine an end, they no longer look upon it as an end but deal with it as a means to attain a still higher end. All other ends are but provisional. They turn into means as soon as they are weighed against other ends and means.
>
> (Mises 1966: 14)

This paragraph points to the essence of the economic act. The allocation of the means does not suppose that the desire for and the evaluation of other ends are deactivated. The ends are considered as such, while the evaluation does not consider a change in them to be pertinent. The ends and the means of the assigned act are not realities external to the person because they are determined by a set of rules that are outside his volition. It is the person who believes that he discovers the possibility of obtaining an end through the use of the real properties of such external things. The end and the means are active possibilities, which the person creates, based on the real characteristics of things. That is to say, *the assignable act is active; it has dynamism.*

The assignment is produced because the human agent has maintained an end activated for a period of time, considering what is the maximum benefit that may be obtained with the resources at his disposal. The phenomenon of the exchange is produced through money and is the result of behaviour conducive to the attainment of the desired end. This behaviour is what the person voluntarily maintains over time and which supposes the justification of the end. The changes produced by the mere passage of time introduce new information that the person evaluates. As Mises defines the axiom of action, the person acts because he wants to change an unsatisfactory situation for another more satisfactory one. The assigned act is active because the person prefers those acts of greater value to those of lesser value. The logical consistency implies that in order to understand the assigned act we must consider that the person pursues an end. However, the fact that the person acts with an end in mind does not suppose that the end being pursued is always the same. In Mises' words:

> If one's valuations have changed, unremitting faithfulness to the once espoused principles of action merely for the sake of constancy would not be rational but simply stubborn. Only in one respect can acting be constant: in preferring the more valuable to the less valuable. If the valuations change, acting must change also. . . . In acting, which is necessarily in the temporal order, there cannot be any question of such consistency. Acting must be suited to purpose, and purposefulness requires adjustment to changing conditions.
>
> (Mises 1996: 103)

These considerations lead us to the essence of the economic phenomenon as we advance in our understanding of it through employing methodological subjectivism. The economic phenomenon which we observe is that the historical fact of exchange is the result of a process of creation and discovery of ends and means, as well as their constant evaluation and execution. Each economic act has a full explanation as an integral part of a dynamic process, in which desiderative, cognitive and evaluative elements intervene. There cannot be a full explanation of the act if it is not embedded in the process that generates it. Therefore, the economic phenomenon acquires its full meaning when it is considered not as an isolated act, but within the active process of the person who performs it. This dynamic character of the economic action demonstrates that these phenomena are really constitutive parts of a more complex dynamic process, that is, human interactions. The economic phenomenon is the result of a dynamic process in which the assignation is only a constituent part: the economic phenomenon is not reducible to its assignable aspect. The assignation is produced when the person decides the end and he proceeds to adjust the means to this end. In daily life there exist millions of situations of undoubted economic importance that are assignable acts. For example: assigning the working shifts in a factory when we are given the number of workers and their wage costs; assigning a certain sum of money for different ends; filling a truck with as many packets as possible.

Investigating the ultimate defining characteristic of the assignation, both of the ends and the means, shows the active character of both economic elements. The end will be considered as such while a more satisfactory situation is not observed and it is known how to transform the situation of the starting point. The means will be considered as such while the person does not consider that the cost of its utilization exceeds its yield in the attainment of the end. This active character points to a more radical and complex structure of every economic phenomenon than the merely assignable. The evaluation of ends and means is dynamic; it goes on altering, transforming itself in new situations. It does this in such a way that each assignable act forms part of a constituent process voluntarily maintained by the person. The assignable aspect of the economic phenomenon is inserted within the dynamic process of creation and discovery of means and ends within each person's possibilities.[3]

The economic phenomenon as action

Mises defines action in the following way: 'We call such a willfully induced alteration an exchange' (Mises 1996: 97). This mutation takes shape in the different changes as they happen. One situation succeeds another. Another, thus forming a succession, succeeds each act. This process, which generates economics, also generates acts that do not belong to the field of economics in the narrow sense. The same concept of the action as the generator of actions is found in other fields of social study. Thus Professor Leonardo Polo in his study of ethics defines action in the following way: 'human life is intellectually directed action' (Polo 1996: 170). Professor C. Valverde in his study of philosophical anthropology defines action as 'free conscious intervention in a process' (Valverde 1995: 181). The idea of a process is evident in these three definitions. The explanation of any fact, whether it is a market fact or an extra-mercantile fact, lies in the understanding of the process of perception and the constitution of the means and the ends. This process includes and goes beyond the merely assignable: the assignation is another element within the general process of action. The action is initiated with the end of satisfying a desire. To achieve the end it is necessary to know the changes that must be made in the situation and to evaluate the different ways to realize it. It is important to emphasize these agreements among the three definitions of action because, since Mises has improved the understanding of economics, explaining market phenomena with the analytical structure which explains any action, the general tendency in the social sciences is to seek a general framework that makes it possible to study the relations between the different humanist disciplines.[4]

The axiom of action

Mises' breakthrough was to see that the dynamic structure of the action made it possible to explain the active character of the assignable act. If this dynamism in the evaluation of the ends and the means makes them vary over time, it is necessary to abandon the search for an economic principle based on the classification of the means and ends. Within the scope of economics, the pursuable ends and the means used escape all classification. Mises is right when he affirms that economics does not determine the ends and the means: this choice corresponds to the person. With his new approach, Mises enlarges the subjectivist base that encompasses many types of behaviour that the classical paradigm considered irrational. This enlargement of economic rationality makes it possible to include in economics many types of behaviour in which the person is not guided by the accounting principle of selling at the most expensive price and buying at the cheapest price. If we focus on the person's subjective evaluations, we find he uses the information transmitted through prices to adapt the means to the end. So, we can use Mises' example again, of the German nationalist who lives in Czechoslovakia. He buys clothes from the German shopkeeper which are more expensive than those of Czech origin because this market purchase is a means to boost support among the citizens of German origin. This person is using the mechanisms of the market to achieve his specific end. This is a market action and it is perfectly rational, although to the external observer the fact that is recorded is a purchase at a higher price. Therefore, concludes Mises, rationality is present in every evaluation of the means.

The scope of 'economics in the narrow sense' is not the only one where there is an evaluation of the means and ends. Any action which uses means, even if these do not include market prices, supposes a cost. These actions have an evaluative system and therefore are rational. Besides this, they have a cost when an alternative has to be chosen, and therefore they are economic actions. Mises establishes, in this way, the axiom of action with its two characteristics: (1) every action supposes an evaluation and is therefore rational, and (2) every action supposes a choice with a cost and therefore is economic. If the evaluation uses prices, we are within the scope of 'economics in the narrow sense'. In the opposite case, we are within the scope of 'economics in the broad sense'.

Rationality in all human behaviour

If we concern ourselves with the etymology, the word reason comes from the Latin *ratio*, the word for the Greek term *lógos*, translatable as argument or measure. For the Greeks a thing had *lógos* if it had a measure. What was the measure of all things? Protagoras defined man as the measure of all things.[5] This statement has a very precise meaning. Following the classification of Emilio Lledó (Lledó 1995), the *lógos* has to do with objects whose principles can be of distinct types. The rational, the *lógos*, has a 'rationalizing' aspect which is integral to the human psyche. The discussion about the different types of principles of things had to be carried out among those who possessed this faculty: human beings. They discuss the principles of things because individual intelligence is not sufficient. Personal evidence is not sufficient. As J. A. Marina commented, '[we look to base the evidence] on universal truths which may be perceived by any intelligent human subject and intelligence becomes reason. The *lógos* has been transformed into *dia-logos*, in communicable thinking' (Marina 1993: 230).

Modern rationality is the endeavour initiated by Greek philosophy of going beyond mythology, of constructing a body of transmissible theories based on the rational capability of humans. The myths constitute a way of confronting things without appealing to reason. As Professor S. Rábade points out:

> The myths rather than convincing, attempt to clarify, insinuate, and provoke a vital attitude. The myths rather than justifying or giving the whys and

wherefores of a thing, wish to present us with a real situation. They are not a web of reasons but a type of reproduction of something that is unreal but which must be accepted as it is.

(Rábade 1965: 188)

This paragraph underlines the dialogic character of reason as against that of the myths: reasonings convince, they are not imposed by force. This process, this march of *lógos* begun by science, has not reached all the fields of reality. The field that remains in darkness despite the light shone by reason constitutes the field of irrationality, which exhibits two fundamental features: theoretical and practical irrationality.

The field of the irrational is what is inaccessible to intelligence. This incapacity may be understood as an indeterminate incapacity of our understanding regarding an object or an order of things. It is important to underline the essence of theoretical irrationality: although we do not know totally or partially the nature of things which we consider irrational, at least we have knowledge of its existence.[6] It must be realized that this reality delimits fields which have varied throughout history. Many realities, known for centuries, have only been able to be explained rationally after a long process of investigation. When Mises affirms that every action is rational, he is referring to the fact that with the enlargement of the subjectivist base of economics, whether in its narrow or broad sense, we have at our disposition a theory that makes it possible to explain every action as a process of discovery, evaluation and choice. What the classical economists consider the area of irrationality disappears in Mises' theory. The following demonstrates Mises' thought to perfection: 'in earlier days people were prepared to assume that there was no sense at all in the exceptional behavior of neurotics. Freud demonstrated that the seemingly senseless acts of the neurotic are designed to attain definite ends' (Mises 1966: 268).

According to Mises, the concept that must be introduced is the error in the evaluation of the means and the ends: 'error, inefficiency, and failure must not be confused with irrationality. . . . The doctor who chooses the wrong method to treat a patient is not irrational; he may be an incompetent physician' (Mises 1966: 268). Within Mises' theory, error is a possibility as valid as correctness and success in the action.[7] The Misian consideration that every action is rational must be understood in its theoretical aspect. Effectively, the enlargement of the subjective base of economics means that there is a theoretical explanation of every action, like the deliberate changes that the human agent introduces in his situation in order to substitute an unsatisfactory situation with a more satisfactory situation.

Mises' theoretical endeavour has provided us with a rational explanation of every action. But this does not imply that irrational actions do not exist in daily life. Let us consider a person who adopts some means to attain an end. If better evidence exists which considers these means to be inadequate and the person knows about this evidence and in spite of this uses the means, then his behaviour is irrational. H. H. Hoppe makes the same additions to the concept of rationality in Mises. He demonstrates this with the use of the theories:

If a superior tool were available, for example, a theory or a paradigm that allowed one to reach a goal that could not be reached equally successfully by applying another, incompatible theory, it would be irrational for an actor not to adopt it. To be sure, such irrational behaviour is empirically possible.

(Hoppe 1993: 212)

The Misian economic principle

In enlarging the field of economics Mises was seeking an economic principle that did not concern itself with the classification of the ends and the means. The solution he provided consists in equating the ineradicable choice between the different alternatives with the economic principle. The Misian economic principle is based on the discovery of means and in the creation of possibilities; the Misian economization is based on the perception of the structure of ends and means. In this approach it is important to explain the dynamic process of discovering means and creating ends:

1   The scheme has its starting point in human reality where we discover the means, and the execution of the action reverts to the same reality, transforming it into another reality. The action is the procedural change of reality. The subjective discovery of means is the beginning of the transforming activity of man about reality.

2   This discovering of means is inseparable from the person's creative ability. Within the axiom of action it is necessary to highlight the ability to embark on new possibilities of action created by the human agent. The concept of pure entrepreneurship developed by Kirzner allows us to understand the active role of the person in the perception of the system of means and ends. It is of fundamental importance to emphasize that *in this model the economic principle does not suppose a maximizing principle*. The idea of the need of a maximizing principle in economics comes from the attempt to copy the mechanistic model of physics (cf. Koslowski 1985). In physics, the use of the infinitesimal calculus establishes the laws of conservation and infinite movement in empty spaces. With both concepts a mechanist model of the world is constructed which explains the interdependence of bodies moving in empty space. This physical model is very attractive for resolving economic problems. It is enough to identify the infinite movement of the bodies in empty space with the limitless human ability for generating new needs and with the need to coordinate the actions of individuals with the interdependence of bodies in space. In this way, it is possible to pose the economic problem with a question: how can individuals coordinate their actions in order to obtain a maximum result in their *individual* actions when their resources and time are limited?

We are not going to enter into the suitability of this mechanistic model for the development of physics.[8] Here we are going to analyse the problem that is fundamental for economics. In Mises' work the action is structured around the ends and the means and there exists a clear distinction between the former and the latter. The appropriate question is, does the distinction between ends and means imply the need for a maximizing principle? In other words: *does the economic principle necessarily have to be a maximizing principle?* This is a crucial issue in the analysis of the works of Mises and Becker. For Mises, who continues the work of Menger (cf. Chapter 7, p. 111), the economic principle cannot be reduced to a mathematical optimizing principle, on penalty of losing the dynamism of the person. His economic principle is based on pure entrepreneurship, understood as the human ability to create and discover new means and ends of action (cf. Chapter 4). On the other hand, for Becker the hypothesis of optimizing behaviour has a precise mathematical meaning. He conceives it in its formal mathematical sense and it is a condition sine qua non for the marginalist approach to economics.[9,10]

The action and the sociocultural framework

To begin to study the relations existing between the person, the sociocultural framework, the ethics and the individual action, let us return to Figure 2.1 (see Chapter 2, p. 18) to represent the division of fields of 'economics' made by Mises.

Mises limits the scope in the 'narrow sense' to actions that use prices as a method of calculation. This method must not be extrapolated in Mises' words to *res extra commercium*. It is important to stop and examine this expression. Mises made an analysis of human action which follows a precise order: (1) he establishes the axiom of action: its prerequisites, requisites and praxeological categories. (2) He analyses human action within the social framework that generates human interactions. (3) He is focused on a precise type of interaction: exchanges. (4) He studies the exchange in which the evaluation of what can be exchanged does not use prices because they do not exist. (5) He analyses the exchanges whose method of evaluation is market prices. The line of investigation to reach the *res commercium* can be summarized thus: individual action; action within the social framework: the interactions; the exchanges: the consolidation of the exchanges in the markets; the use of money as the means of payment: market prices.

This line of investigation analyses the phenomena as they have arisen in human reality. The first process was the socialization of the person in bigger and bigger groups. In the interaction between the members of the tribes or clans, there began the sporadic exchange of food and tools for hunting, etc. These exchanges were isolated until the understanding of the mutual benefits of the exchanges became generalized. It was at that moment that economics arose. It was an incipient economy, where there existed markets of direct exchange in which there did not exist any generalized means of payment. The consolidation of the markets came from the understanding of the benefits of accepting a widespread means of payment. In economic behaviour this was a qualitative advance: passing from merchandise–merchandise exchange to merchandise–money–merchandise exchange. Now it is necessary to introduce some slight shades of meaning into the Misian division of economics of the two scopes. If we bear in mind that 'economics in the broad sense' includes 'economics in the narrow sense', two questions arise:

(1) what is the relation between society, culture and market phenomena? and
(2) what is the relation between ethics and economics?

The market and the sociocultural framework

In the explanation of the economic phenomenon as action, we have concluded that
its basis of study is the field of social interactions, and in this very broad field
we have differentiated between non-monetizable interactions and mercantile
exchanges. However, the praxeological categories that explain any type of action
are the same. It cannot be any other way if we take into account that it is the entrepreneurial function, understood as creative ability, that is the essence of human
dynamism. Within praxeology the concept of entrepreneurship is not limited to
a certain group of persons. It acquires the character of the function that *every person*
makes, when acting. In Chapter four we will develop the concept of entrepreneurship based on the foundations constructed by Kirzner. This development will
make it possible to explain the relation that exists between society, culture and
individual action. The field of application of pure entrepreneurship is the totality
of reality that surrounds man. Anything that arouses the attention of the person
can be converted into a suggestive possibility and become an attractive project.
This human capacity is the element that makes it possible to concentrate on
a fundamental social aspect: the social interrelations that fashion society. Thus, if
we concentrate on the action we can define society, following Professor Huerta
de Soto, as:

> A process (that is to say, a dynamic structure) of a spontaneous sort, that is
> to say, not consciously designed by anybody; it is very complex as it is made
> up of thousands of millions of people, of objectives, likes, valuations and
> practical knowledge; of human interactions (which are basically relations of
> exchange and which on many occasions take the form of monetary prices) and
> are always brought about in accordance with some norms, habits, or patterns
> of conduct, all of these being moved by the force of *the entrepreneurial function*,
> which constantly creates, discovers, and transmits information, adapting and
> coordinating competitively the contradictory plans of individuals.
>
> (Huerta de Soto 1992: 84)

Seizing on such a rich definition, we can tease out the following points:

1   The separation between social interactions and monetary exchanges is
    maintained. The former include the latter.
2   It concentrates on the fundamental problem that every sociocultural frame-
    work has to resolve: how to permit the development of the persons who live
    in it. This poses the problem of the coordination among people. Therefore, in
    Chapter four we shall use the concept of pure entrepreneurship to give
    an explanation of social maintenance and transformation starting from social
    interactions.

3   If we concentrate on society as a process, we confront the problem of the transmission of information. We will pose the problem of the knowledge that every society must resolve for its correct functioning. If we start from individual action we find that each member has at his disposition exclusive scattered information, which refers us to the role played by culture in the triad society–culture–individual action. This widespread information, which is transmitted culturally, allows us to understand culture as the enormous precipitate of possibilities of action that past generations pass on to the future generations.

4   As the definition indicates, the social interrelations are effected in accordance with some norms or patterns of behaviour. That is to say, the coordination of the expectations of thousands of people is only possible within a standardized institutional framework, that is, the relation that exists between individual action and each person's value judgements. We can establish this relation on two levels: on a general level, we can propose the study of ethics as part of a system of philosophical anthropology. However, this proposal goes beyond the limits of this study, in which we concentrate on a more concrete relation: and this is the importance of moral norms for the functioning of the market. In other words, we shall concentrate on the relation between ethics and the market.

Ethics and the market

In his work Mises wants to remain outside what he considers to be the world of value judgements in order to maintain a praxeological theory that does not admit value judgements. The people who have continued his work have criticized this attitude. Israel Kirzner says:

> In most of his work Mises never did confront the challenges of those who would question the *moral* justifiability of pure profit. It was enough to point to the wealth-and-welfare-enhancing consequences of the entrepreneur-driven market process.
>
> (Kirzner 1989: 63)

This commentary by Kirzner on Mises' position is totally appropriate and poses a serious objection to Mises' theory. Mises' utilitarian position considers that the acceptance of market economics because of its results is sufficient in itself. This position poses two problems.

Mises' work, as we demonstrated in Chapter two, has the aim of safeguarding the teachings of the economists because he considers that it is the economists who have made possible the progress of the West over the last two centuries. To defend these teachings he wrote *Theory and History*, a book which must be considered a praxeological analysis of the value systems that are not price systems. Even though he does not recognize it explicitly, all his theoretical labours are orientated to defending the existence of the market against theories which propose its disappearance through the use of arguments about social equality and distributive justice. These are all arguments based on moral considerations. Mises did not consider it necessary to use ethical arguments in defence of the market but focused his defence on demonstrating the advantages of adopting the market.

As Hoppe points out, the exclusion of ethics from the foundations of economics forces a utilitarian choice on the laws of economics: the market is accepted because it produces greater well-being. If economics is separated from its sociocultural base, then its only justification is its utilitarian acceptance of the maximum benefit. In his own words, '[if there is not a foundation in ethics] Liberalism is based on nothing but an arbitrary act of faith (however popular)' (Hoppe 1993: 204) – *an act of faith that is based on the belief that markets always tend to coordinate the actions of economic agents.* Rothbard offers the following example in order to refute this assumption:

> Let us for example assume again – and this assumption is not very far fetched in view of the record of human history – that the great majority of a society hate and revile redheads. Let us further assume that there are very few redheads in the society. This large majority then decides that it would like very much to murder all redheads. Here they are; the murder of redheads is high on the value-scales of the great majority of the public; there are few redheads so that there will be little loss in production on the market. How can Mises rebut this proposed policy either as a praxeologist or as a utilitarian liberal? . . . Neither praxeological economics *nor* Mises's utilitarian liberalism is sufficient to make the case for laissez faire and the free-market economy.
>
> (Rothbard 1998: 213)

Mises was one of the economists who insisted on demonstrating the universality of temporal preference in all human behaviour. His theory of capital was built on the measure of temporal preference that determines the rate of interest. The process of capitalist accumulation is explained as a deepening of the capital structure, which implies a low temporal preference in order for long-term projects to be undertaken. Using his theory of capital Mises recommends that investment plans should be undertaken which postpone consumption to an increasingly distant future because in that way capital is increased. But this recommendation contradicts his utilitarian position because as the value-free scientist he considers himself to be, he cannot try to criticize the measure or the proportion of temporal preference of each person.

Murray Rothbard in his book *The Ethics of Liberty* makes the following comment in this respect:

> And certainly, Mises, as a value-free scientist, could never presume to criticize anyone's *rate* of time preference, to say that A's was 'too high' or B's 'too low'. But, in that case and in the light of the high time-preference, the citizens of a community may reply to the praxeologist: 'perhaps this high tax and subsidy

policy will lead to the decline of capital; perhaps even the price control will lead to shortages, but I don't care. Having a high time-preference, I value more highly short-run subsidies, or the short-run enjoyment of buying the current goods at cheaper prices, than the prospect of suffering the future consequences'. And Mises, as a value-free scientist and opponent of any concept of objective ethics, *cannot* call them wrong.

(Rothbard 1998: 209)

These two objections indicate the line of logical development of praxeology. If it is necessary to admit social interrelations as a constituent part of the dynamic structure, then it is necessary to study the relation between ethics and the market using praxeology. The way to guarantee that the markets coordinate people's plans is to study the formation of the markets from the phenomena that originated them: human interrelations. This approach demonstrates that the markets function while they comply with a series of minimum norms. In other words, the markets have to institutionalize themselves in order to survive. In parallel with the origin of the markets there exist some moral norms that make it possible for the markets to emerge. These considerations, which will be treated in depth in Chapter five, make it possible to differentiate three aspects of social reality. Professor Huerta de Soto (1994) has made a scheme integrating the three levels of study of social reality:

- First level: interpretation of the results of the evolution.
- Second level: formal theory of the social process.
- Third level: formal ethical theory.

Within the Austrian School, there are often misunderstandings because a person does not specify on what level he is developing the analysis: historical studies are mixed with theories about action and with ethical theories. The three levels are related because reality, the object of study, is the union of the three: the person acts in a determined historical context, which provides himself with an ethical model of evaluation.

This book is developed on the second level. We are not going to study any determined historical period, nor are we going to present a determined ethical model of a way of life, showing how good it is and inviting people to adopt it. This study is going to concentrate on analysing the elements that are necessary and sufficient to explain the dynamic structure of the action. It is true that when analysing the evaluative element we have to deal with the ethical evaluative method. Our analysis is going to concentrate on determining the necessary analytical elements present in every ethical evaluation. But at no time are we going to present a model of the person which should be followed. To do this would be to focus on the third level. It is also true that the analysis of the structure of the action must emphasize the historicity of man. Time is a praxeological category that is basic for understanding the action as change over time, but this does not imply that we have to explain determined historical situations: we would pass to the first level if we did. Staying on the theoretical level, the praxeological theories allow us to explain the formation of markets, based on the ethical valuations prevailing in the historical contexts in which the markets arise.

In Chapter five we will analyse the theoretical advances proposed by Kirzner and Hoppe, who use praxeological models to explain the connection between ethics and the market. We will concentrate on the following two problems: (1) the criticisms of Kirzner, Hoppe and Rothbard of the utilitarianism of Mises. They develop the elements which Mises himself did not develop in his books: the role which value judgements play in the formation of the plans of persons. Value judgements are a constituent element in the perception of the system of ends and means. As J. A. Marina points out:

> The development of moral thought is parallel to the development of logical reasoning: a march toward the most stable equilibrium between intelligence and reality. Piaget sums up this idea in a spectacular and excessive statement, like all his statements: *logic is a moral of thought, as the moral is the logic of the action.*
>
> (Marina 1995: 51, my italics)

The evaluative element heeds the ethical criterion that the person learns in the sociocultural framework. The relation between social interrelations and market relations appears as a necessary element for the constitution of markets. The relation between markets and their sociocultural framework is fundamental because it constitutes the original framework of markets.

The praxeological categories: causality and time

The elements of the principal body of Mises' theory of action have already been expounded and we have sketched the developments which, starting from Mises' work, have made it possible to relate society, culture and individual action and to integrate ethics and the market. We now have to deal with the ramifications that arise from the axiom of action: causality and time as praxeological categories.

Causality

Chapter six presents the Misian study of causality. The treatment of causality undertaken by Mises starts by recognizing that the category of means and ends presupposes the cause–effect relation. This relation responds to the question: 'where and how must I interfere in order to divert the course of events from the way it would go in the absence of my interference in a direction which better suits my wishes?' (Mises 1996: 22) That is to say, the axiom of action implies causality as a praxeological category. Man has to know the causal relation in order to act. But this does not imply that we know for sure the cause of every phenomenon. The principle of causality has been posed in the search for the regularity of the phenomena, that is, in the search for laws, if A then B. However, Mises argues:

Sometimes we succeed in acquiring a partial knowledge so that we are able to say: in 70 per cent of all cases *A* results in *B*, in the remaining cases in *C*, or even in *D, E, F,* and so on.

(Mises 1996: 23)

When we do not know the cause for sure, we deal with probabilities. When Mises deals with probability he distinguishes two types of probability – of class or of frequency – and the probability of case.

Probability of class

Probability of class is used in the natural sciences. It deals with simple statements about the frequency with which the different results are often produced. Mises uses the following clarifying example:

> A doctor may determine the chances for the full recovery of his patient if he knows that 70 per cent of those afflicted with the same disease recover. If he expresses his judgment correctly, he will not say more than that the probability of recovery is 0.7, that is, that out of ten patients not more than three on the average die.

(Mises 1996: 110)

Probability of case

Probability of case, unlike the previous probability, supposes that we know some specific circumstances whose presence or absence give rise to the fact that a certain event is produced or not. Outside the field of probability of class, everything that is commonly understood under the term probability is concerned with that special way of reasoning employed to examine singular and individualized facts. This is the specific material of the historical sciences. This second type of probability appears in the sphere of human action, 'entirely ruled by teleology' (Mises 1996: 107).

This conception of causality represents a vicious circle between causality and the axiom of action. If on the one hand, causality is needed as a requisite of its axiom of action, then on the other hand it does not have at its disposition the causal relation until the event has finished:

> We are fully aware that in asserting this we are moving in a circle. For the evidence that we have correctly perceived a causal relation is provided only by the fact that action guided by this knowledge results in the expected outcome.

(Mises 1996: 23)

What solution does Mises offer? None, as can be deduced from the following: 'but we cannot avoid this vicious circular evidence precisely because causality is a category of action. And because it is such a category, praxeology cannot help bestowing some attention on this fundamental problem of philosophy' (Mises 1996: 23). In order to resolve the vicious circle of causality, we will use the dynamic structure of causation developed by Zubiri (2003), who undertook the study of causality from the point of view of the cause and not of the effect, as is often done in economics. Zubiri's study of causality makes it possible to break the vicious circle in which the axiom of action and the principle of causality find themselves in Mises's work. This last author takes as his starting point the Kantian theory of causality, according to which the temporal form of causality is the condition why the principle of causality is applied to real things. The knowledge of what has occurred beforehand is the first step to knowledge of the cause. In this temporal form of causality, the principle of causality is prior to the action. This situation originates Mises's vicious circle of causality: the causal principle precedes the action; but in order to know the cause which produces an effect, the action must be finished.

The vicious circle comes from placing the antecedents of the action in a time prior to the action. Let us look again at the following statement, which has already appeared in this chapter: *the person acts motivated by a future that exerts its effects on the present*. The antecedent of action, the cause does not precede the action in time, but the cause of the action is the desired reality which is projected into the future and to whose attainment we dedicate our present endeavour. In other words, in human action, the cause does not precede the action but is founded on the projective activity of man. Zubiri says:

> As I see the matter, it is essential that we introduce a type of what we might call 'personal causality'. The classical idea of causality (the four causes) is essentially molded upon natural things; it is a natural causality. But nature is just one mode of reality; there are also personal realities. And a metaphysical conceptualization of personal causality is necessary. The causality between persons *qua* persons cannot be fitted into the four classical causes. Nonetheless, it is strict causality.
>
> (Zubiri 1997c: 339)

The study of causality from the point of view of the effect and trying to seek the cause in a prior time is fully valid in the natural sciences. But in the social sciences, the field in which man acts, it is necessary to take into account that man pursues a future end, and it this end which exerts its effects on the present. With the concept of personal causality developed by Zubiri, the vicious circle between causality and the action disappears. *The cause is constituted within the dynamic structure of the action.* It is fundamental to emphasize that personal causality is not reducible to final causality. If we consider the final cause, we take it for granted that the end of the action is given. On the other hand, in personal causality the end is not given. It is constituted together with the discovery of the means in the process of the action. The use of the final cause makes it possible to create models in which the given ends are achieved mechanically with the given means. In these models there is no place for error and failure. Both possibilities are fully integrated, if we propose causality from the point of view of the person who generates his own ends as a further element in the process.

Time

It now remains for us to deal with time as a praxeological category. All of Becker's economic models represent the different points of equilibrium of a process and the balancing mechanism of the changes in the equilibrium. They are atemporal mathematical representations and in these models the historicity and futurity of man is not taken into account. The point of departure is a situation of equilibrium, and as many assumptions as may be necessary for the attainment of the equilibrium are introduced as logical antecedents. These models are a clear deformation of man's projective capacity. This human capacity is represented as the result of a monetary calculation. Kirzner points out in this respect:

> The analysis of equilibrium is identical with the Pure Logic of Choice; it consists essentially of tautologies that are necessarily true because they are merely transformations of the assumptions from which we start. These tautologies by themselves tell us nothing about the real world; they merely elaborate the conditions logically required for the equilibrium state to exist.
>
> (Kirzner 1979: 22)

These models work with the assumption of the self-fulfilment of the plans. To desire an end and to achieve it is all one and the same thing. They start from the given situation and analyse those antecedents in the past which prompted this situation.

It is true that every action is the result of a project, so we can explain, a posteriori, each fact as the logical result of its antecedents. But this explanation does not tell us anything about the origin and formation of the antecedents; about the dynamics of the process themselves. In order to explain the process it is necessary to distinguish two temporal aspects of the action: (1) the historicity of the person and (2) the temporal structure of the project. In Mises' work the analysis of action starts from the fluid reality of the person. He points out: 'the concepts of change and of time are inseparably linked together. Action aims at change and is therefore in the temporal order' (Mises 1996: 99). When we say that time flows, we are referring to the fact that there only exists the present time of the action. The past does not exist any more; the future is *yet to be done*, there only exists the present. Reality is flowing. It goes precisely from the past to the future. Mises notes that 'action is as such in the real present because it utilizes the instant and thus embodies its reality' (Mises 1996: 100). If we pay heed to this fluid reality, man is pure historicity.

However, man can leave the present and project himself into the future in order to make a representation of his own acts. Man forms a future project because, being a fluid reality, he is counting on the totality of time. In the project, the person is represented sequentially, that is, in temporal order, the ordering of the means for the securing of the end. These two elements allow us to explain the structure of the project. In Chapter seven we shall see its temporal and informative structure. The first structure is very closely linked with the second. On the one hand, the projection is based on the fluidity of the action; the relevant information is created during the same action, but this information is projected into the future to plan the system of means and ends. In short, the temporal structure of the project is erected on the historicity of the person.

4 The discovery of means and the creation of possibilities

Introduction

In this chapter we are going to introduce the concept of pure entrepreneurship. Israel Kirzner recognizes that his theory is based on the existence of an entrepreneurial element in *all human action*. The whole critique of the neoclassical characterization of economic behaviour that Kirzner makes in his book *Competition and Entrepreneurship* has its starting point in the sentence 'My identification of an entrepreneurial element within human action which is by definition excluded from economizing simply repeats Mises's assertion that the entrepreneurial function – the action seen from its *speculative* aspect – is inherent in *every* action' (Kirzner 1973: 86). Kirzner's point of departure can be found in Mises' *Human Action* (1996). The following paragraph is taken from this book:

> Economics, in speaking of entrepreneurs, has in view not men, but a definite function. This function is not the particular feature of a special group or class of men; it is inherent in every action and burdens every actor. In embodying this function in an imaginary figure, we resort to a methodological makeshift. The term entrepreneur as used by catallactic theory means: acting man exclusively seen from the aspect of the uncertainty inherent in every action. In using this term one must never forget that every action is embedded in the flux of time and therefore involves a speculation. The capitalists, the landowners, and the laborers are by necessity speculators. So is the consumer in providing for anticipated future needs. There's many a slip 'twixt cup and lip.
>
> (Mises 1996: 252)

All the elements that make up the action are mentioned in this paragraph: projection into the future, the historicity of the person, evaluation and error. The person, by the fact of being the actor of his own life, anticipates, evaluates and commits errors. If we have started from the man of flesh and blood to study economic behaviour, then the key to understanding him depends on us having a clear idea of what we are referring to, when we talk about the entrepreneurial ability of human beings.

This chapter will be developed in the following way: first, it is necessary to introduce the concept of pure entrepreneurship, as I. Kirzner has developed it in his work, in order to understand that entrepreneurship is the creative ability of people. This ability can be understood as ranging from the mere realization of the price differences existing in the market to a more general view in which entrepreneurship is understood as the ability of every person to make projections of new means and ends of action, regarding the totality of the reality that surrounds him. We will explain how this creative ability, which everybody possesses to a greater or lesser degree, can be defined as the ability to create new possibilities of action. Thus pure entrepreneurship cannot be reduced to a productive factor because it is not something that is given as a variable of a production function, but rather it is something prior and more radical. Entrepreneurship is the perception that undertaking this productive action may be profitable.

Second, entrepreneurship cannot be reduced to objective knowledge, like scientific knowledge. Entrepreneurship is the subjective ability to use objective knowledge. It is not objective knowledge of market conditions because this data is known with absolute certainty. Pure entrepreneurship is the ability to make future projections from the information given and to imagine the possibilities of profit. It is knowledge about what to do with the information. To sum up, in this part of the book we will expound the concept of entrepreneurship as being the ability of every person to make projections about the ends of action and to generate the means necessary to undertake the said action.

If we understand entrepreneurship as being the key concept, we can then ask the following question: if this entrepreneurship is universal, that is to say, if man exercises it every time he acts, will not its use be appropriate in all social interactions? If entrepreneurship serves to explain the process of the coordination of individual actions in the market process, will not this concept be necessary to understand the coordination process of any social institution? These questions are clearly encompassed within the line of research initiated by Hayek on the essence of the economic order. For the first time, he defines the economic problem as the search for coordination among the thousands of people who interact in the market. They are people who have at their disposal incomplete information about what they want and the way to achieve their ends. This ability to manage this dispersed, imperfect, tacit information, in order to make projections of the ends and means of action, is what we identify as the pure entrepreneurship of every person. Thus the economic problem cannot be reduced to the allocation of *given* resources.[1] Starting with these seminal ideas, Hayek developed valuable contributions to the social sciences, establishing what has been called 'the knowledge problem'. This poses the general social problem of explaining the evolutionary process of social institutions, and this process can be defined as the coordination of the persons who act with their limited knowledge. In this chapter we are going to make an outline sketch that will allow us to understand this process of social coordination by using pure entrepreneurship. We will redevelop the problem of knowledge, taking as our starting point the concept of pure entrepreneurship as we have defined it, and then we will explain the process of institutional coordination as a process of interaction among thousands of people, who by exercising their entrepreneurial function create new possibilities of action, which are culturally transmitted. These developments will occupy the fifth section, entitled 'The entrepreneurial function and the sociocultural framework of individual action'.

Kirzner severely criticizes the viability of this line of investigation. In fact, he goes so far as to state clearly that it is not viable (Kirzner 1992: 179; 2000: 264–5). To provide a basis for his statement, Kirzner proposes significant differences regarding the problem of knowledge that limits the coordinating role of the entrepreneurial function in the market. In my opinion, his statement is paradoxical for the following reason: the fact that every institution evolves is unquestionable. So, continual opportunities for profit arise in the market, and similarly in other social institutions there arise new possibilities of action, whether they are new words that enrich the vocabulary, new fashion trends or new forms of cultural expression, etc. Second, if we accept that entrepreneurship is the creative ability that is exercised in every human action, which is to say, if we accept that this ability is exercised constantly in the search for new ends and means, why limit its scope of application to the market? Do the praxeological categories, which lay claim to be universals, as Mises has established, now only have partial value for the market?

In my opinion, the objective that Kirzner is pursuing when he distinguishes between 'the knowledge problem A' and 'the knowledge problem B' is directed to the real fundamental problem, that is, the mechanism that each institution has developed, so that each person can appropriate the benefits of his entrepreneurial function. Kirzner poses the real problem in the following terms: 'in order to "switch on" the alertness of a potential discoverer to socially significant opportunities, they must offer gain to the potential discoverer himself' (Kirzner 1985: 29). So for example in the market, this mechanism is the price system. However, the way in which he proposes the difference between the two knowledge problems, starting with static market situations, conceals the dynamism of transmission and the formation of expectations that is necessary for the coordination of individual actions in any social institution. That is, starting from the fact that the social institutions serve to establish norms and coordinate the actions of people, will it not be necessary to inquire into praxeology to understand this coordinating process and also to understand the price mechanism as a particular case of institutional coordination? Therefore, in the fourth section the distinctions posed by Kirzner will be expounded; that is, the real problem that he poses and the re-elaboration of the relation between the knowledge problems 'A' and 'B' which, in my opinion, would make it possible to begin a theoretical line of explanation into the coordination process of any social institution based on the concept of entrepreneurial function. This will serve as an introduction to the explanation of the process of institutional coordination, expounded in the fifth section, as has already been mentioned.

In the last part of this chapter we will analyse the relation that exists between the market and its institutional framework in the light of what has been described in the previous sections. We will analyse the institutional framework of the market from the point of view of the requirements that are necessary in the process of social coordination. This approach will serve as an introduction to the discussion of the relation between ethics and the market, which is developed in Chapter five.

Kirzner's pure entrepreneurship

Kirzner defines pure entrepreneurship as 'that element of alertness to possible newly worthwhile goals and to possibly new available resources' (Kirzner 1973: 35). He uses this meaning to define pure entrepreneurship as being alert to opportunities which previously remained concealed (Kirzner 1973: 36).

This entrepreneurship makes the action something active, creative and human. The perception of the system of ends and means is none other than the result of the person's entrepreneurial activity. In this section we are going to concentrate on this concept because, as Kirzner points out:

> Once the entrepreneurial element in human action is perceived, one can no longer interpret the decision as merely calculative – capable in principle of being yielded by mechanical manipulation of the 'data' or already *completely implied* in these data. One must now recognize that the human decision cannot be explained purely in terms of maximization of 'passive' reaction that takes the form of adopting the 'best' course of action as marked out by the circumstances.
>
> (Kirzner 1973: 35)

Mises' economic principle becomes the principle of action because by means of pure entrepreneurship we can explain how it is constituted and how it varies the system of means and ends. However, the concept of pure entrepreneurship in Kirzner's work has been continually enriched and it gives the impression of referring to different human situations and abilities:

1   There are times when he understands entrepreneurship as the discovery of opportunities: dis-cover is to find an outlet for something that is there. As Kirzner says: 'entrepreneurship is discovering opportunities which are there, "just round the corner"' (Kirzner 1979: 7). According to this version, the person only has 'to know where these unexploited opportunities exist' (Kirzner 1973: 41). He realizes that the opportunities are there and that the person only has to find them, like someone looking for a hidden object. So we can understand his following text: 'I view the entrepreneur not as a source of innovative ideas ex nihilo, but as a being *alert* to the opportunities that exist *already* and that are waiting to be noticed' (Kirzner 1973: 74).

2   Starting from Kirzner (1985), the concept of pure entrepreneurship has been enlarged. Until that book, entrepreneurship was reduced to arbitrating price differences in a given situation. In this situation, entrepreneurship does not take into account the passage of time and is reduced to realizing the existence of something that already exists. It is clear that entrepreneurship is alertness to the opportunities for profit.[2] But Kirzner goes on to ask the question, what

happens when we introduce the passage of time? What is entrepreneurship when we analyse the market over different periods? A fundamental praxe-ological category appears: the passage of time, that is to say, the future.[3] When we enlarge the basic framework of a given situation, typical of the neoclassical model, and we introduce basic anthropological characteristics of the person, such as the future, we need concepts that draw together the richness that persons manifest in the action. The concept of entrepreneurship has to be enriched by making room for the inherent characteristics of every action. In our case, entrepreneurship must include creativity. As Kirzner points out: 'in particular the futurity that entrepreneurship must confront introduces the possibility that the entrepreneur may, by his own creative actions, in fact *construct* the future as *he* wishes it to be' (Kirzner 1985: 63).

This enriching of the concept of entrepreneurship was consolidated in his later works, principally in Kirzner (1989). The following text is proof of this:

> The producer is not, that is, seen as entitled to the product because he pro-duced it by transforming and combining inputs over which he had just title. Rather, the producer is seen as entitled to the product because he genuinely originated the product *ex nihilo*; he originated it by 'discovering', in entre-preneurial fashion, an opportunity to fashion a product out of items (which themselves, up until this discovery, did not at all constitute that product, even in inchoate form). Jones, the producer of a ladder out of lumber found at the bottom of his deep hole, originated that ladder out of nothing but a gleam in his eye.
>
> (Kirzner 1989: 150)

In the light of these two texts the question arises, is pure entrepreneurship creative or not? Because, as we have seen, we can use this concept in a reduced version, like arbitrage, or we can amplify it to include creativity.[4] A practical reply would indicate that we employ the concept according to the problem we are dealing with. So, for example, if we propose a choice at a given moment, it is advisable to use the reduced version. In this situation, we do not need creativity as a determin-ing element in the choice. At first sight, this reply appears to be correct, provided that we are aware that this reduction prevents us from explaining the dynamic process that has originated it. That is, although only for practical reasons, we have reduced real human action to the neoclassical *homo economicus*. This however is no longer admissible, because if we want to enrich *homo economicus* with the inherent characteristics of human action, like futurity, then the basic hypotheses of the model, namely the stability of preferences over time, maximizing behaviour and market equilibrium, must be abandoned.[5] Therefore the reduced version of the concept of entrepreneurship must be abandoned right away. This practical decision has the extremely high cost of sacrificing the theoretical model that explains the real process that originates prices. In consequence, for praxeology the concept of entrepreneurship that is suitable for approaching all human behaviour has to include creativity because this allows us to differentiate, with precision, two subjects that are closely linked but are analytically distinct.

The first subject that appears when dealing with entrepreneurship is its creative ability. The person transcends the reality around him and *creates possibilities about the real properties of things.* There are realities that have been known for a long time. For example, in the nineteenth century in the North American State of Texas, it was known that the grasslands, where a black viscous substance oozed, were very poor as pasture. It was enough for man to discover that with the physical-chemical properties of oil he could propel mechanical motors, for these grasslands to make Texas the richest state in the USA.[6]

Let us return to the example that Kirzner offered us of a certain Jones. He invents the ladder using the actual properties of wood. The wood, as a physical reality, already existed before Jones noticed it. It was a reality with certain physical-chemical properties. But Jones does not concern himself with the properties of wood, *rather he imagines what he can do with them, and on the basis of that reality, he creates the ladder.*

The following example allows us to understand more clearly the difference between discovery as the creation of possibilities and the existing reality about which the possibility is discovered (Kirzner 1989: 152). A person loses a coin in the street. For this person, the loss of the money means that the possibility of buying a loaf of bread, which he had in mind, disappears, even though the coin as a physical reality continues existing. However, if another person, by his alertness, discovers the coin on a corner of the pavement, he does not discover the physical-chemical reality of the coin – which interests him very little; rather, at the actual moment of seeing the coin, he imagines the different goods he could buy with it. In other words, this second person imagines the different ends that he can achieve with that recently discovered monetary means.

The second subject that appears when dealing with the discovery of means is the scope for deploying the person's alertness. Reality in its widest sense is susceptible to becoming the means. Anything, whether material or immaterial, can become a means as soon as anyone perceives that it can be an opportunity for profit. In this sense, Kirzner talks about the world as a reality surrounding us full of opportunities for profit. The opportunities are there. The following extract corroborates this view of entrepreneurship:

> our world *is* a grossly inefficient world. What is inefficient about the world is surely that, at each instant, enormous scope exits for improvements that are in one way or another ready to hand and yet are simply not noticed.
>
> (Kirzner 1979: 135)

If we bear in mind these two aspects – the creative ability of the entrepreneurial function and the world ambit in which it is deployed – *we can define pure entrepreneurship as the deployment of the creative capacity of the person in the reality around him.* The title of this chapter refers to these two pillars on which pure entrepreneurship rests: the creative capacity of man and the ambit in which this activity is deployed. In the following section we will develop the concept of creativity inherent in pure entrepreneurship and its implications so that, second, we can concentrate on the ambit in which the person exercises his entrepreneurial function. This ambit is not reduced only to the market. All reality that has meaning for the human agent is the field of action for entrepreneurship. Therefore the importance of society and culture, as constituent elements of individual action (*Lebenswelt*), is based not on external considerations, but on the fact that both elements, together with individual action, constitute 'the human', where the human agent develops the entrepreneurial function.

Development of the concept of pure entrepreneurship

Pure entrepreneurship and productive resources

In order to comprehend pure entrepreneurship as the creative ability of man it is necessary to overcome a series of obstacles. The first is to consider that the productive resources that we have at our disposal limit production. In this interpretation there is a tendency to consider entrepreneurship as a mere productive factor. Thus the opportunity for profit does not depend on the person, but on the fact that the production of this profit is the result of the activity of the resource. The only thing that the person has to do is to realize that there are certain resources that have some inherent possibilities of development. The following example is quite clear: fruit trees are the result of the development of their fruits. The oak tree is already implicit in the acorn: the activity for why there are oak trees has its origin in nature itself. Man can only profit from the fruits that nature offers; the possibilities depend entirely on the resources. In this view it is the material resources that determine the result of the action. The whole result of the production is attributed to the resources themselves. In this interpretation man has a passive role.

If we hold to this passive interpretation of entrepreneurship, there is no way we can explain productive improvements. Must we interpret the agricultural revolution of the seventeenth century as an action of nature itself? The human element based on the rationalization of the crops – the use of rotation and fallow land – cannot be explained by reducing these facts to the power of nature, because this improvement in production was an action which nature received. In other words, nature was a passive object of the improvements actively introduced by man. This reflection admits entrepreneurial capacity. But how do we admit it? We can consider that this entrepreneurial capacity is another necessary productive factor. Thus we will consider that entrepreneurship is a transforming factor that the producer needs in order to transform the resource into the final product. However, this consideration ignores the fact that entrepreneurial talent is not one more instrument within the reach of the decision-maker, that is, something that is employed consciously and deliberately to achieve an objective that has previously been noticed and desired. Kirzner points out that this view ignores the fact that entrepreneurial talent is not an instrument for the attainment of an end:

[entrepreneurship] *is* the perception of the worthwhile possibility and desirability of that objective . . . entrepreneurial decision making is not the conversion of inputs into outputs; it is the determination that an attempt to convert inputs into outputs is worthwhile and desirable.

(Kirzner 1989: 148)

The essence of entrepreneurship is in the active alertness of the person. Alertness, as Kirzner says, 'does not refer to a passive vulnerability to the impressions impinging on his consciousness during experience in the manner of a piece of film exposed to the light' (Kirzner 1979: 29). Therefore the role of the person in the discovery of the means is active. It is not possible to consider this activity as a productive factor, because entrepreneurship is not manifested in the production, but rather it is implicit in this. Before undertaking a project, the person must perceive the opportunity for profit. In Kirzner's words:

The essence of individual entrepreneurship is that it consists of an alertness in which the decision is *embedded* rather than being one of the ingredients *deployed* in the course of decision making. This sets it altogether apart from being a class of productive factor.

(Kirzner 1979: 181)

Entrepreneurial function and knowledge

There are times when Kirzner uses, as an example of entrepreneurial function, a situation in which a person realizes that in one place a product is being sold too expensively and in another place too cheaply. This person perceives an opportunity for a profit if he buys a little more expensively where the product is sold cheaply, and sells it a little more cheaply where it is sold expensively. Given this example, it is very tempting to conceive pure entrepreneurship as being a greater knowledge of the opportunities for profit. Thus the person with a greater knowledge of the products and prices is considered a better entrepreneur than the person who has less knowledge of market conditions. The entrepreneur obtains certain benefits by exploiting this greater knowledge.

This reduction of entrepreneurship to mere knowledge is not acceptable because entrepreneurship is not a productive factor, as we have seen in the previous paragraph. Knowledge, understood as scientific knowledge of the world, can be employed as a productive factor in the market: the most important expert in whatever the material may be can be hired or the best book on the subject can be bought. Entrepreneurship, therefore, is not the objective, scientific knowledge that can be obtained in the market. The difference between entrepreneurship and objective knowledge lies in the fact that alertness is a *human activity*. Entrepreneurship serves to define economic behaviour in a world without perfect knowledge. Although Kirzner defines alertness as 'the abstract, very general and rarefied kind of knowledge' (Kirzner 1973: 69), strictly speaking, the entrepreneurial function is not knowledge, but the human ability to make projections into the future and to create new possibilities of action. It is an ability that is not exhausted with the discovery of new means or a new end.

Within the neoclassical model of complete information there is no room for pure entrepreneurship. In a world of objective information, the decision to exploit a production is implicit in the market data. On the other hand, the creative ability of the person is played out in a world full of uncertainty and errors. It is these errors, once they have been discovered, that make it possible to realize the opportunities that are being wasted. Referring to the use of the entrepreneurial function in the market, Kirzner states:

> We can hardly deny that the opportunities for pure entrepreneurial profit are generated by the imperfection of knowledge on the part of market participants; that these opportunities can be seized by anyone discovering their existence before others have done so; and that the process of winning these profits is at the same time a process of correcting market ignorance.
>
> (Kirzner 1973: 67)

Entrepreneurship in all Kirzner's works is the search for a profit. It should not be interpreted as in the neoclassical model, where profit is the result of comparing known alternatives. In Kirzner's context the comparisons are totally distinct. In the perception of a possibility, there is no comparison of known alternatives because these do not exist; they are in a future imagined by the human agent. As Kirzner says: 'the incentive of entrepreneurship is to try to get something for nothing, if only one can see what it is that can be done' (Kirzner 1979: 11). This is the defining characteristic that Kirzner's theoretical advance implies. The action is the result of the individual's ability at making projections and his ability to imagine the future. The antecedents of the action should be looked for not in the past but in the attempt to extract from a future, that does not exist, a more profitable present.

Every person, when undertaking a project, ventures on an enterprise. As Marina explains in his book:

> The creator ventures on an enterprise. My admirable Covarrubias defined the word venture: to be determined to deal with some arduous and difficult business *and because the knights used to paint these signs on their shields, they were called enterprises. In this way the enterprise is a certain symbol or enigmatic figure, made with a particular end in view, directed to attaining what he wants.* What is unleashed in the entrepreneurial activity of the human agent is that symbol or enigmatic figure that only he knows how to decipher.
>
> (Marina 1993: 161, my italics)

Each person, however ordinary he may be, undertakes a project outside his zone of immediate development. Human beings have the ability to find information that motivates them to act. If we reduce the entrepreneurial function to mere knowledge, there is no place for creative ability. This ability consists in seeing more possibilities where apparently there are none. It does not mean, as is often said, that people with great creative ability need little information to carry out great enterprises, but rather it should be understood as being the other way round: these people are able to create more practical information than the rest of the people. This does not mean limiting the entrepreneurial function only to the great geniuses. Every person, by the fact of being a person, has that capacity which is not reducible to knowledge.

The following example shows clearly the essence of the entrepreneurial function: the human hand is a perfect example of the creative ability of man. The hand is the transformation of an animal hoof into an instrument of instruments (Aristotle, *On the Soul*, III, 432a; Hamlyn 1968). In reality, the hand is a capacity for action. Let us pick up a stick (Polo 1993: 64). With a stick I can hit harder than with my hand. But a stick is useless against a big animal like a buffalo, for example. The stick itself does not offer the solution. But man's inventiveness makes it possible to sharpen the stick, so that it can be used to wound the animal and reach its vital organs. So man transforms the stick into a lance. The lance is not the stick. The origin of the lance is the transformation of the stick into a cultural symbol. The stick is nature, but the lance is a symbol of intelligent behaviour. It is culture. The process of making something possible is only explicable through the creative ability of the entrepreneurial function. The possibility of hunting bigger animals demands sticks of a certain thickness. Research is done into new ways of strengthening the point by using fire. The most important thing is that the stick's use prompts new questions. Why is a lance suitable for hunting a buffalo but inefficient with faster animals? The lance is too heavy for hunting gazelles. One needs something lighter. The solution was to be found in reducing the weight of the lance, so creating the javelin. Man applies his intelligence when he practises his manual skills: his hands become the inventors of increasingly complex instruments. The bow and arrow appears and animals are domesticated, etc.[7] Against Kirzner's position of limiting the scope of the entrepreneurial function to the market, the extension of this concept to all fields of human activity enables us to understand social interrelations and the emergence of social institutions as human creations.

The scope of pure entrepreneurship in Kirzner's work

Introduction

In Kirzner's famous article 'Knowledge problems and their solutions: some relevant distinctions' (Kirzner 1992: 163–79) he limits the scope of application of pure entrepreneurship to market phenomena. In his opinion the creative ability, the essence of pure entrepreneurship, only allows us to understand the functioning of the markets and does not throw any light on the formation and maintenance of social institutions, such as language and law, etc. The entrepreneurial function serves to explain the spontaneous coordination which occurs in markets, but he states that the explanation of the coordinating role of social institutions, if it exists, must be found elsewhere (Kirzner 1992: 179). This idea of limiting the coordinating role of the entrepreneurial function to the market is maintained in his later work. In his very interesting article 'Rationality, entrepreneurship, and economic "imperialism"' (Kirzner 2000: 258–71) he states:

> Outside the market context we have nothing, within the realm of economic theory, upon which we can rely to generate any systematically rapid processes of mutual discovery that might tend to eliminate episodes of social sub optimality (caused by sheer ignorance).
>
> (Kirzner 2000: 265)

There are two important points to comment on here concerning the limitation of entrepreneurship as the coordinating force in the market: first, the importance of the real problem which Kirzner indicates, and second, the theoretical way of posing this problem. With regard to the importance of the real problem which is dealt with by Professor Kirzner, it is necessary to state that it is very important. In any institution there must exist an incentive that enables the person to appropriate for himself the results of his actions. This incentive, which stimulates the attainment of the ends and the search for the means of the action, is guaranteed in the market by the price system. This is because each human agent projects his actions into the future by means of a cost–benefit calculation. Besides, the price system transmits, rapidly and efficiently, the profit opportunities that are constantly generated in the market. Therefore, the price system is essential for the coordination of individual plans in the market. Outside the market, what guarantees that the plans tend to coordinate, and that each human agent can appropriate the results of his actions for himself? This is a real and important problem that occurs all the time.

Second, to pose this real problem in theory leads us to a paradoxical situation which can be described in the following way:[8] if, in order to explain the behaviour of a multi-period market, we have had to admit creative ability and we also recognize that this entrepreneurial function is found in every human action, how can its scope of application be limited to a particular case of actions? Is it not paradoxical that the universality of Mises' praxeology only has a partial application? If we recognize, as Kirzner does (Kirzner 2000: 264), that the social institutions tend to coordinate, what is the praxeological element needed in order to explain this coordinating process? In my opinion, this apparent paradox has a solution when we analyse the role of prices in the market. As Kirzner explains lucidly, the market needs institutional prerequisites to function. They constitute the limits of the market (Kirzner 2000: 77–88). But is not this institutional framework the result of social interrelations? And in its turn, are not the prices the results of social interactions? These questions suggest that prices are a necessary element, but that they are not sufficient for the market to coordinate. The sufficient condition is the creation of an institutional framework and so there exist in the market two types of institutional conditions: the external ones that guarantee a stable framework for the individual action, and the internal ones, which guarantee the appropriation of the exercise of entrepreneurship.

We are not involved, therefore, in looking for a substitute for prices in order to understand the coordinating force in the social institutions, but rather in the need to analyse the dynamic process which constitutes the institutions as a basic element of individual action. It is necessary to start from the primary reality of the personal action in the historical context with some determined institutions and culture, in order to understand the coordination process of the social interactions. One should then apply this knowledge to verify if the market manages to generate a stable institutional framework that allows for individual action. In other words, the market does not coordinate only because it has a price system. The market tends to coordinate if the development of the entrepreneurial function generates an institutional framework that guarantees the development of people's creative ability. Our apparent paradox can be expressed in the following way: the individual action needs an institutional framework which is in its turn the result of individual actions. And its solution is proposed by recognizing one sole problem of knowledge: *the coordinating tendency of social interactions*, in which each individual exercises his entrepreneurial function for the attainment of his ends. So it is necessary to extend the scope of the application of the entrepreneurial function to every institutional process and this enlargement will allow us, at the end of the chapter, to understand the relation between the external and internal limits of the market and to introduce the relation between the market and ethics, which is dealt with in the fifth chapter.

'The Knowledge Problem' in Kirzner

Kirzner's position, which causes him to limit entrepreneurship to the market, starts by differentiating two distinct problems within what has been called 'the problem of knowledge'. He gives this name to study of the role of knowledge in the economy, following on from the pioneering works of Hayek. Kirzner differentiates two different situations in the problem posed by the use of subjective information:

1   He defines what he calls 'the knowledge problem A'. This first situation is described like this because in the market there are situations of disequilibrium that are known and are therefore self-correcting. For example: let us suppose that the sellers hope to sell at higher prices than those which the buyers are willing to pay, and that for their part, the buyers hope to buy at lower prices than those at which the sellers are willing to sell. This market situation is characterized 'by the unrealism of over-optimistic expectations (both for the sellers and for buyers)' (Kirzner 1992: 171). This situation tends to be *self-revealing* as the buyers and sellers adjust their price expectations to the real conditions of the market. Economic theory explains this situation by means of the general conditions of market functioning: with excess supply, prices fall and with excess demand, they rise. Therefore, 'the process whereby Knowledge Problem A is solved is a process which, without relying on entrepreneurial, profit-motivated alertness arises from well-high inevitable learning of the unrealism of over-optimistic expectations' (Kirzner 1992: 171).

2   'The knowledge problem B' is different. This second situation arises from
     ignorance of the disequilibriums in the market. Let us suppose there is a market
     divided into two parts. Each of the parts has an equilibrium situation, so that
     each half has a different price. The existence of two prices for the same good
     means that those people who pay the higher price ignore the possibility of
     buying more cheaply in the other market; and those people who sell at a lower
     price ignore the possibility of selling at a higher price in the other market.
     According to Kirzner, this second problem can be resolved in a different way
     from the previous one: 'whereas Knowledge Problem A was self-correcting,
     Knowledge Problem B created *an incentive for its solution by discovery in the activity
     of profit-alert entrepreneurs*' (Kirzner 1992: 170). The process for resolving this
     situation depends entirely on the discovery of the opportunities for profit by
     the entrepreneurs.

To sum up, Kirzner proposes the study of the knowledge problem in the markets
by differentiating between two situations: (1) Situations where the disequilibriums disappear without pure entrepreneurship having to intervene: the market
is self-regulating. This situation corresponds to 'the knowledge problem A'.
(2) Situations where there exist constant disequilibriums that the market does
not tend to correct. The correction of these situations depends on entrepreneurs discovering the latent opportunities for profit in the disequilibriums. There
is room for pure entrepreneurship: this situation corresponds to 'the knowledge
problem B'.

    These two situations, which appear in the market, are also found in more
extensive ambits where people act. Kirzner offers the example of the old non-
metric measuring system in Britain to illustrate 'the knowledge problem' in its two
versions outside the market context: we will consider the generalized use of a
pattern of measures. Let us take the British system of measures in feet and inches.
This system is more complex than the metric system but because of its generalized
use in Great Britain, people in the area where it is in use expect that other people
will measure with this system. The system of feet and inches prevails only when
each person expects the others to use this system. People learn to use the British
system of measures without any central direction and they expect the rest of
the people to use it too. The use of this system of measures consists of a system
of expectations that tend to coordinate mutually one with another. As Kirzner
points out:

> The system is based on the concurrence of expectations on the part of millions
> of members of society. No one of them is disappointed in his expectations that
> the others will employ the system. The usefulness of the system depends
> entirely and solely upon the successful solution of Knowledge Problem A.
>
> (Kirzner 1992: 172)

The resolution of 'the knowledge problem A' is vital for the survival of the
institutions. The fulfilment of the expectations, which are to be found in the use of

the institution, generates a coordinating tendency that guarantees that everybody maintains the institutional order. In our example, the generalized use of the British system of measures guarantees its maintenance and the resolution of the problem 'A'.

Let us suppose that starting from this situation, a series of people realize that the decimal metric system is superior to the British one because it enables the number of units of measurement to be reduced as well as reducing costs. With this possibility of entrepreneurial profit, Kirzner wonders if there exists any co-ordinating force which makes it possible to impose the decimal system over the British one. He argues that no grounds exist that will guarantee the adoption of the new system, because 'even if some (or all) were to become so aware, they (correctly) believe others (even where they are so aware) not to be using the metric system (because they *believe* that nobody is using the system)' (Kirzner 1992: 174). And what profit would the entrepreneur make by using the metric system? How could he convince the population, which uses the British system without any problems, of the advantages of the decimal system, or at least, generate expectations that other people would want to use only the metric system from that moment on? There are no grounds, concludes Kirzner, that could guarantee that 'the knowledge problem B' could be resolved. In the market this problem has a guaranteed solution because the profits from the discovery of opportunities can be attributed to the entrepreneur; on the other hand, in the most general case of the system of measures, there is no way to guarantee attractive private profits for the entrepreneurs because the profit would be diluted among all the members who adopt the new system. In Kirzner's opinion there exists a clear situation of externality that blocks the solution to 'the knowledge problem B'. To sum up, the market resolves both problems because the profits of the entrepreneurial activity are always attributable to the individual entrepreneur. But this situation cannot be extrapolated to the institutions in general because, though it is true that their maintenance depends on the resolution of the problem 'A', there is no guarantee for the solution to problem 'B'. There is no method that makes it possible to attribute the profits of the entrepreneurial function to the individual entrepreneur. Kirzner states:

> If this contention of ours be accepted, we will surely have established grounds for challenging any assertion that spontaneous processes are able, in general, to generate not only stable institutions expressing mutually sustaining expectations, but also tendencies, parallel to those operating in markets to solve Knowledge Problem B.
>
> (Kirzner 1992: 173)

The relation between 'the knowledge problems A and B'

As we have seen, Mises' work has gaps which it is necessary to eliminate, and Kirzner's contribution of the concept of pure entrepreneurship has been a funda-mental step in doing this. However, in my opinion the treatment that he offers of 'the knowledge problem' not only means reducing praxeology as an explanatory theory of market phenomena but also reduces pure entrepreneurship to a merely passive and mechanical allocation of given ends and means.

Faced with this situation, it is appropriate to proceed to a detailed analysis of Kirzner's article. He begins with a study of the market in static equilibrium: 'consider a single commodity market in competitive equilibrium. A market clearing price prevails' (Kirzner 1992: 166). Surprisingly, Kirzner begins with a neoclassical model of an equilibrium situation under perfect competition! Given this model of perfect competition, 'the knowledge problem A' consists of the disappearance of the excesses of supply and demand, depending on the complete information that the buyers and the sellers possess of the functioning of the market. The problem 'A' is resolved on reaching Pareto's Optimum. The second problem arises when introducing the concept of pure entrepreneurship, starting from a situation of equilibrium under perfect competition, and admitting man's ability to make projections and the discovery of opportunities for profit. This second problem is resolved in the market because the entrepreneurs perceive the opportunities for profit which the Paretian Suboptimums offer to entrepreneurial alertness. These are profits that the entrepreneur can award himself in their totality within the mechanism of the market. Therefore, Kirzner says: '"the knowledge problem B" is solved by means of the attainment of a Paretian Optimum in the equilibrium of the market' (Kirzner 1992: 174).

This starting point is problematic as a development of praxeology for one fundamental reason. In this article Kirzner begins with market equilibrium under perfect competition and then introduces pure entrepreneurship. This basis demonstrates that a pre-existing sociocultural framework sustains markets. This dependence of the markets on a framework of general rules for their functioning, rules which are known by all the participants, is what Kirzner identifies as 'the knowledge problem A'. This problem is real and supposes a key discovery by Kirzner, when he demonstrates the relation between markets and their extra-economic basis. Another of Kirzner's key discoveries is recognizing that markets and institutions must find a place for people's creative ability. The ability to make projections must have some channels which allow it to develop. Therefore, the survival of markets and institutions depends on the solution that is given to 'the knowledge problem B'. In short, Kirzner is right when he identifies the reality that he wants to analyse: *the relation which exists in every institution between the framework of general rules which sustain the interrelations, and the development of the creative ability of the person in the institutional context.*

In my opinion, it is not enough to consider that the guarantee of a solution in the market to the two problems is that, through prices, the entrepreneur can award himself the whole profit from the exercise of his activity. The price system is a necessary condition, but it is not enough. The reality is that the market resolves both problems because, like any institution that wants to survive, it offers channels for the development of people's creative ability. The key to understanding the two problems is the role that pure entrepreneurship plays in any ambit where the human being acts. If the market has a coordinating effect, it is due to the fact that it becomes an institution where people's creative ability can be developed. If we apply this concept, we immediately detect that the creative ability of the person acts in all the ambits of action and that both problems of knowledge are very closely linked. Although we can separate them analytically, the existence of problem 'B' presupposes the solution to problem 'A' *and we are going to demonstrate that the solution to the problem 'A' implies the solution to problem 'B'.*[9] So Kirzner's conclusion to limit the coordinating role of the entrepreneurial function in the solution of both problems only to market phenomena prevents the fact from being understood that in every institution, including the market, the solutions to the two problems are inseparable. The fact that both problems are solved in the market depends entirely on the same elements that solve the two problems in other institutions.

If we accept the Misian theory, Kirzner's conclusions are troublesome. His analysis inverts the lines of investigation proposed by Mises' methodological subjectivism. In order to demonstrate that in any institution the solution to problem 'A' implies the solution to problem 'B', it is necessary to carry out the opposite process. Kirzner begins with market phenomena when the correct way is to begin with social interactions. In Misian orthodoxy, the first step in the analysis is to study the action of the entrepreneurial function on the sociocultural framework. People's creative ability discovers ends and means of action in every ambit in which man acts. The fact that the entrepreneurial function can be exercised (to solve problem 'B') institutionalizes a person's expectations (to solve problem 'A'). But the opposite is also true: an institutional framework is necessary (to solve problem 'A') in order that the entrepreneurial function can be exercised (to resolve problem 'B'). To unravel this apparent paradox, we will analyse the relation that exists between society, culture and the person who acts. These relations are only comprehensible because of man's ability to create new possibilities of action starting from given situations. But to undertake this enterprise it is necessary to use the concept of pure entrepreneurship, as we have developed it in the previous sections.

The knowledge problem looked at anew

It is of fundamental importance to maintain the Misian characterization of economic behaviour without introducing any reduction that would place us, as the starting point, in a hypothetical equilibrium situation. This is the same criticism that Kirzner makes of the neoclassical model, for not explaining the market process, and for concentrating on static situations without explaining where these situations emerge. However, the same criticism can be made of Kirzner for starting from a situation of market equilibrium without explaining the process of how the institutions emerge in the market. Once we have explained the way in which the entrepreneurial function solves both knowledge problems in any institution, we will concentrate on the market as a particular case. In the market the creative ability is guaranteed while the social norms which generate and sustain it are complied with. The market on its own does not guarantee the coordination of the concurrent expectations. Market transactions must be subject to a sociocultural framework in order for the market to work. We have called this institutional framework the external limit of the market. In other words, 'the knowledge problems

A and B' are resolved not because the market guarantees the gains to the entrepreneur, but because the gains which the person discovers in the market are
adjusted to the ethical principles that regulate people's behaviour. Expressed
in other words, when problem 'B' is resolved, it is necessary for problem 'A' to be
resolved.

The institutional order is not a fact that is external to the action: the institutions
are transformed by people's actions. Society and culture are realities that we know
from childhood but this does not mean that they are unchangeable. The survival
of both culture and society depends on their offering the person the means to realize
his life. A social institution survives so long as it allows people to develop, otherwise
it suffers a crisis. In other words, 'the knowledge problem A' has a solution while
it simultaneously resolves 'the knowledge problem B'. The definition of pure
entrepreneurship as man's creative ability implies that the person goes beyond the
existing condition and projects imagined realities in the future. Each possibility of
action means updating the institutional framework. The institutions are transformed in accordance with the new concurrent expectations that are created, but
in order to be able to create new expectations it is necessary to solve 'the knowledge
problem B'. Therefore, the two knowledge problems demonstrate the dynamic
character of the social institutions.

In reality, there are not two problems but only one: *the study, with praxeological*
models, of the concurrence of entrepreneurship of different persons, both in the formation of markets
and in the emergence and the evolution of the institutions. In praxeology itself, to differentiate
between 'the knowledge problem A' and 'the knowledge problem B' is misleading
as a consequence of starting from a situation of perfect competition. In that
approach to the problem, the future disappears, and the temporality of the action
disappears. In reality, 'the knowledge problem A' only makes sense in a model
which always represents the same situation, where there is not any change, nor is
there any place for the man of flesh and blood. In this part of our study of Mises'
work, we cannot renounce man's temporality because it is a praxeological category.
We cannot renounce the view of action as a constant change. Every action implies
making a projection about oneself beyond the present and choosing between the
alternatives that are constructed in these projections about the future. Kirzner
accepts that every person has this ability, that is, pure entrepreneurship is present
in every human action (Kirzner 1973: 86). Therefore, no action is a repetition of
the past. As we have seen, only to accept 'the problem A' is to accept a static view
of the world where there is no room for creativity. This means the elimination of
man from our study. In my opinion, to accept the hypothesis of the neoclassical
model, if only for dialectic reasons, always has the same consequence: the study of
man disappears. The reality, which originates the phenomena being studied,
disappears.

In short, in praxeology the real problem that is analysed is how the person,
through the action, supports the sociocultural framework and its relation with the
market creativity. The problem, which problem 'A' refers to (i.e. the need for a
sociocultural framework, which makes possible the concurrence of individual
expectations), acquires all its richness when it assumes the creativity of the

entrepreneurial function. The institutions are not supported passively, as something that is just there. Their support and transformation depend on the actions of each and every one of the people. Therefore, the knowledge problem does not refer to objective knowledge, but to the coordination of concurrent expectations through pure entrepreneurship. The problem is posed in the following way: every action starts from a sociocultural framework (problem A); but at the same time, every sociocultural framework is transformed by individual actions (problem B). Following the Misian methodology, we are going to analyse, first, the problem in its most general context and then the particular case of the market.

The entrepreneurial function and the sociocultural framework of individual action

Introduction

Our study of social institutions and culture is strictly limited to a certain ambit. We rigorously and methodically limit ourselves in describing what things patently are, that is to say, how they manifest themselves to us in the ambit of the primary radical reality that is our life. We show that individual action is carried out in a certain society and culture. It is the coexistence and common participation in determined values and beliefs, where the means and ends which constitute individual action are configured. It is entirely suitable therefore to define man as *with-being*. With this expression we indicate the person's essential openness to his fellow men by means of society and culture. Thus every individual action is social and has a cultural significance.[10] Figure 4.1 illustrates what I wish to say. Individual action appears intimately related to social institutions and culture. The entrepreneurial function that the person exercises in the action is projected in an institutional and cultural framework. We can say that society is *a process of the creation of possibilities of action that are realized in social institutions and culturally transmitted*. To explain this statement, let us analyse each one of the components of this triad.

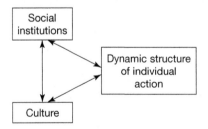

Figure 4.1 Sociocultural framework and individual action

Social institutions

In this section we are going to analyse the importance of the existence of institutions for the action. This importance is based on the fact of people's recognition of recurring expectations prior to every action. As we have seen in the previous section, the person develops his entrepreneurial function in a framework where the expectations come together. The framework of reference constitutes what Kirzner calls 'the knowledge problem A'. Pannenberg defines this framework of reference as 'the regular forms of life in common of individuals, which are called institutions' (Pannenberg 1983: 385).[11] There are two currents in the study of institutions: the first consists of considering society as superior to the person. The superiority of *human nature* over the private individual can be seen in society. Society acquires substance at the price of making the individual and personal characteristics disappear. People, as individuals, are absolutely interchangeable. The whole personal element disappears under the superiority of *human nature*. The second current concentrates on reducing institutions to the singular activity of people. Institutions are considered as a product of human action.

The first current highlights the transcendental character of institutions. It points up Kirzner's 'knowledge problem A'. Every action is developed in the framework of institutions that coordinate the recurrent expectations, but this approach does not question the origin of institutions. It considers them necessary and, therefore, they are a fact that is external to the action. In this approach, people's creative activity (Kirzner's problem B) is not even considered. Holding to the first position, without recognizing any active role for man in the evolution of institutions, has a very high price: the person disappears. Without people, how can one explain the origin, continuity and the transformation of institutions? The second approach is necessary to explain the institutions as basic pieces of human action. Being a basic piece does not imply that the maintenance of the institution can be reducible to the action of one particular person. Both approaches are needed. The second approach hits the nail on the head when it points out that institutions are maintained while they offer a solution to 'knowledge problem B'. As we showed in the previous section, the two problems are intrinsically linked. The solution to problem 'A' implies the solution to problem 'B' and vice versa.

The social system and its organization in institutions start from individual action in its primary aspect: coexistence. Institutions are derived from human interaction. The study of institutions in this dimension begins with the interaction of individuals. The analysis of the interaction of individuals as the basis of institutions has three constituent components: the first aspect is the satisfaction of needs; the second, the stabilization of behaviour; and the third, the objectivization of institutions.

The first constituent: the satisfaction of needs

The study of institutions begins with the work done by B. Malinowski (1944). The approach to the institutions was carried out by basing their diversity on the satisfaction of man's fundamental needs. These were such needs as feeding, reproduction, security, hygiene and growth. All these needs have the basic characteristics of deriving from a person belonging to the human species. A person cannot stop providing for his basic needs if he wishes to preserve his life. The success of these institutions will be measured by the degree to which they satisfy these needs. This success makes the development and emergence of new needs possible, which in turn originates auxiliary institutions. So the institutions are coordinated for the satisfaction of more than one need at the same time. Malinowski states that the formation and maintenance of auxiliary institutions, which coordinate the others, is the best means for the simultaneous satisfaction of a whole series of needs (Malinowski 1944: 142).

Pannenberg poses two problems with this statement by Malinowski: (1) if it is not possible to identify the satisfaction of a particular need with a certain institution, 'the singular institutions cannot be correlated exclusively with singular necessities. Evidently, their existence also has to rely on other causes' (Pannenberg 1983: 389).[12] He shows, with this criticism, the impossibility of studying institutions based on the end that they make it possible to achieve. In the study of institutions the same problem is posed which arises in economics, if we propose the study of the needs that people want satisfying. The classification of institutions according to needs does not permit us to link each institution to a need, and in economics there is no way of separating economic behaviour from extra-economic behaviour depending on the ends that are being pursued. Therefore, for the understanding of both market phenomena and institutions, it is necessary to start from human action. (2) The needs for food, shelter and sexual union are obtained without the necessity of institutions. A society may be built on robbery, piracy or the systematic sacking of neighbouring peoples. Therefore, the explanation of social institutions cannot be reduced to the satisfaction of needs. In reality, what do the institutions provide for the satisfaction of man's needs? What is their special contribution? The answer to these questions introduces us to the next constituent of institutions.

The second constituent: the stabilization of behaviour

Basing himself on the work of Parsons and Shills (1962), and Berger and Luckmann (1966), Pannenberg develops the importance that the stability of institutions has for the social system. The cause of the stability of institutions is based on people's patterns of behaviour. Parsons bases the cohesion of the social system on the role: the role or rather the roles which a person may play are defined as 'the organized system of interaction between the ego and the alter' (Parsons and Shills 1962: 19). Simultaneously with the role, there emerge the expectations *of the role*: 'they are the reciprocal expectations with regards to the mutual actions' (Parsons and Shills 1962: 19). The inherent characteristic of institutions is 'the integration of the expectations of the human agents in an appropriate system of interactive roles which have a pattern of rules and a sharing of values' (Parsons and Shills 1962: 20, note 26).

In this model, institutions constitute an integrated system where the expectations of the roles are rule-governed. This rule must be interpreted as a reciprocal stabilization of conduct. This conduct becomes a habit. As Berger and Luckmann point out: 'from this perspective, an institutionalization is always reached where the habits of behavior of a multiplicity of individuals are co-ordinated in a typified and constant way' (Berger and Luckmann 1966: 51). To explain this process, Pannenberg uses the following example, taken from Berger and Luckmann:

Let there be two individuals, A and B. A observes the conduct of B. He attributes motives to B's actions and in view of the repetitions of those actions, he typifies the motives as recurrent. The same thing occurs with A with respect to B. This means that A and B begin to interpret roles with regard to the other. (Pannenberg 1983: 392)[13]

With this conception of expectations, one can explain the origin of the division of labour, which is the basis of economic progress. The division of labour is an *expectation of the role*. It is a particular case of great importance in the process of institutionalization. The division of labour is a role insofar as it enables people to specialize in a task, and to expect the exchange of the goods produced by each person. This possibility of exchange is what the market economy is based on; this typification of the expectation in the exchange is based on the fact that the division of labour has become rule-governed, it has become institutionalized. The relation between the two knowledge problems is clearly seen. *The decision to become specialized (knowledge problem B) is based on the fact that the division of labour is the behavioural norm (knowledge problem A).*

Pannenberg highlights the importance of the division of labour in the general process of interaction. In his analysis of the different theories of institutions, he emphasizes the importance that Gehlen (1977) gives to the division of labour as the determinant of the duration of and the resistance to the passage in time of the institutions. What does he base this statement on? On the satisfaction of basic needs, which is the basis for the formation of institutions. He states: 'such needs cause the process of becoming accustomed to the actions, immediately to give place to cooperation in the division of labour, which is directed towards the object of satisfying the needs' (Pannenberg 1983: 391).[14] There is a fundamental element here: *the concurrence of the expectations of the people is a dynamic process.*[15] With a dynamic framework, one can appreciate that the expectations concur because the entrepreneurial function, which impels the action, has channels in which to develop.

The basis of the fundamental categories of economics, such as production based on the division of labour, is extra-economic.[16] Its explanation requires the interpretation of economics within a wider anthropological framework. In Mises' work there exist the bases for making this extension. It is true that in Mises' model there are errors, but he also offers the elements necessary to correct them. The importance of the division of labour in Mises is extended and becomes the division of information. The division of labour is not so important in itself as the division of knowledge necessary to produce it. It is this division that obliges man to adapt certain patterns of behaviour with other men in order to share knowledge and to become specialized, with the consequent increase in production. This idea is practically the same as that expounded by Gehlen and picked up by Pannenberg. This idea of the importance of the division of information in Mises' work has been expounded and developed by J. Huerta de Soto (1992). When dealing with the basic character and content of Mises' contribution, he says: 'Mises' essential contribution is limited now, for the first time within the theoretical analysis of the processes of creation and transmission of practical information, which constitutes society' (Huerta de Soto 1992: 172). As Huerta de Soto indicates, Mises speaks of an intellectual division of work and shows that this idea was already present in Mises (1920). Huerta de Soto takes up the following paragraph:

> The distribution of administrative control over economic goods between the individuals of the society, who participate in the production of these goods, demands a type of intellectual division of labour, which is not possible without a system for making calculations and without a market.
>
> (Mises 1920: 102)

Starting from Mises' work, there is no necessary logic in reaching the same conclusions as Professor Kirzner.

There is no theoretical justification for limiting pure entrepreneurship to a limited number of people or to certain ambits of action. With the creative activity of the entrepreneurial function, we can explain the coordination of the actions in the institutions and in the market. One could consider that the institution is constituted when the conduct is rule-governed. The stability of the culture lies in the rule governing *the expectations of the role*. But one can ask the question, what permits the person to classify a form of behaviour as recurrent? The repetitive process of the behaviour makes it possible for the expectation and the wait to be typified. The reiteration of the behaviour explains how the institutionalization is produced, but it does not include the integration of an expectation of role within the social system. In order to classify an act as recurrent it is assumed that the primary motivation is repeated. The motivation leads us back to the meaning that a person gives to a thing. We recognize a form of behaviour as recurrent when we attribute recurrent motivations to it. The recognition of a pattern of behaviour implies being able to give it a meaning. The person must be capable of identifying motivations and responses. In other words, in order to recognize a pattern of behaviour, it is necessary to distinguish between means and ends. However, this distinction does not imply a criterion of maximization. The only thing necessary is to recognize that in order to achieve the ends, whatever they may be, society offers the means for their attainment.

The following extract, taken by Pannenberg from the work of Berger and Luckmann, makes the point quite clear:

> Individuals perform discrete institutionalized actions within the context of their biography. This biography is a reflected-upon whole in which the discrete actions are thought of not as isolated events, but as related parts in a subjectively meaningful universe whose meanings are not specific to the individual, but socially articulated and shared. Only by way of this detour of socially shared universes of meaning do we arrive at the need for institutional integration.
>
> (Berger and Luckmann 1966: 61)

Summing up what we have explained so far: the study of institutions started from the satisfaction of primary needs. The success in the provision of the satisfactions originates the appearance of auxiliary institutions. The relation between the institutions does not make it possible to relate univocally the singular needs with each one of the institutions. The simultaneity in the satisfaction of needs denotes a greater complexity in the institutions. The second constituent centred on the study of the institutions on its role of rule-governing behaviour. The interpretation of behaviour as recurrent needed a framework of common sense in which it could integrate its activities. To study the importance of the unity of meaning as the agglutinator of the social system, we introduced the third constituent of institutions.

The third constituent: the objectivization of social institutions

When a person recognizes another person's behaviour as recurrent and changes his own conduct in consequence, both persons create a nexus of meaning, but this nexus of meaning is only possible when both persons agree on the common consciousness of the meaning. What is this consciousness of meaning? Pannenberg indicates:

> They are lasting configurations of sense for the common life of men . . . evidently they have something to do with the reciprocity of men's conduct in concrete, concurrent situations, or in relations which go on extending themselves temporarily without a solution of continuity.
>
> (Pannenberg 1983: 394)[17]

This configuration is formed, for example, in language. When the reciprocity of the conduct is articulated, it acquires its independence of the individual and enters the symbolic world. It acquires a cultural meaning. This is how institutions, in spite of its specific differences, exist in all cultures by taking as its points of departure the existence of primary needs.

This cultural dimension of social institutions is of maximum importance. The unity of meaning of the institutions enables them to be dynamic: the institution not only has made it possible to achieve the ends desired in the past, but it has to make it possible, in each present action, to achieve the ends that each person determines. Using Kirzner's terminology, 'knowledge problem A' is solved because the institutions solve, in the present of each action, 'knowledge problem B'. The unity of meaning gives the stability and independence of particular people to the social system. Our objective then is to explain how the institutions resolve the 'knowledge problem B' in the dynamism of the action.

Culture

The second component of the triad, culture, demonstrates that persons do not simply live in the natural world. The inherent characteristic of human beings is interpreting and organizing nature. Living in common and the existence of relations among the members of the group are not exclusive to persons. The difference between human beings and animals is the interpretation of nature. In the previous section, we saw how from birth persons are immersed in an institutional order that provides them with the means of action. Pannenberg states: 'the specific human form of life in common is already constituted by the concept of a common world which we call culture' (Pannenberg 1983: 305).[18] Therefore, every institutional order must resolve 'knowledge problem A'. But this support is only possible if the entrepreneurial function can be developed. This creative ability, which interprets the world, is cultured behaviour. In other words, *culture is the creative ability of human beings in action*.

The first approach to this subject is to define the term culture. C. Kluckhohn, a collaborator of T. Parsons in *Towards a General Theory of Action*, together with his colleague L. Kroeber, made a compilation of the meanings of the term culture. This situation, rather than providing a framework within which the action can be discussed, demonstrates the complexity of the problem and the inadequacy of the proposal (Kroeber and Kluckhohn 1952). We can consider the attitudes, knowledge, values, language, technology, food and educational norms as cultural elements. What is the common element in all of these? We could consider that the common characteristic is the transformation of nature. This approach seems to be too limited: what is the transformation of the means that is implied in language and dress? Of course, there are cultural elements whose declared objective is the transformation of the means, as in the case of technology, but it is not the radical elements that unify culture. The search for what qualifies diverse vital forms, like culture, leads us to wonder about what fundamental things give unity to a lifestyle. Mises considered that the unifying element of culture was not knowledge of every sort, but the internalization of what tradition has bestowed, so as to use it in the process of individual humanization. He points clearly to two aspects, tradition and the individual, and to the historical dimension of culture as the tradition that is offered to an individual to live his life.

From the exposition in the previous paragraph, it appears that society reaches its fullness when the social institutions acquire a cultural dimension. The social system, formed by the institutions among which the most prominent are blood, territory, teamwork and the specialization of abilities, has a cultural aspect. As Malinowski points out: 'culture is a complete thing constructed on a basis of institutions, which are partly autonomous, and are partly co-ordinated' (Malinowski 1944: 79). According to this view, the social system is reducible to the cultural system. Society acquires its cohesion through culture. Parsons shares this idea:

> The correct proceeding, is to deal with the system of cultural orientation as an integrating part of the real system of action, from which it can only be separated analytically. Culture in the anthropological sense, is the condition, the component and the product of the systems of action.
>
> (Parsons and Shills 1962: 279)

We could conclude, if we stopped our study at this level, that society is reducible to culture. However, as Pannenberg indicates, the reverse is also valid:

'the interpretation of the concept of culture cannot make an abstraction either, that this always acquires its configuration in the ordering of social reality' (Pannenberg 1983: 308).[19] Therefore, *culture is not reducible to social institutions and social institutions are not reducible to culture.* We need culture and social institutions in order to explain the concept of pure entrepreneurship and to understand how pure entrepreneurship discovers means of action in society. The creative activity is formation and transformation of something that has been received. It is not absolute *ex-nihilo* creation.[20] The transformation of institutions is the process of change of existing things. In other words, 'knowledge problem A' exists because 'B' exists. Pannenberg points out:

> The creativity of man basically serves to obtain and explain states of things that are only obtainable and explicable in that *medium* (culture), but which do not however owe their reality to the whim of human creation. What is accumulated in the process of tradition in the culture is the treasure of access to reality; and it is only in tradition that there is conserved what promises to continue amplifying and deepening the dealings with experimentable reality.
>
> (Pannenberg 1983: 305)[21]

That is to say, culture is a re-updating of the approaches to reality offered by tradition to the person. And this leads us to concentrate on the form in which a society resolves 'knowledge problem B'.

This problem is not developed in Mises' work, though it is defined with clarity and precision. In Mises (1966) we find the following paragraph:

> [The fundamental thing about culture] is the assimilation of ideas that roused mankind from the inert routine of a merely animal existence to a life of reasoning and speculating. *It is the individual's effort to humanize himself by partaking in the tradition of all the best things that earlier generations have bequeathed.*
>
> (Mises 1966: 294, my italics)

This text suggests that tradition is the handing on of ways of being within a reality; and of the possibilities of action that the person receives. Curiously, the word tradition comes from *paradósis, traditio*, whose meaning is 'bequeathal'. Tradition is not the uncritical acceptance of past usages. So, just as the bequeathal of physical characteristics is transmitted genetically, the radically human element, the ways of being in the world, are handed on by tradition. When a person is born, he is placed in the world and given some ways of being in the world. The bequeathal, inasmuch as it comes from the ancestors, 'is formally a continuation of that part of themselves that these ancestors have wanted to bestow on man' (Zubiri 1974: 25). The bequeathal by the parents of what they consider the best or simply what they have known has a recipient who in himself is living another reality. The son, by the mere fact of being a man, is another reality that is distinct from that of the parents. When we say distinct, we are referring not only to the specific corporeal differences between the son and his parents, but also to the distinct social spheres in which he lives his life. The survival of institutions as means that are offered to the son so that he can achieve his ends, depends on its acceptance by the recipient. That is to say, the recipient decides on the continuity of the institutions. Zubiri says: 'continuity is the result of a positive act of receiving something that is bestowed: the act of receiving something and of reviving the thing received from within' (Zubiri 1974: 25). The maintenance of the institutions depends on the entrepreneurial function.[22] It is the heir who decides if what he has received allows him to face up to reality. When a culture does not offer acceptable answers for future generations is when it begins its transformation.

Because he belongs to the human species, the individual must respond to the same problems that his ancestors had to face: food, clothing, education, social relations, etc. With the progressive opening up of the person to greater spheres of activity, he has to ask himself if he accepts the received solution, if he transforms it or if he rejects it. The fact that he is receiving the traditions or looking for solutions in history to problems that arise, implies a progressive transformation of tradition. The key problem is the fact that the person opts for the possibilities that he has already received, or transforms these possibilities or creates new possibilities from what he has received.[23] It is important to emphasize that the possibilities of action are possibilities in the plural, because we never have only one possibility of action: the elements of the culture can be combined in another way from the way they are combined by tradition. A simple but clear example would be a young poet's dissatisfaction with the existing poetic forms. The same language allows for new combinations which give rise to new compositions of rhyme, rhythm and new verses.

Faced with an object from a previous century, the first question is, what was it? Or what did it mean? We wonder about the meaning it had for a human action. When we look at utensils whose use we cannot understand, tradition tells us what human activity could be carried out with each utensil. The object acquires meaning within an action. It becomes a means of action. Let us take, for example, Roman ploughs. It is true that they had a meaning. They were the means used in agriculture. But in praxeology, the key question is: Does it have any meaning in my present reality? If what I really want to do is obtain the maximum yield from the soil, does it make any sense to use a Roman plough nowadays? Certainly not. Therefore, the meaning that past institutions had for our forebears is not fundamental in praxeology. That an institution was a means in the past does not imply that it will continue to be so in the present. In praxeology the institutions must have a present meaning. As Zubiri says:

> [The sense of the institutions] would not worry us if it was not the sense of some human actions, which not only have to have a *had* sense, but also that because of their own nature, they must *have* some sense in order to be what they are: human actions. Therefore, the sense is not then the *had* sense, but the sense that it must have, the *having* sense. Thus, the sense is not the sense that it appears to have, but *the very reality of having sense*.
>
> (Zubiri 1974: 36)

It is with explanation that Pannenberg's phrase 'tradition as the treasure of access to reality' acquires importance. Tradition not only bequeaths the meaning *had* but also a possibility to the present reality. This possibility must have real meaning for the recipients. When what has been received has no meaning as a real possibility, it is transformed. The solution to 'the problem of knowledge B' lies in the fact that people have the possibility of developing their creative ability. If they do not consider that they are going to achieve their ends with the existing institutions, they transform them creatively.

This meaning that an institution acquires enables it to survive even though the reality that originated the meaning has disappeared. Many institutions become a tradition, but in a pejorative sense. They are not a bestowal on the coming generations, which must be re-updated. They become the repetition of types of apparently unreasoned behaviour. This possibility poses for us the problem of the maintenance and disappearance of institutions. There may be a case where the disappearance of an institution does not create any problem.[24] This situation will occur provided that the primary needs are covered and that the institution has lost its meaning as a possibility of real action. Other changes or transformations will create tensions in the social system.

It is important to stress that there is no collectively possessed tradition: tradition limits its bequeathal to the individual. Each individual action is a solution to 'knowledge problem B' and in consequence it is also a solution to 'A'. The problem 'A' proposes the stability of social institutions and the problem 'B' proposes the independence of particular people from the social system. Taking Mises' work as a starting point, and using Kirzner's concept of pure entrepreneurship, we can explain the relation that exists between society, culture and the person who acts, and we can resolve from praxeology the paradoxical conclusions which Kirzner reaches. Disagreeing with Kirzner, we can extend the scope of application of entrepreneurship.

We are going to introduce a concept used by Huerta de Soto: the *Social Big Bang* (Huerta de Soto 1992: 84). It refers to the expansion of means and ends that are produced in a society by the interaction of millions of people. In this section we have seen how the cultural transmission of the possibilities of action from generation to generation expands people's present scope of acting. Through individual actions, what has been received is altered, expanding the field of social interactions and market exchanges (solution to 'knowledge problem B').

This concept is very appropriate for understanding the definition of society that we gave in the previous chapter, as a process or dynamic structure. It is perfectly adequate because the evolution of this process is what we have called the *Social Big Bang*. This expansion of possible interrelations of every type is the result of the concurrence of thousands of people exercising their entrepreneurial function in the solution to 'knowledge problems A and B', as we have already explained.

Individual action

Having reached this point in the exposition, we hope that we have provided sufficient elements to clarify the essential relations that exist between individual action, society and culture. Each one of these elements can only be separated analytically, since the only reality that we observe is individual action. In this section we are not going to concentrate on the analysis of the dynamic structure of the action. The analysis of the praxeological concepts which explain individual action is developed throughout the first part of the book. We are going to concentrate on a subject that concerns the activity of the entrepreneurial function.

At the beginning of this section we stated that society *is a process of the creation of possibilities of action, and that these are achieved in the social institutions and culturally transmitted.* Now we can reformulate this premise and postulate the following: *an institutional and cultural framework will be more efficient, the more there are individual possibilities of action generated.* That is to say, Hayek's problem of knowledge allows us to venture a criterion of social coordination in accordance with the possibilities of action (cf. Huerta de Soto 2004). Let us introduce the definition of coordination provided by Kirzner: 'we use the word coordination to refer to the process in the course of which a state of discoordinatedness gradually comes to be replaced by successive states of greater and greater degrees of coordinatedness' (Kirzner 2000: 141).

The first aspect of this criterion is that it is dynamic. The coordination lies in the process of social interaction that progressively eliminates inefficient situations. So, *a social and cultural situation will be more efficient if it increases the possibilities of individual actions.* That is, a situation will more efficient when a person's expectations of action increase. And vice versa, a social and cultural situation will be more inefficient if the possibilities of action that are permitted to the individual are more limited. If we are referring to knowledge problem 'A', we can say that we have at our disposal a criterion for the evaluation of social institutions and different cultures. However, we can turn this criterion around and state that individual action will be more efficient, the greater the degree of social coordination that is generated. So, if we only state the first part and we remain with the increment in the personal possibilities, then we could understand that a society is more coordinated, the greater the freedom of action that we have. Thus we could reach the paradoxical situation of stating that a society is more coordinated, the greater the number of murderers, drunks, thieves, etc. there are – something that nobody accepts. This first formulation of the criterion proposes an element that is necessary, but is not sufficient. This first aspect sends us back to knowledge problem 'A' and proposes the valuation of the institutional order, but throughout this chapter we have demonstrated that this first problem demands the solution to knowledge problem 'B'. That is, the institutional order is maintained by individual actions, which poses the second problem. Therefore, it is necessary to complete the criterion of coordination from the viewpoint of the individual and state: *individual action will be more efficient, the greater the degree of social coordination it generates.* So, we can state that all the types of behaviour that we normally consider antisocial or prejudicial like robbery, murder, fraud or drug addiction are inefficient because it is impossible for a society to function with them. As with such behaviour, it is impossible to resolve knowledge problem 'B' and as a result there is no institutional order; that is, it does not resolve the problem 'A' either.

A first conclusion to this section is that this criterion of coordination is systemic. Given that we have developed the relations between individual action, institutions and culture, the criterion admits three formulations. Each one of them refers to the contribution of each element to the system. So, as M. Csikszentmihalyi (1996) points out, when speaking of creativity, one should adopt a systemic vision. Instead of asking ourselves about isolated individual creativity, one should ask about the way to stimulate creativity in individual action, in culture and in social institutions. We can formulate the criterion by referring to each one of these elements:

1   As regards the social institutions, the criterion is: *the social institutions will be more efficient, the more possibilities of action they permit the individual to have.*
2   As regards culture: *the mechanisms of cultural transmission will be more efficient, the more possibilities of action they foment.*
3   As regards individual action: *the action will be more efficient, the greater its contribution to the institutions and culture.*

If we bear in mind that each separation is analytical and that the only existing reality is man in action, we can summarize the three criteria in one: the co-ordination improves *if the process of the creation of individual possibilities of action, which is carried out in the social institutions and culturally transmitted, is extended.*

Second, this systemic criterion enables us to deal with a frequent criticism. Normally, the criticism is that the results of an institution and a culture are only admissible from within these institutional and cultural prerequisites (Kirzner 2000: 138–9). So, for example, the functioning of the market is accepted, provided that we accept as valid private property as an institutional prerequisite. If we reject private property on moral grounds, the market result is unacceptable and it is necessary to consider that its supposed efficiency is false and, above all, unjust. Is this objection valid? From the point of view of the dynamic and systemic criterion that we have expounded, it is objectionable, since the institutional prerequisites are an essential part of the individual action. The institutions and the culture are not facts external to the action and therefore they are susceptible to valuation. Clearly some institutions and cultures are superior to others. The only irreducible fact that is axiomatic is the action as a primary reality (cf. Hoppe 1993). This primary reality is human action that consists of the intentional pursuit of certain beneficial ends with scarce resources. In this way, it is understood that all of Mises' criticism of socialism does not only lie in its impossibility, because without prices a cost–benefit calculation is impossible and the only thing that is generated is productive chaos. This criticism is extended with the criterion of coordination, which we have expounded, and one can state that socialism is inefficient because it limits people's possibilities of action. Further, in this system, as people cannot freely exercise their creativity owing to State legislation, they cannot generate more open institutions

– by open institution, we understand that institution that is a fundamental part of the open society as defined by Popper (1950).

Therefore, the criterion of efficiency based on human action is perfectly valid for institutional evaluation (cf. Koslowski 1982). Obviously, when we are dealing with human action, value judgements are involved, but this criterion of coordination based on the primary reality of human action is independent of moral judgements (Kirzner 2000: 136). To put it in other words, it is prior to a moral judgement. This judgement will come as a result of a historical evaluation of a given society and culture, although this historical evaluation allows us to make value judgements about the suitability of social institutions for human development. This criterion allows us, as Kirzner says: 'a possible norm of coordination in the sense of the ability to detect and to move towards correcting situations in which activities have until now been discoordinated' (Kirzner 2000: 190). If this is true, we have the analytical elements at our disposal for making an evaluation of a very particular institution: the market.

The market as a social institution

In this last section we are going to analyse the market in the light of what we have expounded previously. The objective is to demonstrate that the market coordinates when it acquires its institutional character. That is, the institutional prerequisites of the market, namely private property and fulfilment of contracts, are the result of social interactions. Therefore, all the elements which explain the dynamic process that underlies the creation and maintenance of any institution are present in the market. Kirzner disagrees with this opinion, and considers that the prerequisites of the market are not explicable from the starting point of the coordinating processes which exist in the market, and states:

> These limits on the market are imposed by its institutional prerequisites. Without these institutional prerequisites – primarily, private property rights and freedom and enforceability of contract – the market can operate. It follows that the market itself cannot create those institutions. The institutions upon which the market must depend must have been created or have evolved through processes different from those spontaneous coordinative processes, which we have seen to constitute the essence of the market's operation.
>
> (Kirzner 2000: 83)

This statement is the result of the proposals expounded in his article 'Knowledge problems and their solutions: some relevant distinctions', which we have already commented on. Therefore, to finish this chapter it is necessary to deal with a difficult subject which in my opinion clearly contradicts the whole of Kirzner's theoretical work. In accordance with what we have expounded in the previous section, social institutions must meet three requirements in order to act as supports for individual action: (1) to furnish needs; (2) to establish behavioural norms; and (3) to develop a formal structure that is culturally transmitted. The market, as a social institution, functions provided that it fulfils these three requirements. The market has been developed in keeping with the rate at which it has renounced aggression against other people. As Roepke (1968) explains, the social form of struggle against scarcity can be organized in three ways. The first is the ethically negative one of violence and fraud. The second is the ethically positively one of altruistic gifting, for which the means are provided without there being anything received in exchange. The third relation is based neither on egoism, in the sense that one's own well-being is favoured to the detriment of a third party, nor on altruistic gifting in the sense that one's own well-being is neglected to the benefit of others.

Rather, it is an ethically neutral relation, in which by virtue of contractual reciprocity, the aim of increasing one's well-being is pursued with the end of augmenting one's own well-being with the means for augmenting the other's. A person who establishes a business with the firm intention of deceiving his clients will not last for very long. At the opposite extreme, a person who bases his business on the charitable gifting of his product will not have much future. His only possibility of success is to provide quality service, a service that will find a response in a mutual service being offered. This ethically neutral form has a clear rule-governed component. In the first case, it may be that robbery is considered acceptable when it is perpetrated against a person of another clan, association or social class, while maintaining a strict morality among the members of one's group. In this case, there is a strong internal morality, accompanied by a total lack of any external morality when dealing with strangers, who are not considered equals.

The process of secularization of basic Christian morality has enlarged the sphere of internal morality, while reducing its content. The principle of counter-offers has become generalized as the basis of social relations, while fraud and altruistic behaviour have slowly been decreasing. The idea of the equality of man has enlarged the sphere of activity in which fraud is considered immoral and at the same time the profit motive has replaced charity, erasing its Christian origins. In this way, the market has been configured as an institution with a minimal ethical content, but with a universal norm which has facilitated its present-day implantation: *the principle of mutual benefits*. Therefore, the market has a rule-governed component, which is inherent in every institution, consisting of rule-governing behaviour. Exchanges are possible because mutual benefit is expected as the basis of cooperation. However, the principle of mutual benefits can be broken in the market; that is to say, ethically negative behaviour may occur. This situation can only degenerate into anomie, in the lack of rules. So just as language provides the means and the rules for the formation of thought, but does not determine the person's speech, which falls within his sphere of responsibility, so the market establishes the rules of exchange, but does not determine the person's behaviour; this falls within his sphere of freedom. The price system is necessary for this task. It is the essential element for the person to be able to project the sequence of means and ends and to make his cost–benefit calculations. Therefore, the price system is a fundamental institutional element for the market to function.

The process of cultural transmission in the market is the third element that guarantees the survival of the institution over time. So we can say, the price system is a necessary condition, but it is not sufficient alone for the survival of the market as an institution. The durability will be determined by the success of the market as a means of developing people's creative ability. The market will be successful while it offers real possibilities of action. When the cultural meaning of the market is not realized, strains develop. It is considered an imposition, a tradition imposed without any sense for the life of the present generations. To understand this dynamism of the market we need the two approaches presented in knowledge problems 'A' and 'B', which, as we have explained, are very closely linked in social reality but which we differentiate analytically. The first demonstrates the importance of the consolidated market structures, which tend to perpetuate themselves. It presents us with the market as an institution, already given to individual action. It is the enterprises that have a market share and that want to maintain their situation by offering a competitive product. Within the market process, this first approach represents the tendency towards homogenization of the goods, and to competition through the reduction of costs. The second approach demonstrates the difficulties in innovating, of introducing or developing a new product, service or entrepreneurial organization, etc. This second approach represents the tendency to innovation. Both encompass diverse phenomena, which we can represent in Table 4.1.

We are going to introduce the concept of 'market tolerance' to analyse the tension between homogeneity and variation, which converge in market forces. This may expand and, in fact, market globalization is in fashion today, but the limit of market tolerance lies in the fact that it continues to be an institution; that gives people stability. The great entrepreneurial creators force the limits of the market, introducing new products and new technologies which expand the possibility of the instrumental plexus that constitutes the economy. The constant change forces the assimilation of new information and little by little configures the information society. This dynamizing force, the core of the market, implies a disposition to change in the enterprise, in the city and in the activity. It is highly significant that in the United States, the average number of jobs that a person has throughout his professional life is much greater than in Europe. In Europe, on the other hand, stability and homogenization predominate over creativity and change. Society

Table 4.1 Forces of the market

Homogenization	Variation
Knowledge problem 'A'	Knowledge problem 'B'
Satisfaction of needs	Need for change
The impersonal	The person
Tendency to line production	Tendency to innovation
Social division at work	Personal fulfilment at work
Security	Risk
Consolidated markets	Markets in expansion

needs stability in its institutions: some minimal expectations must exist in every institution so that they can provide people with a pattern of behaviour. Nobody in his right mind would devote six years' training for a profession that only had the possibility of surviving for three years. When he finished his training, he would already be obsolete! That is, in order to project his vital possibilities into the future, a person must have a fixed point from which to glance at that future. There is a need for stability in the division of labour so that people can develop their projects. Creativity, therefore, is not a mere whirlwind, *but rather it transcends the established social framework*. Every innovation needs an established market in which it can highlight its individuality.

We would consider that a novelty is successful if it manages to be sold rapidly in the market. That would be to value the novelties only by monetary criteria. This is true, as nobody could undertake a project if he did not have the monetary means to finance it, but this monetary criterion is not sufficient to guarantee the survival of the novelty and its use. Individual creation will be successful and will survive over time when the new possibility of action is absorbed in the undivided institutional estate and increases the future possibilities, so that when this new possibility is totally institutionalized and its use generalized, one tends to forget the name of the person who created it. How many utensils do we use every day without knowing the names of their creators! However, independently of our ignorance of the names of these creators, we know perfectly the possibility of action that these useful things permit us. These useful things have become real possibilities of action. In other words, the human forces that move the market acquire all their nuances when they are explained with praxeological categories – praxeological categories that cannot be reduced to a mere maximization of benefits.

Schumpeter (1961), the Austrian economist, spoke of creative destruction, implying with this concept that every economic innovation was an abandonment of economic equilibrium. Each change impels the relations in the market, making it impossible to reach the state of rest which characterizes economic stability. This expression has had enormous success, but it does not capture the essence of the problem. Rather than destruction, one should speak of the retention and expansion of possibilities. The destruction would occur when a previously satisfied need could not be met with the new product. Creative innovation cannot be a reduction, but rather it is an enlargement of the satisfaction of needs and an enlargement in the possibilities of action (Kirzner 2000: 239–58). There is a retention of possibilities that is formed in the institutions and is transmitted culturally. These possibilities of action, already institutionalized, are transmitted to people so that they can carry out their projects. In that moment there emerges the creative tension that expands, maintains or diminishes the possibilities of action. Then, there enter into action all the praxeological elements that characterize the action as a dynamic, historical process, open to the future and, of course, subject to error and failure.

5 The evaluative system

In the previous chapter we developed the concept of pure entrepreneurship, which is inherent in every human action. This field, in which man deploys his creative capacity, encompasses and transcends exchanges in the market. Human beings undertake actions which go beyond what they have been given in the here and now, in all social interactions. They project different possibilities of action into the future and they evaluate them. It is important to point out that there never exists only one possibility of action: a person may opt for a multiplicity of ends. Even in the simplest case, that of binary choice, the person has to decide between action and passivity, and after all, this is also a form of acting. Therefore, in every situation the person evaluates the different possibilities of action. As we have seen in the previous chapter, the expectations that each person projects into the future concur with the expectations realized by other persons, because these persons abide by the norms that guarantee the working of the institutions. In the specific case of the market, the expectations concur whenever they abide by some extra-mercantile norm, thus posing the relation between ethics and the market. Although Kirzner limited his work to the market, if we bear in mind that entrepreneurship is an indispensable element in every action, the relation between ethics and the market must be posed within the wider framework of the relation between ethics and individual action. Whether in the market or in a social inter-action, every person acts in accordance with some moral norms, whose study establishes the importance of the evaluative system in the theory of action. It is not surprising therefore that Rothbard, Kirzner and Hoppe have done praxeological research on the role of value judgements – research directed to demonstrating the ineradicable unity between the existence of the market and the acceptance of certain moral systems.

The praxeological relation between ethics and the market

In this section we are going to set out the contributions of I. Kirzner, M. Rothbard and H. H. Hoppe. Essentially, these three authors present the same criticism of Mises. They criticize him because, in spite of the brilliance of his contribution to the defence of the market economy and private property, his arguments are centred on the acceptance of capitalism because of its monetary consequences. However, he does not deal with the relation between ethics and the market, and the three authors, while considering Mises' arguments insufficient, offer some new praxeological developments which enable them to mount a more effective defence of the market economy than that offered by Mises.

Kirzner's Discovery, Capitalism and Distributive Justice

We will first set out Kirzner's contribution, as it is a continuation of what we expounded in the previous chapter. Kirzner analyses the ethical connotations of considering market exchanges as a result of pure entrepreneurship. In *Discovery, Capitalism and Distributive Justice*, Kirzner criticizes Mises for never confronting the pretensions of those people who questioned the moral justification of pure profit resulting from the discovery of means. As Kirzner points out: 'Mises did not feel called upon to argue the justice of entrepreneurially-won profits on the basis of any conceivable discovery of the means' (Kirzner 1989: 64). However, he accepts that Mises was the pioneer in the recognition of entrepreneurship in each and every one of the actions undertaken in the market.

Kirzner's objective is to show that from the perspective of entrepreneurship, the discovery tends to confer a title of legitimacy to property ownership over what is possessed. If we take discovery as our starting point, we can define the following generally accepted rule: *who discovers it, keeps it* (or colloquially *finders keepers*). This rule states that an object without an owner becomes the legitimate property of the person who, having discovered its availability and its potential value, takes possession of it. It is of fundamental importance to explain in detail what this discovery means. As we have explained in the previous chapter, this discovery is the subjective perception of a possibility of action. It is not a question of discovering its physical-chemical existence, which in our study is unimportant. If we remember the example of the coin lost in the street, the person who finds it does not discover its physical existence but its economic value, that is, the goods that can be bought with this coin. Kirzner makes the point specifically when he says:

> The prior existence of the inputs [in our example, the coin] does not contradict our perception of the creativity of the entrepreneurial decision to produce. Inputs do not ensure output in a world of open-ended uncertainty. More to the point, inputs do not ensure the worthwhileness of the economic value they may generate.
>
> (Kirzner 1989: 153)

Discovery is, therefore, human activity and it cannot be explained without resorting to the active role of man. Generally, when one hears about discovery, it is understood that the object that is acquired is already there; that the resources are given and the only thing that one has to do is to seize them. For example, wooded land is waiting for someone to convert it into a fertile farm. This interpretation is true to a certain extent since, as we have seen, human creation is not creation from absolutely nothing. It is creation from something that is there, *but whose value does not exist until it is created*. Therefore, the creation of the possibility confers value and existence on the resource as a means of action. As Kirzner points out: 'each decision is a creative act, a leap of faith expressing the decision maker's vision of an essentially uncertain future. Inputs by themselves do not ensure the production of anything – certainly not of anything valuable' (1989: 147). If we agreed with the first interpretation of a world with given resources, whose only problem was to assign them efficiently, we would consider man in a passive way. Value in general and economic value in particular would be totally independent of human actions. Kirzner is right when he states:

> Such a treatment can never permit us to see an individual as having *originated* anything of value – since these valuable things do not owe their existence to any decision of his. . . . This is so because, on this view, the output really existed, even before the decision to produce, in the form of the resource mix from which the output is transformed.
>
> (Kirzner 1989: 148)

If we define persons as passive optants facing given situations, the only way to admit entrepreneurship is as another factor of production. If the producer does not originate the product, then his right to property must derive from the right he had to the resources starting from those as a first cause. This scheme leads to an endless regression, seeking to determine whether the first acquisition was just or not: what this scheme of *homo economicus* cannot explain is how the first acquisition of original resources, without an owner, was produced.[1]

For praxeology, the essential feature of entrepreneurship is that the decision-making occurs prior to the acquisition of the factors of production. It is the perception itself that attempting production is going to be more profitable. It is the same entrepreneurial decision which causes the objectives to exist so that the resources can be means of action. In other words, it is the perception of the end that causes the resources to become the means. Professor Kirzner says:

> We can no longer be satisfied with a moral philosophy which, in its considera-tion of property rights and property institutions, treats the world as if the future consists in an unending series of fully perceived manna-deposits waiting to be assigned and distributed.
>
> (Kirzner 1989: 150)

If we bear in mind all these considerations, the rule *who discovers it, keeps it (finders keepers)* has a moral component that is difficult to reject: everybody has the right to the results of his creative capacity. One cannot argue against this by saying that the resources already existed, because until they are valued as means of action it is as if they did not exist – and there are no rights to property over something that does not exist. If this rule is admitted, we must also admit the ethical coherence of the application of this rule in the market. Kirzner concludes:

If an undiscovered resource is, in the moral sense, a non-existent resource, then it will turn out to be crucially important in the moral appraisal of the institution of property, to recognize that resources come into existence as a result of discoveries, of purely entrepreneurial hunches and vision.

(Kirzner 1989: 149)

Kirzner's argument throws new light on the importance of private property. In praxeology, Kirzner begins with human action and its motive power: entrepreneurship. It is the exercise of a person's creative capacity that discovers the means of action, which until their discovery were non-existent, in the sense that they did not have any value until the human agent decided to use them in an action projected into an uncertain future. In this view, property is not reduced to monetary fortune, that is, to the market valuation of a person's material possessions. Kirzner points to the origin of private property in the action itself. It is the discovery that tends to confer in the eyes of many people the legitimate title to property of the thing possessed. The essence of private property, in Kirzner's scheme, is not that it possesses things; rather it is the ineradicable right of every person to exercise his creative capacity and to claim the profit generated by his discoveries for himself. Therefore, the study of the ethical connotations of the market should not be posed from the point of view of the results that are obtained: rather it should be based on the fact that the participants in market exchanges have the right to exercise their entrepreneurship, and the duty to recognize the same right in the other participants. From this point of view, market exchanges are not just because they are beneficial, but rather because they comply with the rule, *who discovers it, keeps it*.

Murray Rothbard and The Ethics of Liberty

Rothbard criticizes Mises because he does not consider that his utilitarianism is adequate for defending the free market. For Rothbard: 'one must go beyond economics and utilitarianism to establish an objective ethics which affirms the overriding value of liberty' (Rothbard 1998: 214). The case of Mises is of singular interest for Rothbard because the former has been the most intransigent defender of free market economics and the most inflexible defender of value-free economics of all the twentieth-century economists. This contradictory situation intrigues Rothbard and makes him wonder about the ways that Mises offered in order to reconcile the two positions. Mises presented two solutions to this problem:

The praxeologist cannot describe a policy as good or bad. According to Mises, he cannot say, per se, whether certain government programmes are good or bad. However, if a certain policy leads to results which all the supporters of this policy agree are bad, then the neutral economist has sufficient justification to describe such a policy as bad. For Rothbard, this first solution is an ingenious attempt to decide if something is good or bad without the need for making value judgements. This first solution, presented by Mises, starts from the assumption that any defender of interventionist policies will abandon his defence as soon as an economist informs him of the consequences of the interventionism. Let us frame the question, how does Mises know what the supporters of this concrete policy consider desirable? According to Mises, one of the great contributions of praxeological economics is that economists have pointed out that they do not know of any scale of values, except the preferences that each person demonstrates through his concrete actions. Scales of values do not exist independently of the actual conduct of individuals. If this analysis of Mises' is admitted, the economist can show that the control of prices will lead to an unforeseen shortage of the offer of consumer goods. Rothbard wonders: 'how does Mises know that some advocates of price controls do not *want* shortages?' (Rothbard 1998: 208). There are thousands of examples of people who, after having studied economics and being aware that price restrictions produce scarcity, continue supporting such measures.[2] Rothbard states:

> In fact, once Mises concedes that even a *single* advocate of price control or any other interventionist measure may acknowledge the economic consequences and *still* favor it, *for whatever reason*, then Mises, as a praxeologist and economist, can no longer call any of these measures 'bad' or 'good', or even 'appropriate' or 'inappropriate', without inserting into his economic policy pronouncements the very value judgments that Mises himself holds to be inadmissible in a scientist of human action.
>
> (Rothbard 1998: 208)

With this example Rothbard demonstrates that there is no reason to assume that all the supporters of government intervention will abandon their positions when they know the consequences of such intervention. So the primary solution offered by Mises for defending the free market, without emitting any value judgements, must be considered a failure.

Mises offers a second solution. In his defence of the free market he takes a totally different route which leads him to concede that the economist, as a scientist, cannot advocate free market economics *but he can do this as a citizen*. As Rothbard points out: 'what Mises does is to make *only one* narrow value judgment: that he desires to fulfill the goals of the majority of the public' (Rothbard 1998: 210). This position is very poor. The only thing that he recognizes is that he is in favour of most people achieving the aims that they desire. As we have seen in Chapter three, Rothbard offers the following example to explain the problems that this position poses:

> Let us for example assume again – and this assumption is not very far fetched in view of the record of human history – that the great majority of a society hate and revile redheads. Let us further assume that there are very few redheads in the society. This large majority then decides that it would like very much to murder all redheads. Here they are; the murder of redheads is high on the value-scales of the great majority of the public; there are few redheads so that there will be little loss in production on the market. How can Mises rebut this proposed policy either as a praxeologist or as a utilitarian liberal?
>
> (Rothbard 1998: 213)

This second solution proposed by Mises is not free of problems. The only value judgement he makes is his emotional support for the majority of the population in favour of peace and prosperity, while he reduces the value judgements to their most basic level. He does no more than state that it is desirable that the majority of the citizens attain their objectives.

Mises' utilitarian position causes another problem. He was one of the economists most determined to demonstrate the universality of temporal preference in all human behaviour. His theory of capital was built on the rate of temporal preference, which determines the rate of interest. His explanation of the process of capitalist accumulation is based on a deepening of capital structure, which implies the need for low temporal preference for long-term projects to be undertaken. Using his theory of capital, Mises recommends carrying out investment plans that put off consumption to an increasingly distant time because in this way the person increases his capital. However, this recommendation contradicts his utilitarian position, because as the scientist without value judgements that he considers himself to be, he cannot try to criticize the rate or the proportion of each person's temporal preference. Rothbard makes the following commentary with this regard to this matter:

> And certainly, Mises, as a value-free scientist, could never presume to criticize anyone's *rate* of time preference, to say that A's was 'too high' or B's 'too low'. But, in that case, what about the high-time-preference people in society who may retort to the praxeologist: 'perhaps this high tax and subsidy policy will lead to a decline of capital; perhaps even the price control will lead to shortages, but I don't care. Having a high time-preference, I value more highly the short-run subsidies, or the short-run enjoyment of buying the current goods at cheaper prices, than the prospect of suffering the future consequences'. And Mises, as a value-free scientist and opponent of any concept of objective ethics, *cannot* call them wrong.
>
> (Rothbard 1998: 209)

Mises does not offer any arguments that enable him to recommend investments that put off consumption to a long time in the future. As Rothbard indicates, it is necessary to go beyond utilitarianism in order to sustain the process of capitalist accumulation. Having made these pertinent criticisms of Mises' work, Rothbard establishes the principles of the relation between ethics and economics. For this author, the relation between ethics and economic is based on natural law. It starts from the study of human nature in order to know the inherent private nature of man. Rothbard bases his study of man on liberty. He points out that:

> The individual man, in introspecting the fact of his own consciousness, also discovers the primordial natural fact of his freedom: his freedom to choose, his freedom to use or not to use his reason about any given subject. In short, the natural fact of his 'free will'. He also discovers the natural fact of his mind's command over his body and its actions: that is, of his natural *ownership* over his self.
>
> (Rothbard 1998: 31)

The freedom of man is revealed by the fact that the knowledge necessary for survival and progress is not innate, nor is it determined by external events; the fact is that man has to employ his mind to acquire this knowledge. In short, Rothbard's first basic assumption is that *each individual is naturally the owner of himself.* Rothbard extends this result to the interaction of various persons and states: 'economics has revealed a great truth about the natural law of human interaction: that not only is *production* essential to man's prosperity and survival, but so also is exchange' (Rothbard 1998: 35). For Rothbard, it is fundamental to bear in mind that the only two ways to have ownership over goods are through production and exchange. In his own words: 'ownership rights are acquired in two ways and two ways only: (a) by finding and transforming resources ("producing"), and (b) by exchanging one's produce for someone else's product' (Rothbard 1998: 37). Rothbard refers to these two ways to justify private property as 'the rules of natural property' and he postulates: (1) every individual is the owner of himself, and (2) ownership is based on production and exchange. Therefore in the free market all ownership is based: (a) on the ownership that each person has over his own body and over his work; (b) on the ownership that the individual has over the land he has discovered and transformed through his own work; (c) on the exchange in the market from the products from the mixture of ways (a) and (b) and with the products from other people, who have obtained them in these same ways. Rothbard concludes: 'in the free society we have been describing, then, all owner-ship reduces ultimately back to each man's naturally given ownership over himself, *and* of the land resources that man transforms and brings into production' (Rothbard 1998: 40).

Rothbard's study reveals complementary elements to those explained by Kirzner's theory. For Kirzner, ownership is based on the fact that every person has the right to the results of the exercise of this entrepreneurship. In his turn, Rothbard bases his study on self-possession as the essence of the person and starting from self-possession he explains ownership as the result of production and exchange. Any productive act is the result of the creative capacity of the person. Then, self-possession and entrepreneurship are analytical concepts that are applied to the same human reality, that is, the action. Kirzner himself points out that his theory:

> In the first place, presents a novel perspective on the original acquisition of property, seeing it more as the discovery and origination of an ownerless natural resource, than as a question of combining it with man's own work. In second place, when he reinforces his premise of self-possession, he also offers support for the Lockean theory of the original acquisition of property, which is based on the combination of a resource with man's own work.
>
> (Kirzner 1989: 163)

The two theories are mutually reinforcing: Rothbard emphasizes liberty as an essential characteristic of man and Kirzner emphasizes the development of liberty through entrepreneurship.

Mises' utilitarian position poses some serious problems for his theory of capital (Mises 1980). For Mises, the structure of capital is formed by the intermediate stages between the first productive act and the consumption of the product. If we use Hoppe's definitions (Hoppe 1988: 14), we define the consumer decision as the decision to undertake projects in which priority is given to immediate consumption. The investment decision is the decision to undertake projects in which consumption is put off to a more or less distant future. In the way we have defined consumption, to consume is to give priority to the immediate satisfaction of needs, and investment is to postpone the satisfaction of needs to a more or less distant future. In accordance with this criterion, an investment in capital structure will appear on many layers. With greater investment, consumption will occur in an increasingly distant future. So, for example, the capital structure of a car, nowadays, appears as a very long-term capital structure. All the productive techniques are considered in the structure, such as the time employed in developing various technologies, research into assembly line automation, etc. The car, as capital, is the result of prolonged investment. Curiously, this structure, this accumulation of information, enables cars to be produced in less than half an hour. The accumulation of investment in the capital structure makes it possible for a car to be produced in a time that was unthinkable 50 years ago. The capital investment makes it possible to save time.

The problem of utilitarian ethics is that the goods acquire a value in themselves. They are desired for the satisfaction that they provide. The perception of the goods begins to be emotive. They are valued for their power of immediate satisfaction. The goods acquire this power depending on the waiting time before they can be enjoyed. There is no sense in putting off this enjoyment. Utilitarian ethics has two fundamental effects: (1) the norms, in utilitarian ethics, are complied with because they have a *useful value*. The following paragraph by Mises is quite revealing:

> The ultimate yardstick of justice is conduciveness to the preservation of social cooperation. Conduct suited to preserve social cooperation is just, conduct detrimental to the preservation of society is unjust. . . . Social utility is the only standard of justice. It is the sole guide of legislation.
>
> (Mises 1966: 54)

As Rothbard indicates, in utilitarianism it is impossible to criticize a society in which consumer decisions predominate. In a society dominated by utilitarianism there is no reason to put off present consumption to a distant future. Utilitarianism does not present any arguments in favour of low measures of temporal preference, which make it possible to make investment decisions whose results will be seen in an uncertain long-term future. The direct consequence of utilitarianism is that long-term projects are never undertaken.

The new praxeological developments make it possible to go beyond Mises' utilitarianism and indicate a direct relation between investment as a saving of time and ethics as a system which enables man to save time. The development in the last two hundred years to which Mises attaches such importance, and which was made possible, he says, because people paid attention to the teachings of the economists, was not only an increase in useful values. This process was based on investment, in the increase of resources and, therefore, in the increase in the possibilities of action. Mises' utilitarianism cannot explain the internal cohesion of this process. It is only possible to explain the development by going deeper into methodological subjectivism. Capitalism cannot be reduced to a utilitarian view that gives pre-eminence to consumption: this attitude supposes its own destruction. Pre-eminence must be given to man in all his dimensions. Pre-eminence must be given to the internal consistency of the person. It is the only way to increase human capital, which is the basis of all economic development. Rothbard's work with his contributions – which he was not able to develop owing to his early death – points to the transcending of utilitarianism. He introduces the sphere of personal liberty and the importance of ethics as a necessary element for increasingly long-term projects to be undertaken.[3] As he points out: 'there is no way that [Mises] can assert the superiority of the long-run over the short-run without overriding the values of the high time-preference people; and this cannot be cogently done without abandoning his own subjectivist ethics' (Rothbard 1998: 209).

H. H. Hoppe and the axiom of argumentation

Rothbard's work has served as the basis for a later elaboration by H. H. Hoppe, whose own work has made it possible to highlight the most important aspects of that of Rothbard and to clarify its complementariness to Kirzner's work. Hoppe (1993) proposes to improve Mises' work by following the contributions made by Rothbard (Hoppe 1993: 204). His aim is to classify the concept of self-possession as the essence of the person. To reach his objective Hoppe takes the axiom of action as his starting point and adds the axiom of argumentation. What does this second action consist of? There are two essential ideas: (1) Hoppe considers that in order to know what is just or unjust, and even to know what is a true sentence, one must be capable of exchanging propositions, that is, of arguing. There is no way of justifying an idea other than arguing (Hoppe 1993: 205). What is more, it is impossible to refute this principle without incurring a contradiction. If a person wants to argue the impossibility of argumentation, that is in itself an argument. In other words, in the same way that Mises considers action to be a self-evident axiom, so Hoppe considers that argumentation is also a self-evident axiom. (2) All argumentation needs some scarce resources to be effective. In Hoppe's words: 'the resources that are necessary for argumentation are those of private owner-ship' (Hoppe 1993: 205). No person has the possibility of proposing, nor will he be convinced of any proposition, through argumentation, if the right of this person to the exclusive use of his own body were not assumed. Self-possession is the requisite of the axiom of argumentation.

For Hoppe, private ownership is justified a priori with the following reasoning: any person who wants to justify a norm has to presuppose, beforehand, an exclusive control over his body as a valid norm, although only in order to say: *I propose this or that*. However, argumentation would not be possible if only control over one's own body were recognized. It is necessary to permit the appropriation of things by the use of scarce means with the body. This appropriation is the result of personal work and the accumulation of the surpluses of production. According to Hoppe: 'by the virtue of the fact of being alive then, property rights to other things must be assumed to be valid' (Hoppe 1993: 206). There must be an objective relation between a particular person and a scarce resource in order for argumentation to be possible. This objective rule is the following principle: the first in using, the first in possessing (*first user–first owner*). Thus, every person who through his action in a certain place and at a certain time appropriates a thing as a productive resource, becomes the owner of the thing and is objectively recognized as such by other persons. To deny this right is to deny the possibility of arguing: if a person had to argue with the person who tried to obtain possession of the resource after him, then the action would become impossible. Possession of resources would turn into an endless argument, outside the time and space of each concrete action. Therefore, as a requisite for action, every person must have prior consent to the exclusivity of the goods that he generates.

In short, the structure of the union of the axiom of argumentation and the axiom of action is the following: first, every justification is validated with arguments. The axiom of action and the axiom of argumentation are self-evident. Second, argumentation presupposes the ownership of the body and of the goods appropriated by the principle of accumulation. With this second step we achieve two objectives: (a) integrating the axiom of action with the concept of self-possession, as Rothbard expounds in his *The Ethics of Liberty*. Once the assumption of self-possession is integrated, the exercise of individual action must be respected. (b) Hoppe with his rule, *first user–first owner*, establishes an objective relation between the person and the axiom of argumentation. This rule establishes nothing more than the right of each person to use his own body as he thinks fit and to exercise his creative capacity. In other words, argumentation is the exercise of entrepreneurship. Hoppe manages very concisely to integrate the contributions of Rothbard and to clarify the complementarity of his axiom of argumentation with the right to obtain profits in Kirzner's entrepreneurship.

Private property in praxeology

In the previous chapter we studied the market as a social institution and analysed how the market resolves Kirzner's 'problems of knowledge A and B'. As we saw, the market solves both problems because it complies with the functions attributable to all institutions. In this chapter it is pertinent to introduce a new approach, which will enable us to highlight the importance of the theoretical contributions of Kirzner, Rothbard and Hoppe to gain a greater understanding of private property as the basis of market economics.

According to W. Pannenberg, institutions unite two different structural moments in the conduct of individuals: (1) each one seeks to maintain himself against the other one; this is the aspect of particularity; (2) each individual seeks to adapt himself to the other one; this is the aspect of community. On its own, particularity is not enough to form lasting relations, as sooner or later it is necessary for the individual to adapt himself to the other individual. On the other hand, stabilization is achieved when there exists a certain degree of particularity between individuals. These two spheres are separated with greater sharpness in the institutions of the family and property. In the family, the aspect of community takes precedence; the members, while still being persons, are subordinated to the community; the aspect of community has precedence over individuality. The conduct of a member of a family is based not on reciprocity among equals, 'but on everyone belonging to the community and on the particular contribution of each one of the members; it is this contribution which establishes inward relations of mutual recognition and esteem, and outward relations of solidarity' (Pannenberg 1983: 400).[4] On the other hand, in property and in economic life, what takes precedence is the aspect of particularity. Each person seeks his particular interest in self-assertion. However, the two aspects cannot be differentiated in reality. Neither in the family is everything submission to the community nor in the enterprise is everything the self-assertion of each individual. In the social system both aspects are necessary. It may be that in an institution like the family the aspect of particularity is subordinate, but the family as an institution is destroyed when oppression is exercised over the independence of the members. Inversely, private property is not able to forget the aspect of community.

These two aspects which can be found in the conduct of individuals, that is, the particularity and the community, will enable us to understand the importance of private property as the institution where the self-affirmation of each person takes precedence over that of all the others, without forgetting the aspect of community. To demonstrate this statement we will synthesize the contributions of our three Austrian authors and we will prove how private property, in its praxeological interpretation, complies with the three functions that Pannenberg attributes to every institution.

Private property and the provision of needs

Rothbard is the author who puts most emphasis on the idea that things are possessed because of their attachment to the body. This consideration of the body as a resource is special to man; the body is understood as a reality capable of being transformed. Unlike the animal, which is adapted to the medium, man transforms his medium. The sensation of perfection in every baby animal is curious; the animal body is a catalogue of responses that are already established. Persons come into the world, on the other hand, in the process of being established. Economic science is popularly understood as the way to make money; that is, chrematistics. But this popular interpretation does not take into account the fact that the word chrematistics comes from *khrêma*, which in its turn comes from the verb *krháo*, which means to have in the hand. According to Professor L. Polo: 'the primitive sense of this word alludes to the fact that man is a being with hands' (Polo 1996: 91). Productive activity is possible because man is capable of manual activity. Rothbard hits the nail on the head when he points out as the first assumption of the right of property the right of possession of one's own body and the transformation of the medium through work.

This corporal attachment is fundamental for the satisfaction of primary needs, but the attachment has a characteristic feature: exclusivity. The possession by a person of any good excludes other people. Property is the right to dispose of a thing on one's own, while excluding other people. As Pannenberg indicates: 'the relinquishing of the characteristic feature of exclusivity in the concept of property, which would make this a mere right to have access to or participate in something, would result in the elimination of ownership itself' (Pannenberg 1983: 404).[5] The very characteristic of human ownership is derived, as Kirzner tells us, from the discovery of the means through the exercise of entrepreneurship. The transformation of the means through individual work is the origin of ownership. Ownership does not originate because a person may have access to a thing but because he can exercise his creative ability with it and use it for a productive activity.

However, the aspect of exclusivity is not particular to human possession – animals also possess things. Every predatory animal has its hunting ground and dominates other members of its group. Even a domestic dog has its favourite bone. Animals graze in order to feed themselves, but we do not say that they work. A lion hunts to eat, but we do not say the work of a lion is to hunt. All work is a tiring activity. It cannot be otherwise, given the corporate reality of man. As well as the tiredness, the other characteristic feature of human work is to give a meaning to the activity that human beings carry out. As Kirzner points out, an action is undertaken because it is considered that its results will be beneficial. For example, picking fruit is intelligent conduct. Fruit is collected not only for the needs of the present moment but also in order to use it later. Unlike the animal, which only grazes to satiate its present hunger, man collects for the future. Pannenberg offers as an example of work, the preparation of food (Pannenberg 1983: 406). Food can be prepared to conserve it better or to satisfy one's taste – Professor Polo considers the culinary art as one of the primary manifestations of cultured behaviour. As Pannenberg indicates: 'work provides a means of living, not only in the present instant, but as a precaution for the future, and so, incipiently, as a precaution for the whole life' (Pannenberg 1983: 406).[6] These considerations introduce us to the second function of private property as an institution.

Private property and reciprocal behaviour[7]

By producing more than is needed persons demonstrate the socializing aspect of work. A person produces more than he needs of one product, but at the same time he lacks other products. In a common world, man realizes that another person makes the thing that he desires available and that he has something to offer in exchange for it. The exchange happens because both perceive it as a gain. Each person values the thing that he receives more highly than the thing that he gives.[8] The typification of this behaviour makes possible the division of labour and the increase in production. Rothbard emphasizes that the exchange is always beneficial, even though one of the persons who takes part is more productive than the other in absolute terms. He comments:

> This insight into the advantages of exchange, discovered by David Ricardo in his Law of Comparative Advantage, means that, in the free market of voluntary exchanges, the 'strong' do not devour or crush the 'weak', contrary to common assumptions about the nature of the free-market economy. On the contrary, it is precisely on the free market where the 'weak' reap the advantages of productivity because it benefits the 'strong' to exchange with them.
>
> (Rothbard 1998: 36)

We can consider that the division of labour is the consequence of the reciprocity of the expectations of behaviour among private owners. Each person can utilize his property:

> cooperation under the principle of the division of labor is favorable to all participants. It is an advantage for every man to cooperate with other men, even if these others are in every respect – mental and bodily capacities and skills, diligence and moral worth – inferior.
>
> (Mises 1966: 40)

By means of the division of labour the process of production is accelerated. If, following Rothbard, we bear in mind that the two ways to legitimize private property are personal work and exchanges, then the greater the development of the division of labour, the greater the increase in the possibilities of production through private property.

The objectivization of private property as an institution

The necessity of covering needs by means of reciprocal behaviour, which implies being able to dispose exclusively of one's goods, is the origin of property. As Rothbard says, work and property form the sphere of liberty. Property as an institution recognizes the right of every individual to dispose of his resources for an action. This is the recognition of a mutual condition that cannot be denied without grave consequences. Rothbard refers to this objective recognition, saying: 'it is necessary to establish an objective ethic which affirms the overriding value of liberty' (Rothbard 1998: 214). As Hoppe puts it, property as a possession reaches its full meaning in self-possession as the essence of individual liberty. His axiom of argumentation demonstrates the objective value of private property as the basis for market economics. The work of Kirzner, Rothbard and Hoppe shows that the importance of private property *is the social recognition of personal autonomy, is the social recognition of the exercise of each person's creative capacity and the usufruct of the results.*

6 Causality as a praxeological category

Causality in the work of Mises

In this chapter we are going to analyse the treatment that Mises gives to causality and the problems that it presents. The study of the relation between causality and the axiom of action is perfectly delimited. The objective of this study is not to give a general treatment of causality, which would mean a study of the philosophical problems that arise and the solution provided by the different philosophical systems. Mises' objective is much more limited; focusing on the study of human action, he wonders about the relation between human action and causality. Mises never ceases repeating: 'we must restrict our endeavors to the study of human action' (Mises 1996: 25). In his study of causality Mises differentiates very clearly between the basis of causality and the determination of the cause.

The basis of causality

Causality, as a praxeological category, is based on the intrinsic unity of two specific features of man, thinking and acting. Mises takes the Kantian theory of knowledge and considers that causality is a logical imperative of the human mind. It is an a priori structure, that is, prior to every experience that shapes the act of thinking itself. In other words, causality is a principle of knowledge for the mental understanding of reality. It is sufficient, for the development of the praxeology, to bear in mind that 'there is only one logic that is intelligible to the human mind and that there is only one mode of action which is human and comprehensible to the human' (Mises 1996: 25). Therefore, the starting point of Mises' analysis is that man has to know the causal relation in order to act; causality is a category of action. Human action, which is intrinsically connected to thought, is conditioned by causality. Mises' treatment of causality starts by recognizing that the category of ends and means presupposes the cause–effect relation. This relation answers the question, where and how must I intervene in order to divert the course that events would adopt without my interference and which is capable of impelling those events towards objectives that best satisfy my desires? In other words, Mises' study of causality is limited to the study of the relation of causality to the axiom of action. In Mises' work the study is focused on this relation because 'man is in a position to act because he has the ability to discover causal relations which determine change and mutations in the universe' (Mises 1996: 22).

The determination of the cause

In the previous section we have seen that Mises considered that causality was a praxeological principle of action. Causality is based on the fact that action and knowledge are two realities inherent in man. But the fact that we know on what the cause–effect relation is based does not imply that we know for sure the cause of each event. Mises separates two problems which generally are combined: what causality is and how we determine the cause.

We have already seen that Mises establishes causality in the reality of the action, but there are many mutations whose causes are unknown to us, at least for the present moment. The determination of the causes, argues Mises, has been posed in the search for the regularity of the phenomena and in the search for laws: if A then B. However, continues Mises: 'sometimes we succeed in acquiring a partial knowledge so that we are able to say: in 70 per cent of all cases *A* results in *B*, in the remaining cases in *C*, or even in *D*, *E*, *F*, and so on' (Mises 1996: 23). When we do not know the cause for sure, we deal with probabilities. Mises distinguishes two types of probability: the probability of class or probability of frequency, and the probability of case. The probability of class is used in the natural sciences. It is concerned with simple statements about the frequency with which different results are usually produced. Mises uses the following illuminating example:

> A doctor may determine the chances for the full recovery of his patient if he knows that 70 per cent of those afflicted with the same disease recover. If he expresses his judgment correctly, he will not say more than that the probability of recovery is 0.7, that is, that out of ten patients not more than three on the average die.
>
> (Mises 1996: 110)

The probability of case, unlike the previous one, supposes that we know some specific circumstances whose presence or absence causes a certain event to be produced or not produced. Beyond the field of probability of class, everything that is generally understood by the term probability has to do with that special mode of reasoning employed when examining singular and individualized facts. This material is specific to the historical sciences. This second type of probability appears in the ground of human action, 'entirely ruled by teleology' (Mises 1996: 107).

In short, the Misian conception of causality is built upon two pillars: (1) causality is a principle of human knowledge. It is a principle of the mental understanding of reality. Causality is based on the mental structure of the person. (2) The determination of the cause in human action is based on the probability of case. These two pillars, although they are not fundamental for praxeology, since its basic support is the axiom of action, enable us to develop a very interesting series of implications.

On the Misian basis of causality

There is a vicious circle involving causality and the axiom of action if on the one hand Mises needs causality as a requirement for his axiom of action, while on the other hand he does not have the causal relation at his disposal until the event has finalized. Mises himself recognizes this: 'we are moving in a circle. For the evidence that we have correctly perceived a causal relation is provided only by the fact that action guided by this knowledge results in the expected' (Mises 1996: 23). What solution does Mises offer? None, from what can be deduced from the following: 'we cannot avoid this vicious circular evidence precisely because causality is a category of action. And because it is such a category, praxeology cannot help bestowing some attention on this fundamental problem of philosophy' (Mises 1996: 23). In the next paragraph, we will explain how to break this vicious circle by introducing the dynamic structure of causation in the dynamic structure of action.[1]

On the determination of the cause

The probability of case plays a fundamental role in Misian methodology.[2] Each person when performing an action weighs up the importance that each event may have in the process. Each singular fact is weighed up within the sequence that constitutes the action. The probability of case is based on the personal interpretation of the phenomena that intervene in the process. It is a subjective interpretation which deals with information that is incomplete and cannot be evaluated numerically. In Mises' words: 'case probability is not open to any kind of numerical evaluation' (Mises 1996: 113). It is important to emphasize that Mises' concept of probability does not admit any numerical calculation. He makes this statement to differentiate his concept of probability of case, based on methodological subjectivity, from the theory of subjective probability, which, on the basis of statistical inference, attempts the quantification of human action. If we focus on a comparison of the different probabilistic theories we will go beyond the scope of this book, since the subject of causality is a problem when it generates a vicious circle with the axiom of action. Therefore, our objective is to study action in greater depth in order to rid ourselves of this vicious circle by using praxeological categories.

The Misian basis of causality

The vicious circle of the principle of causality and the axiom of action

The existence of the vicious circle within praxeology is of secondary importance: praxeology maintains its coherence in spite of this flaw. As Mises points out, the philosophical problems posed by causality fall outside praxeology. However, the resolution of this vicious circle is pertinent because as causality is a praxeological category, we cannot avoid alluding to the fundamental philosophical problem in question. The vicious circle begins with the Misian basis of causality in intelligence.

For him, causality is the principle of the intellectuality of reality. Concerning this starting point of Kantian origin, Mises defines the principle of causality as a law. In this way, causality is the search for regularities among events, postulated in the following form: given A then B occurs. But this cause–effect relation has to be known to the human agent before he acts. So causality is a prerequisite for the action. The knowledge of the cause–effect relation precedes the action – in other words, the cause temporally precedes the effect. However, this knowledge, which as a prerequisite of the action is its temporal antecedent, is the result of the said action. We move in a vicious circle, since we show the causal relation after which our acting has caused the expected result.

This vicious circle is based on two assumptions of Kantian origin: (1) causality is a structuring principle of the human mind, and (2) in the cause–effect relation, the cause temporally precedes the effect. The study of the historical formation of these two assumptions will be of great interest because it is going to show us the way to resolving the problem of the vicious circle in which we find ourselves.

Causality in Aristotle

To understand the Misian scheme it is necessary to study its historical genesis. The starting point is the classical one, where the Aristotelian view dominates the whole question. Aristotle bases causality on it being a principle. For Aristotle, this principle 'consists of something arising from something else' (Aristotle, *Metaphysics*, V, I, 1013a 17–18, Ross 1975) and the cause is a mode of principle. Therefore, causality is a case of principle: the causes are principles. This vision has determined the later development of causality. Causality has been limited to being a special case of the principle of being able to provide an explanation for something. In this view, there is causality when the principle that originates the transformation can be determined. Causality is reduced to being able to give an explanation about the origin of a transformation or change. In the Aristotelian scheme of things the problem that represents the basis of causality and the determination of the cause are already identified. This first of these is resolved by defining causality as a principle, which leads us to ask ourselves about the way of acting of each principle to determine each cause.

Therefore, the problem of causality is focused on the study of the principles that act on the natural substances. As soon as we know the principle of why one thing proceeds from another, we will be able to determine its cause. Aristotle said that the substance has powers, *dynámis*, which go into action because of the influence of the other substances which are in the action, and it is precisely these which activate the cause. In this way causality precedes the activity. When we can confirm the cause, when we know what has influenced the substance, there will be activity. Aristotle indicated four types of causation: material, formal, efficient and final. For instance, matter is something that stays intrinsic to the developing being, and enables this being to be engendered from its matter. The form gives it a determination; the efficient cause gives it a principle of change; the final cause, a *télos*, or end. To clarify the distinct Aristotelian meanings of causality let us take the following examples. One example of a material cause would be the bronze within the statue, or the silver in the jewel. The formal cause would be the formal configuration of both the statue and the jewel. However, the material has been given a form, which raises the question, what is the origin of the transformation?[3] What or who has transformed the bronze or the silver? From the reply we get to this question, we obtain the third form of causation. By replying that the artist has transformed the bronze or the silver, we are pointing out the efficient cause. Lastly, the final cause would be to ask the reasons why the artist carried out these works.

Of the four types of causation, the first two, the material and the formal, are more than arguable and over periods of history they have disappeared. Finality is considered something inherent in man and has abandoned the general framework of causality, and is reduced to the efficient cause. The reduction of causality to the efficient cause, starting from the Aristotelian framework, was necessary and it was expressed concretely in the study of movement, since, if causality is the determination of the act or *energeia* which activates a power or *dynámis*, it is then necessary to study the causes of the movement.

Causality in modern times

Causality in the Middle Ages was focused on the study of movement in the universe. Men discussed what was called the fall of the elements: the question of whether, when a body moves in space, the falling movement was or was not in conformity with the rotating movement which the body might have. In Zubiri's opinion, it is Galileo who changes this point of view of causality. Galileo defends a new science in which he is going to tell us how things happen, and he measures some dimensions and some duration of time; he measures a series of things and, giving them some numbers, he sees that there are effectively some results which are expressed in other numbers, which are functions of the first ones. The problem of the basis of causality in reality disappears and the problem for Aristotle of the determination of the causes is transformed into a statistical study of regularities. As Zubiri points out: 'the problem of causality [its basis and the determination of the cause], which had been reduced to the plane of efficient causality, has passed from the plane of efficient causality to the plane of lex' (Zubiri 2003: 50).

Hume criticizes this interpretation of causality as law. His well-known criticism is the following: one can never have experience that the pull on a rope is what produces the sound of a bell. What can be said is that regularly and with perfect normality, whenever there is a pull on the rope, in certain conditions the sound of a bell is produced, but the fact that the first action is the cause of the second is something that completely escapes the senses. What we call laws are purely and simply habits of showing the succession or the coexistence of certain phenomena which are presented to the perception of the senses. Hume concludes that as there is no basic sensation of causality, then causality is a habit or custom.

It is necessary to distinguish two aspects in Hume's criticism: (1) first, Hume again poses the study of causality in its two aspects. He is right when he states that we cannot be sure of knowing the cause of an event. Many times what was considered to be the cause was one that later investigation has refuted. Hume shows that the basis of causality has in reality been reduced to the determination of the cause and, as he points out, knowing the cause is always problematic. (2) One problem is to determine the cause, which is very problematic, and another problem is to consider that causality is based on habits. Can causality be considered a habit, given the difficulty of knowing the cause with certainty? Yes, says Hume.

These two aspects of Hume's criticism are the starting point of the Kantian treatment of causality and also of Mises' treatment of the same subject. The analysis of Kant's work on this problem will offer us the solution to Mises' vicious circle. Kant criticizes the reduction of causality to mere habit, although he recognizes that Hume had awakened him from his dogmatic dream. That is to say, *he accepts Hume's criticism with respect to the problem of the determination of the cause and he rejects the basis of causality in habits.* In order to understand the argument which he uses against Hume, the following is a key text, chosen by Zubiri from Kant's *Kritik der reinen Vernunft*:

> Let us take the proposition, 'everything that happens has its cause. In the concept of something happening, I certainly think of something that exists, prior to which there was a certain time and naturally another time after that and another after that, etc.' From this concept I can deduce as many analytical judgments as I wish. In other words, I can have the concept of a thing that begins, see that the beginning is included within a previous time and a consecutive time, and make all kinds of direct physical and metaphysical analysis of that thing. But the concept of cause is this: the concept that something exists that is different from that which is happening, this can never be obtained from analysis of the concept of what is happening.
>
> (Kant 1930: B13, 9–11)

Kant tells us, in this paragraph, that any analysis can be made about what happens, but we will never find in this appeal to another thing, distinct from what happens, that there would be exactly the cause of the event of the first thing. This cannot be obtained with analytical judgements. Hume demonstrated that it was impossible to determine the cause analytically. One cannot obtain more than synthetic judgements.

So the appeal to a second thing is a synthesis with respect to the analysis of the first one. Therefore, the principle of causality is not a principle of reality; rather it is a mere principle of knowledge. In other words, causality is a principle of the apprehension of reality. Kant establishes causality as a principle of human knowledge. For Kant, the value of causality is not based on an analysis of concepts, nor in a perception of realities, but rather it is a condition of intuition inherent in the human intellect. Starting with Kant, the role of the individual in the act of obtaining knowledge is fundamental. Man acquires an active character in cognition. Up to this point, we have seen the formation of the first assumption of Mises and still there has been no reference to the vicious circle between causality and action. It is necessary, in order for this to emerge, to analyse Mises' second assumption: *in the cause–effect relation, the cause precedes the effect in time.*

The Misian determination of the cause

The determination of the cause in the action

Mises' second assumption relates the cause–effect causal structure to the temporal structure, establishing that the cause temporally precedes the effect. However, if in order to act the human agent must know the effect of his action, causality is prior to the axiom of action. On the other hand, to recognize a certain causal relation, a person must be able to perceive the results of his action, and this produces a vicious circle. To resolve this vicious circle it is necessary to study more deeply the Kantian treatment of causality because Mises adopts it in its entirety. Kant's work gives pre-eminence to the active role of man in knowledge. He makes causality a principle of knowledge, but it is still necessary to explain the method for determining the causes. In this second problem of causality, Kant takes as an example the physics of Newton. In this mechanistic model everything that is in time has an antecedent that determines it rigorously. Therefore, in this model the cause–effect relation is considered from the point of view of the effect and one seeks the temporal antecedent that originates it. In this way, Kant unites causality and temporal determination.

We are not going to involve ourselves in the importance that causal determinism has for physics. We are going to focus on the study of human action, bearing in mind that it is the kingdom of final causality or teleological causality and we are going to ask whether in human action the causes have to be antecedents in time. Mises takes this Kantian premise of causality as his starting point, according to which the temporal form of causality is the condition why the principle of causality is applied to real things. The knowledge of what has happened previously is the step prior to knowledge of the cause. In this temporal form of causality, the principle of causality is prior to the action. This situation causes Mises' vicious circle: the causal principle precedes the action; but in order to know the cause which produces an effect, the action must be finished.

The vicious circle comes from following the Kantian model exactly and placing the antecedents of the action in a time prior to the finished action, which as we shall see is false. Let us go back to the phrase, which has already appeared in this book, the *person acts, motivated by a future that exercises its effects on the present.* The antecedent of the action, the cause, does not precede the action in time, but the cause of the action is the desired reality, which is projected into the future, and we dedicate our present efforts in order to obtain this reality. In other words, in human action the cause does not precede the action but it is based on man's activity of making projections into the future.

We need to make a short digression concerning this paragraph because of the pertinent criticism that an anonymous reviewer made for me.[4] He or she points out quite correctly that in the action, there is the anticipation of the subsequent effect, which constitutes the cause of the action. And the reviewer states: 'even in human action, therefore, and *pace* Aranzadi, causes temporally precede their effects'. Thus, *the project temporally precedes the performance of the action*. This criticism is correct provided that one takes the following into account. Rather than preceding in time, the project is based on the category of anticipation, which is given in the present consciousness of the action, and of the person himself in the course of the action itself. Therefore, the anticipated action and the real action cannot be reduced to a mere extrapolation of past experiences. Provided that we are aware of man's openness to the future, the anticipated project and the present action are co-determined in the reality of the experienced life. That is to say, in the course of the action the project is always in a state of constant revision. Thus the future project exercises its effects on the present time of the action, and at the same time the present performance of the action feeds back to the project. *If we organize this process chronologically, from this point of view we can state that the action precedes the project*. That is, even accepting the premises of the criticism, we have reached the opposite premise. Therefore, I think it is very difficult to consider the project as something given prior to the action. If we simply state that the project precedes the action chronologically, we can separate it analytically from its originating structure and consider it a priori to the action. If this was so, *it would be necessary to consider the sense of the action once it had been realized and we would fall into the Misian circle*, which we have already explained. In short, although I accept that one can consider that the project precedes the action in time, one must take into account that in reality there is a constant feedback between the project and the action. To avoid this problem of the chronological antecedents of some praxeological elements on others, I consider that my position is theoretically solid. And I stand by the statement that in human action the cause does not precede the action, but is based on man's activity of making projections into the future. However, it is necessary to develop a concept of causality that fits in with this dynamic structure of the action. In my opinion, the concept of personal causality, which we are going to introduce shortly, may be most suitable for resolving this problem.

Zubiri says:

> As I see the matter, it is essential that we introduce a type of what we might call 'personal causality'. The classical idea of causality (the four causes) is essentially moulded upon natural things; it is a natural causality. But nature is just one mode of reality; there are also personal realities. And a metaphysical conceptualization of personal causality is necessary. The causality between persons *qua* persons cannot be fitted into the four classical causes. Nonetheless, it is strict causality.
>
> (Zubiri 1997c: 339)

The study of causality in the natural sciences has always been posed from observing the effect and looking for the cause in a previous time, but in the social sciences, the field in which persons act, one has to take into account that persons pursue a future end, which exercises its effects on the present. With the concept of personal causality developed by Zubiri, the vicious circle between causality and action disappears. *The cause is constituted in the dynamic structure of the action.*

The two problems posed by causality – its philosophical basis and the determination of the cause – are resolved. Mises' first supposition is completely valid as a philosophical basis of causality. However, the real problem that the person faces when acting is to know what to do to change his situation. It is this second problem – that is, the determination of the causes of the action – which is the responsibility of praxeology. If we take into account that the person always acts with an end in mind which he projects into the future, then this end is the cause that makes the human agent transform his situation. In short, with regard to the basis of causality, Mises is right when he says that causality is a necessary gnoseological principle so that the person can intuit reality. If the means and the ends were not in causal relation, they would be unintelligible. Regarding the determination of the cause, the perception of the ends that motivate the person to act is the causal dynamism which in the dynamic structure of the action organizes the action in projects. We are going to keep to Zubiri's terminology and denote this causal dynamism as *personal causality* and to differentiate it from final causality. The former refers to personal dynamism par excellence: human action.[5]

Conclusion

Using the concept of personal causality we can verify the importance the probability of case has in Mises' scheme. This probability is the personal valuation of the relative importance of events in the process that constitutes the action. It is the personal valuation of what is singular and unrepeatable that makes up human history.[6] This personal deliberation does not allow for any kind of scientific numerical calculation. As Mises says: 'what is commonly considered as such exhibits, when more closely scrutinized, a different character' (Mises 1996: 113). These quantifications are subjective valuations, which are more or less reasoned and relevant, but cannot be considered at all to be objective scientific knowledge.[7]

The scheme of the laws of natural science, developed by Galileo, cannot be related to the problem of personal causality. In this law everything is reversible. Any of its terms can be taken as the subject of the law. I can pose the law as Y as the function of X or inversely, X as the function of Y. In personal causality this is not possible. Once a cause is given, the effects are irreversible. One can correct the course of the action, but what is a fact is a fact. Causality is applied independently of any idea of scientific law. Reality is much more than a system of regularities. The problem of the reality of the action is to see who provides the motives. Human action is not reducible to the study of some past regularity. As Zubiri indicates, human action is self-positioning: 'and consequently, the antecedents do not fit the scheme "consequent–antecedent"' (Zubiri 2003: 61). The action encompasses the causality, and not the other way round. In the natural sciences, causality is studied from its effect. A phenomenon attracts people's attention and they try to determine its causes. If it is not possible to do this with absolute certainty, at least it can be done in statistical terms. This is the usual scientific utilization of the principle of causality, which works from the effects. However, this principle only explains how things occur. More than causes they are conditions. This principle does not propose the idea that persons do things with reality. He only studies what there is at a certain moment. This principle of the law 'does not pose the problem as to what "beginning" means and what "ceasing to be" signifies in reality' (Zubiri 2003: 63). This principle is not applicable outside the field of repeatable and controllable experiments. It must adapt itself to the laws of probability. But *probability cannot say anything about what does not exist, because what does not exist must be created.*

7   The project

In this chapter, the last one in the first part of this book, we are going to analyse the last two components of action: (1) the projection of the system of means and ends, and (2) the execution of the project. In the first part of this chapter we will analyse the structure of the project. Generally, when talking about the project one understands the organization of the productive factors. In our study we are not going to focus on this view, but rather on something that is anterior and more radical: the way in which entrepreneurship is developed. If, as we have shown, entrepreneurship is not a factor of production but the creative capacity of the person, we cannot reduce the projection to the technical manipulation of the factors of production. Rather than talking about resources in physical terms, we are going to talk about the way of creatively integrating the means for the attainment of the desired end. In other words, we are going to focus on the organization that each person makes of the system of means and ends. We are going to call this dynamism of pure entrepreneurship, the project. It is important to stress this approach, which is our starting point. We are not going to deal here with the inherent technical difficulties in the execution of any economic project. These difficulties are faced because undertaking the project is considered beneficial. The person makes projections from what is given and undertakes the project if he previously perceives the possibility of profit. The future projection of the human dimension interests us because in this projection the creative capacity of each person is manifested. This capacity is demonstrated in the creation of increasingly ambitious ends and in the search for the necessary means for their attainment. We cannot forget another fundamental element in the projection: time as a praxeological category. We are not referring here to the analogical time of a clock, but the way in which each person organizes his time of action; that is, the way of organizing the means in stages. In short, it is the time that each human agent gives himself to achieve his ends. Therefore, the project is the temporal organization of the means to attain the ends.

This chapter finishes the explanation of the dynamic structure of action of Mises. If we began with the concept of pure entrepreneurship to explain the discovery of means and the creation of possibilities, we must finish by explaining the dynamism of this praxeological category to understand how the person modifies his situation through the action. In this way, the dynamic structure of the action has constitutive sufficiency. Each one of the elements that we have been explaining is based on the others and the last one of them, the execution of the project, reverts to the original framework: human reality. However, the final reality is not the same as the reality at the start; the situation has been modified in the process. Each person has modified his situation at the start, by acting. As we defined it at the beginning of this part devoted to Mises, human life is intellectually directed action. But we cannot state anything about the result of the action. It may be that the action is a success or a failure. There is no reason why our efforts should be guaranteed success. In the final section of this chapter we will devote ourselves to analysing the consequences that the execution of the project has for the original framework of the action. This result may be a success or a failure; in praxeology there is no logical restriction that imposes limitations on the result of the processes that we are studying. Failure and error are as feasible and real as success and profit.

The constituents of the project

The possibilities that the person subjectively creates are, from the point of view of entrepreneurship, the result of the intelligent management of reality. Reality is expanded by the possibilities, managed by intelligence, of integrating it into human projects. Man invents possibilities through originating and managing the unreality of the project. If, however, it is true that what is possible is based on real properties of things, it cannot be reduced to them because what is possible, although not yet in existence, arises from the action of intelligence on reality.

The aim of this section is to explain entrepreneurship as the capacity to create information, to elaborate it and to produce efficacious responses. Entrepreneurship acts on the structure of means and ends. It evaluates the distinct possibilities of action, and it decides on one of them. Therefore, the constituents of the project are the end, the means and the evaluative system. In Chapter four we analysed the discovery of the means and the creation of possibilities, and in Chapter five we investigated the evaluative system. Therefore, we have still to analyse the determination of the ends and the structure of the project.

The determination of the end of the action

To project is to anticipate a goal. Every person when tackling a project undertakes a venture – the project is an unreality; it is a projection of the person. He projects himself into the future, transcending the present. The project is a line of action about to be undertaken; it activates, motivates and directs the action. In the origin of all the events, projected into the future, there is a desire to act. Every person undertakes a project, however routine it may be, outside his area of immediate development. The objective is perceived in a diffuse and not very clear way. Rather than being a clear, precise piece of knowledge it is a sensation of lacking something. What does a person know about an objective when he proposes something? He always starts from very vague ideas. J. A. Marina points out that the objective may be any thought-provoking reality about which many possibilities are conjectured.

Let us emphasize again that these possibilities are not properties of things, but initial operations by the people that change the importance of things. They become rich in ideas, interesting and promising. We perceive improvements in the situation in which we find ourselves. As Mises indicates, in the origin of each action there is the perception of a lack of satisfaction and the knowledge, however diffuse it may be, of a more satisfactory situation that becomes the objective of our action.

The end of every action has two essential characteristics:

1   *Every objective is the perception of a need for something, united with the desire to act.* The perception of the goal anticipates the route to follow in order to achieve it. In every project, the person ventures beyond what is given and what is statistically foreseeable, penetrating into the unreal, into what does not yet exist. The person seeks what he has never seen.[1] Human action on projecting itself into the future ventures beyond what it is given in the present. It does not seek a repetition of the past, but rather its improvement. Each individual's personal reality is enlarged with possibilities, which up to that moment he had never attempted. The project is to submit human action to the attainment of an unreality which does not yet exist, but which the person finds very attractive.

2   *The objective is always an individual perception.* Different people conceive the same reality in a totally distinct way. The characteristic of entrepreneurship is to see possibilities where other people see nothing.[2] This end that is projected into the future brings to bear its effects on the present. There is no insurmountable chasm between the end of the action and the present. The project is the plan that makes our end real and up to date, which to begin with appeared distant and unreal. Between the future and the present there is established a nexus which makes our aspirations a reality. Therefore, the future is not something utopian that has no place in this world. On the contrary, the essential note of the objective that we are pursuing is that it is feasible and that it can be attained. In this way, we can state that the objective we mark in the future is not something that is given to us, but something to be realized.[3]

Once we have decided on an end, we adapt the means for its attainment. Therefore, we can state that projecting into the future is an assignable process. However, bearing in mind that the essential thing about the project is its dynamic character, we cannot separate the assignable character from the procedural one and consider that the ends of the action are given. This separation supposes a fundamental anthropological reduction. If we adopt the hypothesis of the given ends, we forget that there never exists only one course of action; we forget that the possibilities are always plural; that there is never only one solution. For this reason, in Chapter four we talked about the *creation of possibilities in plural*. Man is the animal who possesses a future; he is always confronting multiple possibilities of action. The problem he faces is to determine what he can do with each alternative, to determine the importance or the objective of each possibility and compare them, one with another. Although this idea seems obvious, it is important to stress that the dynamic structure of the action, because of its inherent dynamism, determines multiple ends that compete among themselves. In other words, the action does not exist in the singular, but in *the plural system of ends and means*.

In Chapter three we talked about the active character of assignment, and we concluded that we could say that the person acts with an activated end. Among the different ends within his reach, he decides which one he values most, but as soon as the circumstances change, he can change the valuation and activate another end. As Mises points out:

> if one's valuations have changed, unremitting faithfulness to the once espoused principles of action merely for the sake of constancy would not be rational but simply stubborn. Only in one respect can acting be constant: in preferring the more valuable to the less valuable.
>
> (Mises 1996: 103)

If we separate the end from its generating structure, we do not make an unimportant simplification; we make a change in the basis of the study of human problems. We abandon the real person and we focus on *homo economicus*. We will analyse the consequences of this change of basis in the second part of this book. In praxeological economics, it is fundamental to connect the ends to the structure of the action. The multiplicity of these ends and their dynamic character make it advisable that they should be studied from the praxeological categories that we have developed. If we start from the view of the means and the ends as a dynamic structure, the function of the project is to plan the activities that must be undertaken for the attainment of the end. This planning is based on two praxeological elements: time and information.

The temporal structure of the project

The project is not a dream – in a dream there is no way to pass from unreality to reality. In the project, real things that constitute the resources keep us in the real world. The project is always conditioned by the resources of the action. A great part of the creative task is going to consist of managing the restrictions, and time is one of the principal restrictions. Henri Bergson has these beautiful words about time:

> Time is what prevents everything from being done in one go. It retards, or better, it delays. It must, therefore, be elaboration. Is it not a vehicle for creation and choice? Does not the proof of the existence of time mean that there exists the indetermination of things? Is not time this indetermination itself?
>
> (Bergson 1963: 1333)[4]

In the study of time it is necessary to differentiate two aspects: the historicity of the person and the synoptic structure of the project.

The historicity of the person

The first approach to reality based on time is to recognize that human life has duration; it is understood that life lasts a series of years. But it is duration with a well-determined order – time has a past, a present and a future. As Mises says:

> He who acts distinguishes between the time before the action, the time absorbed by the action, and the time after the action has been finished. He cannot be neutral with regard to the lapse of time.
>
> (Mises 1996: 99)

The passage of time – the before, the now and the after – is not only a duration in three parts, but means that these three parts have a certain order. Before and after mean before and after in the ordering.

This temporal ordering is not only an ordering, but an ordering in which in each moment there only exists one of the parts, the present. The past no longer exists; the future does not exist yet. When the ordering of elements of a magnitude is such that the precedence and posterity in the order means that the one thing ceases to exist and is succeeded by the other, then the ordering is flowing. Mises points out: 'for praxeology, between the past and the future, there extends a wide, real present. The action itself is found in the present because it utilizes that instant when it embodies its reality' (Mises 1996: 121). Here is the key to understanding the historicity of the person.[5] Persons do not live in time; their historicity is somewhat more radical: *the present of man is made of the past and the future.*[6] Not only is human reality in time, but time is found in human reality. Therefore, man not only has a past and a future, as in the physical world, but his present is made of the past and the future.

The historicity of man, that is to say, the flowing of time, implies a direction. Time flows from the past to the future. Mises adds:

> In any case action can influence only the future, never the present that with every infinitesimal fraction of a second sinks down into the past. Man becomes conscious of time when he plans to convert a less satisfactory present state into a more satisfactory future state.
>
> (Mises 1996: 100)

The flowing time means that man is inexorably projected into the future. There is no possible reversibility in his historicity. Every moment lived becomes the past. The now of the present continually enters the past, only being retained in the memory. It is the ends that the human agent consciously projects into the future which exercise their effects on the present. But this present is constantly flowing. There is no way to hold back time. The only way that persons have to go beyond what they have been given, that is, from the flow of time, is to imagine a scheme which synthesizes the steps that they have to take to attain their objective. In other words, persons overcome time by means of the project.

The synoptic structure of the project

The time of the project is the time which the individual counts on to lead his life. Man counts on time and counts on his time to do the project. This structure of counting on time is not independent of the flow: a human is a flowing being independent of the project. The life of man flows inexorably in one direction. The first characteristic of the project is its flow. Every project is a succession of activities. The way to venture beyond this flow is through intelligence. The person organizes the information he possesses and forms a mental picture of the activities that he has to carry out in order to achieve his objective. He imagines his own life as a whole in which the stages of the project are the parts that make up his desired reality. This intellectual imagination or projection towards the future that the person possesses is what, following the example of Zubiri, we are going to call *synoptic structure*.

What is this structure? The *synoptic structure* of the project is the way to escape from the flow. It is a perception of the time which the person has available to carry out the project. In Zubiri's words:

> Man has an intelligence and an intelligence, whose flow, therefore, has two distinct dimensions: on the one hand, like a psychic act it is submitted to a flow, exactly like everything else: with its feelings and its volitions and its entire life. It is a flow of acts that is not discerned; each act, with respect to the others, flows in the unity of the torrent of consciousness. That is the truth: But what happens, in unison is that the intelligence sees precisely its own flowing reality and it counts on the entire reality as such, and therefore, is opened to the totality of the field of what is real in its flowing character. It is the synoptic time. *Then this view of the entire field of flowing reality works again on the present moment of its flowing, and this re-working is exactly the project.*
>
> (Zubiri 2003: 307, my italics)

The capacity to make projections in time is an inherent possibility of man and his life. In every project persons have a synoptic view; the different stages of the project appear in sequential order and exercise their effect on the present time of the action. In the previous paragraph we have used italics for the last sentence of the text by Zubiri because it expresses with clarity and precision the nexus that exists between the projected future and the present time of the action. The desired reality the human agent wants to achieve affects his historicity. This influence of the future on the present is the material that manages entrepreneurship. Now we can understand the definition of the project that we gave at the beginning of this chapter. The project is the dynamism of pure entrepreneurship. This creative capacity is not reducible to the information managed by the person, but rather its fundamental mission is to manage information prospectively; that is to say, to generate plans.[7]

The idea of the synoptic structure of the project is present in Mises' work. He expresses this idea very concisely: 'man becomes conscious of time when he plans to convert a less satisfactory present state into a more satisfactory future state' (Mises 1996: 100). With the unity of the synoptic structure of time and the flow of time, the meaning of the Spanish phrase *dar tiempo al tiempo* (awaiting the opportunity to do something; literally, 'to give time to time') can be explained (Zubiri 2003: 201). Here time functions twice. From the synoptic point of view, it is necessary to let time flow; then, in the flow of time, ideas have to mature, they have to be productive. In every project, one tries to save time. But as Mises indicates, 'For this man too, time would be scarce and subject to the aspect of *sooner* and *later*' (Mises 1996: 102).

In praxeology, a lot of importance is given to the synoptic structure of time in the individual preparation of the projects. This structure is measurable. Time is an ordered structure and, as such, admits a metrical structure. The unit of measure of time is a periodic movement and the duration of time is measured with this periodic movement. The important thing about time is that it is measurable, and not the measurement of time itself. To organize the stages of a project it is necessary to count on time for each activity. Time is countable and thus it makes possible an estimation of the approximate duration of the implementation of the project. The person can organize his time of action by means of chronometry.[8]

This measurement enables comparative statistics to be made. For example, if the average time for completing a university degree course is five years, then to take twice as long appears to be a waste of time. All the statistics of average times enable the human agent to form an idea of the activities he has never realized. In this sense, these statistics are of help in the structuring of the project. But as Mises points out: 'time as we measure it by various mechanical devices is always past' (Mises 1996: 100).

The structure of the information in the project

It is generally considered that the works that initiated the study of information by the Austrian School are the famous articles by Hayek (1937, 1945). In these essays, Hayek, for the first time, defines the principal economic problem, the coordination of individuals in social interactions.[9] This problem arises not because of the technical problems of the combination of the factors of production in a society with the division of labour but because of the division between all the members of the society with the relevant information for the solution to the economic problem. This economic scheme originates in Mises.[10] If we use the praxeological categories our problem is based on the recognition that the entrepreneurship of each person is the engine of human activity. Therefore, the economic problem is focused on explaining how each person creates and discovers the information that is relevant for the exercise of his entrepreneurship.[11] In other words, it deals with studying the development of entrepreneurship in the projected perception of the means and the ends.

In the previous section we have analysed the temporal form of the project, but we still have to explain what it is that entrepreneurship manages. There are occasions when Kirzner defines the alertness of the entrepreneur as 'an abstract, very general and rarefied kind of knowledge' (Kirzner 1973: 69). He indicates the subject that is going to occupy us in this section. Entrepreneurship is the capacity of producing, discovering and modifying information. Therefore, the study of the characteristics of the information will enable us to develop the fundamental role played by entrepreneurship in the project.

The characteristics of the information

The information that is managed in the project has its own series of particular characteristics: the information is practical, private, it is tacit and it is transmissible.[12]

Subjective knowledge of a practical, non-scientific type

This is the type of information that one acquires through practice. In Hayek's words: 'there exists a body of very important but unorganized knowledge which cannot possibly be called scientific in the sense of knowledge of general rules: the knowledge of the particular circumstances of time and place' (Hayek 1976a: 80). The important knowledge for the human agent is not, therefore, the objective and atemporal knowledge that is formulated in physical laws. This body of knowledge, which we call scientific, can provide us with very little when it comes to our desires and our volitions. To act we will have to base ourselves on the particular perceptions concerned with concrete human valuations, as regards both the ends that the person wants to attain, and his knowledge about the ends that he believes the other people want to attain.

Private and dispersed knowledge

Every individual who acts does so in a personal way, as he tries to obtain some ends in accordance with a view and a knowledge of the world that only he knows in all its wealth and with its variety of nuances. Therefore, the knowledge to which we are referring is not something that is given, that can be found at the disposition of everybody on an equal basis. This knowledge is a precipitate that the person has in his memory. All past events are kept in his memory as recollections. Mises makes a brief reference to memory in *Human Action*. He considers that memory is 'a phenomenon of consciousness and as such conditioned by *a priori* logic' (Mises 1996: 35). This reference directs us to the true importance of memory in the theory of action.

Memory is a dynamic system: it constitutes the personal and untransferable access to reality. All the information is managed from the memory. J. A. Marina distinguishes three sources of information (Marina 1993: 123): (1) the system of immediate information, the source of direct information. This is the knowledge that man possesses and is what is traditionally termed memory. (2) The system of media information, made up of all the support material of information: books, archives, videos, etc. (3) Man has a third source of information: the whole of reality. Information is obtained from the things that surround him. Memory manages these three sources of information. If memory does not have the information necessary for a project, it activates the search in all types of documents concerned with the subject. If the information retrieved is not sufficient, it turns to reality itself in order to study it. Every piece of information comes from one of the three sources. For example, if a person wants to know the colour of the Infanta Maria Teresa's dress as painted by Velázquez, he can resort to his memory, see it in a photograph, or go to the Prado art gallery to see the picture. All this information about reality settles in the memory. In other words, access to reality lies in the memory. If a person does not know a foreign language, all the information available in this language is as if it did not exist. As J. A. Marina indicates: 'we only see what we are capable of seeing and we only understand what we are capable of understanding . . . this personal world is not an intimate redoubt that isolates us from reality, but is our access to reality' (Marina 1993: 124).

All knowledge of access to reality depends on the meaning that the memory gives to reality. Each person builds his structure of means and ends from the information that he manages from his memory. Neither the memory nor the world is static: a person is a being-in-the-world, living in reality made conscious. What is perceived in the moment is integrated with what is remembered. These are the limits of consciousness: the perceived and the remembered. Knowledge does not constitute a storeroom where pieces of knowledge are piled up. Memory is active; it offers the ways of approaching reality. In short, to remember is to carry out the act that places a piece of information in a conscious state. Remembering a piece of information settled in the memory brings its sense up to date. In the action, the past sense of the information is questioned: it is interrogated to see if it really has sense in the here and now of the activity. Memory is creative, not only because it is a dynamic system, but because it is handled within a project and manages the possibility.

Memory orders the past with views to future action. It organizes the past with the present so that the past is not lost. The creative capacity of man integrates the information that he possesses in his memory with the ends projected into the unreal future.[13] This is the nexus that unites the project with reality. Persons never start from zero; they dispose of their experience, which enables them to cover the gap that exists between the future end and the present.

Tacit knowledge

Saying that information is tacit is to stress its dynamic character. Information appears in the memory in integrated blocks, which assimilate reality. The assimilation is produced by selection from among an enormous amount of information. Here we are facing a ticklish problem: why do we consider a thing attractive? How can we perceive of something that does not exist yet? Tacit knowledge functions like a gigantic anticipatory system. Even the most highly formalized scientific knowledge is always the result of an intuition or an act of creation, which is none other than manifestations of tacit knowledge. The basis of all scientific research is surprise. Surprise, as defined by Marina, 'is the feeling produced by the inadequacy of what is perceived with what is expected' (Marina 1993: 144). Marina cites the work of A. C. S. Peirce, a researcher intrigued by the singular instinct for guessing that man possesses. The number of hypotheses that can be managed in a scientific study is infinite. It is unheard of that absolutely correct hypotheses are chosen. This author is forced to admit the existence of a type of instinct which puts a limit on the number of admissible hypotheses, and this instinct is manifested as a feeling.[14]

Each person's tacit and private information depends on his experience. However perfect our theoretical knowledge may be, the perfection necessary to learn to do a job successfully occupies a lot of our time. Not only is this theoretical training necessary for us, but what is of incalculable value is the knowledge that we obtain about other people's way of life, the particularities of each region and of all those circumstances that Hayek calls 'knowledge of space and time'.

Transmissible knowledge.

Although it is tacit, information is also communicable. It is communicated by means of social interrelations (cf. Huerta de Soto 1992: 60). In Chapter four we gave a solution to 'knowledge problems A and B' posed by Kirzner that makes it possible to extend the scope of application of entrepreneurship to all reality. We are going to take another brief look at the solution we proposed because it is intimately connected with the form of transmitting the practical, private and tacit information, which constitutes the temporal structure of the project. The 'knowledge problem A' proposed the stability of the social institutions and the 'B' proposed the way of guaranteeing the results of entrepreneurship for each person. These problems are proposed in the following manner: every action starts from a sociocultural framework (problem A). However, in its turn, every sociocultural framework is transformed by individual actions (problem B). The solution we offered was based on demonstrating the very close connection that exists between the two problems: an institutional framework is necessary (to solve problem 'A') so that entrepreneurship can be exercised (to resolve problem 'B'). But the reverse is also true: that entrepreneurship can be exercised (to solve problem 'B') and it institutionalizes people's expectations (to solve problem 'A'). We concluded by stating in Chapter four that in Kirzner's terminology, the solution to 'knowledge problem 'A' demanded the previous solution of problem 'B'.

We are going to pose both problems again, focusing on the information: if we start from problem 'A', that is to say, from the stabilization of the social institutions, we recognize that through culture, each person receives the tradition of his society. What are received are the possibilities of life that have served in the past and that the preceding generations hand down to their descendants. These ways of life are a precipitate of responses that society offers to the new generations. With what we have seen in this chapter, we recognize that this accumulation of knowledge, which constitutes 'knowledge problem A', is practical, private and tacit information that is passed on. Through this process of social interrelations, the person receives information about norms, habits and behaviour, which are summaries of the responses used in the past for resolving daily problems. All this knowledge, which the person receives in the course of his mutual relations, settles in his memory.

However, we have already seen that remembering is updating the sense that the received information possesses. Each person wonders if this information is useful to him, here and now, for undertaking his projects. This situation poses the problem of knowledge 'B' for us. We face the problem of guaranteeing the results of entrepreneurship for each person, since the acceptance of the information transmitted depends on the receiver. This information has to make its sense relevant to the present time and to really be a possibility of present action. If the person with this information can alter his initial situation and attain his ends, he will do so; if not, he will modify it or reject it. Therefore, the institutions and norms are maintained while they guarantee the creative capacity of the members of society.

If we unite the results of Chapter four with what we have expounded in this chapter, we observe that the informative structure of the project has an operative structure in two dimensions: in the first dimension, *the information possesses a had sense*. That is, in a past time it made an action possible. It corresponds to 'knowledge problem A', constituted by the precipitate of norms, habits and behaviour that each person receives through tradition. In the second dimension, *all information has to have a projective sense*; that is to say, it really has to make an action possible. This knowledge is the material which develops entrepreneurship and which constitutes 'knowledge problem B'.

The two dimensions are no more than the reformulation of knowledge problems 'A' and 'B' from the point of view of *the dynamic structure of the information*. This new formulation supports the thesis that we defended in Chapter four about the impossibility of separating the two problems. In reality, there only exists one problem: *the social coordination of individuals who act with practical, private, tacit and communicable information*. If we take this view, the problem 'A', which formulates the stability of the institutions, is posed in terms of the past sense that these same institutions represent, and the problem 'B', which formulates personal creativity, is posed in terms of the projective sense that all practical and private information has to have in the present moment of the action.

The execution of the project

The execution of the project closes the structure of the action. Whatever the type of project, its execution transforms its original framework. When the project is formed, the order is given to start it and it is executed. The fluid character of time means that only one activity can be carried out at a time. The execution of an activity has three fundamental characteristics:

1   Information is created. The creative phase encompasses not only the projection, but also the realization. In the first part of this chapter we explained that the information has two dimensions. In the first dimension, information

has a *had* sense. The information about past facts or about new realizable possibilities with the resources is managed in the projection. In the second dimension the information must have a real sense in the execution of the project. For example, if I have a project to buy a jersey taking last week's price as a reference, it may be that when I go to buy the jersey, the price has varied. In this case the activity is stopped and the purchase is not executed. There is a difference between thinking about a project and executing it. One can plan the construction of a house in a certain time and find unexpected problems when beginning the work, or insuperable technical problems. One can study trigonometry in great detail and still be incapable of measuring a distance on the ground exactly. Examples of this type demonstrate the difference between understanding a sense, a *had* sense, and realizing a possibility, that is to say, to show with facts, the current importance of the sense.

2 The information is integrated in perceptive systems. As we have shown, actions do not exist in the singular but there exist a multiplicity of alternative actions. The end that we are pursuing when carrying out an activity is one among the many possible that may be performed by the person. The information that is generated in the implementation of the action does not only modify the project of this initial possibility, it also feeds back all the structure of the action. The whole structure of means and ends is thought out and evaluated in the light of the new information. For this reason, I consider it more suitable to talk of the generation of means and ends rather the assignment of means to an end. With the new information, the projects, which are in a latent state, acquire new perspectives. It may be that as soon as a project is initiated it is advisable to transform it into another project.[15] To persevere in a project when the person has information which makes it advisable to abandon it is, as Mises says, the opposite of practical reason: 'if constancy is viewed as faithfulness to a plan once designed without regard to changes in conditions, then presence of mind and quick reaction are the very opposite of constancy' (Mises 1996: 104).

3 The project that is executed is a new resource. The realization of any project transforms the reality, either of its own characteristics or of the exterior reality.[16] The resources are not given; they are constituted in the activity. The expression that is heard so often, the world is not what it was, establishes the dynamic reality of the resources. The world of the Romans is not the same as the medieval world; nor is the medieval world the same as the world at the present. For present-day man, the Roman or medieval worlds are possibilities to which he can resort to obtain information, but present-day reality has more possibilities than past worlds. This view of the resources, from their origin in human action, enables us to offer a new interpretation of the characteristics that Carl Menger identifies in economic resources.

Interpretation of Carl Menger's definition of the economic resource

In C. Menger's work there appears a list of the requirements for economic resources, or goods, as they are normally called in economics. For Menger, there are four requirements (Menger 1981: 52):

1 A human need.
2 The thing – that is capable of being a resource – must possess those properties that enable it to be located in a causal relation with the satisfaction of a human need.
3 The person's knowledge of the existence of the causal relation.
4 The ability to direct the employment of the thing, so that it can be really used for the satisfaction of this need.

The problem with which we are faced is to determine the process in which a thing, either material or immaterial, becomes an economic resource. The first component, according to Menger, is a human need, the prerequisite of action. As Mises says, it is prior to the axiom of action. In our explanation the need is the dynamism of pure entrepreneurship. The second and the third components point directly to the activity of entrepreneurship. Pure entrepreneurship is the creation of possibilities of action operating on the properties of things. The possibility is an intellectual perception, which is why it is subject to causality. As we saw in Chapter six, causality does not mean that the cause of the action precedes it in time but that the cause–effect relation has to be seen by the person through an intellectual perception. Finally, the projection and the execution of the project as activities of entrepreneurship can be perfectly defined by using the fourth component indicated by Menger: *(entrepreneurship is) the ability to employ the thing in such a way that it can really be used for the satisfaction of this need*. It is important to stress the interpretation of the characteristics of the economic resource indicated by Menger, for three reasons:

1 The determination of the economic resources depends on the person. The valuation that the person makes of a thing, as resource for action, is accidental to it. That is to say, the economic value of a resource does not depend on the thing itself. The study of the properties of the thing, that is, the determination of its properties, is the object of the physical sciences. Economics is concerned with the thing inasmuch as it has value for a person. Economics is a human science because its object of study is the personal valuations of the means to attain the ends. Therefore, the determination of the requirements which a thing must comply with to become a resource poses, at the same time, the problem of the origin of economic value. In other words, *to explain the origin of economic resources through human action is to base the theory of economic value on man.*[17]
The value of any mean of action, although rooted in the object, originates in the perception and creation of the possibilities of action by man. This

entrepreneurial activity of valuing and projecting is not limited solely to one possibility. As we have seen, the execution of the project creates feedback and brings the whole structure of means and ends up to date. The greater the coordination between the different means, the greater the number of possibilities that are generated. Therefore, the greater the capacity of action, the more highly valued the resources will be.[18]

We have considered these things in order to stress the separation that exists in economic praxeology between the theory of value and the theory of prices. There is a very fine difference between value and price. Paying attention to the division between praxeology and catallactics, and the subordination of the latter to the former, the value of a resource is the subjective appreciation of the suitability of a means to obtain an end or the appreciation of the end itself. On the other hand, in the catallactics, that is, in market exchanges, prices are the transmitters of the information that the human agent uses in his cost–benefit calculation. In other words, prices constitute the system that transmits the information to the market. In Chapter ten we will compare Mises' and Becker's theories of prices and we will see the impossibility of distinguishing between value and price in the Beckerian model.

2   Menger's definition of economic resource does not suppose any mathematical maximizing principle (cf. Chapter 3, endnote 10). His work cannot be reduced to the neoclassical scheme of *homo economicus*, the maximizer of utility. The theoretical sources of this author drink from the waters of the philosophical tradition of Christian humanism.[19] Max Alter points out that the four requisites formulated by Menger coincide with the four causes defined by Aristotle. The material cause would correspond to human need (the first requirement). The formal would correspond to the requirement that the thing that is capable of being an economic resource is in such a form that it can be related to the needs of the person (the second requirement). The efficient cause would be the knowledge of this relation by the person (the third requirement). And finally, the final cause would correspond to the ability of managing the employment of the thing in such a way that it could really be used for the satisfaction of this need (the fourth requirement).[20]

Bearing in mind this parallelism, praxeology makes it possible to interpret Menger's conception of economic activity in the philosophical current, which since its Greek origins has focused on the study of man. Economics in Menger is not reduced to a mere theory of choice. It consists of the activity of creating the means for achieving the ends which the person desires. The economic resource is only explicable with reference to human action.[21]

3   It is necessary to emphasize that any resource of action must comply with these four requirements for a resource of action. Not only do monetized market resources fulfil them, so also do any means that a person uses in a social interrelation. This does not mean that Misian praxeology makes it possible to monetize all human behaviour. It must be stressed as many times as necessary that the praxeological definition of the resource differentiates very clearly between non-monetizable and monetizable scopes of human action. Within

praxeology we must distinguish between non-monetizable social interactions and monetizable market exchanges or catallactics. As Mises points out, praxeology encompasses catallactics.

In Chapter five we concentrated on the studies of Kirzner, Rothbard and Hoppe concerning the relation between ethics and the market and reached the conclusion that private property was the social recognition of personal autonomy. This praxeological interpretation of property demonstrates the difference that exists between property as a moral principle and fortune as a monetary expression of the goods of a person. The right to property, as a moral principle, is not reducible, in the least, to its monetary aspect. *The praxeological view of property encompasses and exceeds its monetary or catallactic aspect.* This relation of the subordination of catallactics to praxeology leads us to a clear separation between value and price.

We are making these remarks to differentiate very clearly between the two approaches under study. Economics of a praxeological stamp is founded on an anthropological base which, as we have developed it, constitutes a general theory of action. On enlarging the anthropological base, the phenomena which can be explained by praxeology exceed by many times those of the market, which is why it becomes necessary to differentiate between monetizable and non-monetizable phenomena. On the other hand, Becker's scheme, which, having no theory of value, has to generalize the use of the neoclassical theory of prices to all human behaviour, reduces the individual to *homo economicus*. In opposition to the Misian position, he proposes monetization as a method of valuation for all human activity. The difference between the two authors is not therefore a question of nuances and their two theoretical schemes cannot be mixed.

The error in praxeology

The pioneering treatment of error in praxeology is due to Kirzner (1979: 120–36). If we start from the characteristics of the information there is nothing to guarantee that the human agent will achieve his ends. He may perfectly well not perceive or discern the important from the superficial information. As Kirzner says: 'there is nothing in purposeful action that by itself guarantees that every available opportunity must be instantaneously perceived' (Kirzner 1979: 130). The praxeological approach proposes the action from the historicity of the person. In each moment of the process it is not possible to go back; the action is irreversible. The real person is impelled by circumstances to decide here and now the course of action to follow. He has to make a decision about a structure that is constantly changing. It is not a question, as Becker supposes, of making decisions where the alternatives are given; it is about deciding to do that thing about which we know nothing for sure, among a multiple of attractive alternatives which are constantly changing. The strange thing in a world as complex as our own is not that there exist errors – that would be logical; the surprising thing is that projects are finished. We have already seen the constant feedback in all the dynamic structure of action. In this constant updating it is perfectly feasible to demonstrate that the steps taken do not lead to the objective and it is at that moment that we perceive that the information that we had previously disdained is the important information for attaining the end. This confirmation of having failed in weighing up the information properly constitutes an error.[22]

The error consists in the a posteriori confirmation that, with the information available, the person could have achieved his objective if he had realized the importance of the elements he had ignored. A very simple, but clear, example of this is taking an examination. There is no more disagreeable sensation, when the exam is over, than realizing that one has ignored an important fact or has not interpreted it properly. The sensation is such that very few people want to know the answers on finishing the exam. Obviously in this book we are not going to analyse that sentiment of anguish, frustration and anger we feel about failure. We have a much more limited objective: that is, to prove that error exists in human action and its existence is fundamental for economics itself; and to show that it is always possible to improve and that it is always possible to eliminate inefficiencies and errors.

Part II

The economic approach of Becker

The generalization of *homo economicus*

8 The definition of economic behaviour in the work of Becker

Introduction

Starting from the basis model, which everyone knows and is taught in every introductory course in economics, Becker extends the theory of utility from its original economic field to all human behaviour. He generalizes the use of the assumptions that sustain the definition of *homo economicus* in order to explain human action in general. This process of extension goes beyond the original framework of consumer preferences in the theory of prices to define his economic approach to human behaviour. Gary Stanley Becker's work is, therefore, the development of the neoclassical paradigm taken to its ultimate consequences.

This process supposes an authentic revolution in its paradigm for the neoclassical model. Becker himself differentiates between the classical utilization of the model and his own model. He considers that his work has consisted of obtaining the *extended* utility function, taking the typical utility function as his starting point. This extension is the logical enlargement of the neoclassical model: it does not imply a rupture with the basic contributions of the model, but the generalized utilization of the combined assumptions of maximizing behaviour, market equilibrium and stable preferences. Becker's success comes from questioning the limits of the application of these assumptions from the moment he began his research activities. If the monetized exchanges can be explained with these assumptions, why not use them as the theoretical basis for the explanation of all human behaviour? We can discern three stages in this extension of the economic analysis of human behaviour:

1 The first stage is the application of the neoclassical model in atypical fields of study. He introduces arguments in the utility function that enable him to explain situations that until that moment were not contemplated by researchers. Becker's thesis, published under the title of *The Economics of Discrimination* (1957), is the first systematic study within the neoclassical school of discrimination in the labour markets of the United States. The second book of this period is his celebrated *Human Capital: A Theoretical and Empirical Analysis, with Special Reference to Education* (1964). In this book all the elements that constitute his working method are already present, although he still does not state or define the potential of his analysis. He does something much more practical:

he makes a systematic study of such an important area as education. It is in his third book *Economic Theory* (1971) that, for the first time, he states the universality of his economic model for explaining all human behaviour.

2   His second period represents his maturity as a researcher. The three fundamental works of this period are the books *The Economic Approach to Human Behavior* (1976), *A Treatise on the Family* (1981) and the article 'De gustibus non est disputandum' (Stigler and Becker 1977). These works constitute a unitary framework of analysis of human behaviour and they clearly establish the way to approach every human action from neoclassical economics.

3   In the last few years, and especially since the award of the Nobel Prize for Economics in 1992, Becker's work has become very popular. His approach to human behaviour has become an object of great interest. To meet this demand, Becker has written two basic works in which he explains his economic approach in general terms: they are his speech on receiving the Nobel Prize, entitled 'The economic way of looking at behavior' (1993), and the book *Accounting for Tastes* (1996). In these works, Becker analyses his own course of development and highlights the most important points in his contributions.[1] A third, and the most recent work, is *Social Economics* (Becker and Murphy 2000), in which he presents the theoretical framework for analysing how the social environment affects people's preferences and behaviour.

The extension of the theory of utility

Becker's essential contribution is the conversion of the basic utility function into what he has called the *extended* utility function (Becker 1996: 26). The way of generalizing the maximizing utility hypothesis to all human behaviour is to introduce, as variables of this function, all the elements necessary to assume every human act as a choice between different alternatives known to the economic agent. The classical utility function is:

$$u = \left(x_1, \ldots, x_m \right) \tag{8.1}$$

where x_i represents the i-th consumer good which the consumer may choose. This economic agent will choose that combination of goods which maximizes this function subject to:

$$\sum_{i=1}^{m} p_i x_i \leq M \tag{8.2}$$

that is to say, subject to the fact that this combination is accessible in market prices, p_i, and to the M euros which the consumer has at his disposal to spend.

The way of generalizing the maximization of utility, even without the existence of market prices, is to pose the following maximization problem. Let:

$$U = U\left(Z_1, \ldots, Z_m \right) \tag{8.3}$$

where Z_i represents the i-th commodity[2] that satisfies the economic agent. Each one of these Z_i commodities has the following production function:

$$Z_i = f_i\big(X_{1i},\ldots,X_{ki};t_{1i},\ldots,t_{ki};S_1,\ldots,S_r;Y_i\big), i = 1,2,\ldots,m \tag{8.4}$$

where X_{ji} represents the quantity of the j-th good or service employed in the production of the i-th commodity; t_{ji} is the j-th person's own time input; S_j represents the human capital of the j-th person, and finally, Y_i represents the other non-specified inputs.

Obviously, not all the Z_i have a market price. Some may represent a commodity that only has a subjective value for a person who is dedicated to producing it for his own satisfaction without introducing it on to the market. But Becker does consider that each Z_i has shadow prices π_i *calculable*. Each one of these shadow prices, π_i, can be broken down into two, adding up to:

$$\pi_i = \sum_{j=1}^{k}\alpha_{ji}\left(\frac{p}{\varpi_1},\frac{\varpi}{\varpi_1},S,Y_i\right)P_j + \sum_{j=1}^{l}\beta_{ji}\left(\frac{p}{\varpi_1},\frac{\varpi}{\varpi_1},S,Y_i\right)\varpi_j, \text{ for } i = 1,2,\ldots,m$$

where P_j is the cost of X_j; ϖ_j is the cost of t_j; α_{ji} and β_{ji} are the input–output coefficients, dependent on the relative set of prices, p; costs, ϖ; human capital, S; and other inputs which are involved in the production, Y_i.

With this new scheme, the *extended* utility function is not restricted by the market prices, but the important constraint to equation (8.3) is:

$$\sum_{i=1}^{m}\pi_i Z_i = S \tag{8.5}$$

where each π_i is the *complete* or *extended* price of the i-th commodity produced by the economic agent and S represents the human capital of each person. With the new formulation each human act is the result of maximizing the utility of the m commodities which the person can produce subject to the human capital, S, which each person possesses and the individual valuation of the price of producing each good, π_i. Therefore, all human behaviour can be posed in the following terms:

$$\text{Maximize } U = U\big(Z_1,\ldots,Z_m\big), \quad \text{restricted to: } \sum_{i=1}^{m}\pi_i Z_i = S \tag{8.6}$$

In short, the passage of the primary utility function to the *extended* one is the result of a double process: (1) the conversion of the goods, x_i, in commodities produced by the person, which is to say, Z_i. (2) The conversion of the market prices, p_i, into shadow prices, π_i, which represent the quantification of the valuations which each person makes of the m commodities that produce utility for him. The best way to understand the consequences of this conversion is to show it in its genesis through the stages into which we have divided Becker's production.

First stage: the application of the neoclassical model in atypical fields of study

In this first epoch, Becker proposes the way to analyse non-monetary phenomena with the instruments that the neoclassical theory of prices offers. Becker argues that if with this theory we can explain the relation which exists between quantities of goods and the money that are exchanged, why not seek a way to quantify, and to express in money terms, the non-pecuniary elements which affect the decision-making of the human agents?

This is the objective of his doctoral thesis. In this work he tries to offer a theory that quantifies the non-pecuniary elements that intervene in discrimination at work. As he says: 'money, commonly used as a measuring rod, will also serve as a measure of discrimination' (Becker 1957: 6). The way he proposes to measure discrimination is to consider that an individual who discriminates acts *as if* he wants to pay something to associate himself with some persons rather than others. Becker calls this sum of money, which the individual is prepared to pay, a discrimination coefficient, abbreviated to DC.

In any relation between persons, the monetary costs are a part of the total costs that are incurred. Let us suppose that an entrepreneur is racist. The monetary cost of employing a person of another race, π, does not reflect the total cost which the entrepreneur puts up with in order to 'tolerate' the person in his company. In reality, his total cost is the salary, π, plus his discrimination coefficient (DC), which quantifies, in money terms, the burden he must put up with for employing this person. Therefore, the total or extended cost will be $\pi(1 + d_j)$.

In his turn, the person employed who receives his salary, π_j, does not earn all he could, if the discrimination did not exist; his real salary is $\pi_j(1 - d_j)$. That is to say, the discrimination supposes a cost for the person who is discriminated against, represented by a percentage of the salary that he could earn, but does not receive. A racist consumer who buys a good produced by the person suffering discrimination pays a price p, but this price does not reflect the aversion that is produced in him in buying this good from a despised person. The extended price would be $p(1 + d_k)$, where d_k represents the DC of the buyer. With this very simple formulation we can extend the classical utility function in order to introduce the discrimination coefficients as an explanatory variable.

The utility function of a racist person would be equation (8.3), where each commodity, Z_i, depends not only on the good, but also on the DC, so:

$$Z_i = f(x_i, \text{DC})$$

For its part, the monetary constraint would be extended to admit d_k, becoming:

$$\sum_{i=1}^{m} \left[p_i (1 + d_k) Z_i \right] = M$$

The interpretation of this new formulation makes it possible to supersede the conception of the economic agent as a mere optant between goods that are given, and he becomes the 'producer' of the commodities which give him satisfaction. The choice of the employees is not a decision between different 'given' alternatives, while the entrepreneur does not choose between different persons, but 'produces' the satisfaction of associating with certain persons.

The objective is to quantify, using the neoclassical theory of prices, the non-pecuniary elements that are fundamental in each act. Becker shows that the problem to be faced is the negligence which the neoclassical economists have incurred by ignoring the effect that the productive process itself has on the person. In other words, he points to the essential problem of the neoclassical model; it is a static, atemporal model, in which the structure of the process is not reflected. Therefore, Becker's aim is to explain the passage of one situation of equilibrium to the next, as the result of the inherent dynamism of the maximization of the *extended utility* function.

In Becker (1964) we find the way to pose the problem, which supposes passing from one situation of equilibrium to another. If we focus on the labour market, the equilibrium condition of the profit-maximizing company is equal to the salary and the marginal productivity of labour. In symbols: $MP = W$. In this formulation of the problem, the relation existing between present salaries and present and future working conditions does not appear. It is a valid first approach, but Becker argues that it is very reductionist because we have experience of the importance that training has for present and future salaries. For example, training may give rise to a reduction in present incomes and an increase in present costs. As Becker points out: 'expenditures during each period need not equal wages, receipts need not equal the maximum possible marginal productivity' (Becker 1964: 10). Therefore, for each period, the marginal productivity of labour and the salary do not have to equal each other. In symbols:

$$M P_t \neq W_t$$

To resolve this problem, we can consider that the person in each period acts *as if* he equalled the adjusted values of income and expenses. If E_t and R_t represent the expenses and the income of the period t, respectively, and if i is the rate of the market adjustment, then the equilibrium conditions can be expressed in the following way:

$$\sum_{t=0}^{n-1} \frac{R_t}{\left(1+i\right)^{t+1}} = \sum_{t=0}^{n-1} \frac{E_t}{\left(1+i\right)^{t+1}} \tag{8.7}$$

where n is the number of periods and E_t and R_t depend on all the remaining incomes and expenses. In this way, the equilibrium condition is equal to the adjusted value of the flow of marginal products and the adjusted value of the flow of salaries.

If we suppose that the company incurs training expenses in the first period alone, then the expenses of the initial period would be equal to the salaries plus the training expenses, and the expenses of the remaining periods would be equal to the deferred salaries, and the income of all the periods would be equal to the marginal products. Therefore, equation (8.7) is transformed into:

$$M P_0 + \sum_{t=1}^{n-1} \frac{M P_t}{(1+i)^t} = W_0 + K + \sum_{t=1}^{n-1} \frac{W_t}{(1+i)^t} \tag{8.8}$$

where K represents the training expenses.

If we define a new term in the following way:

$$G = \sum_{t=1}^{n-1} \frac{M P_t - W_t}{(1+i)^t} \tag{8.9}$$

G represents the surplus of future income over the future expenses that the company receives for training its employees, that is, it is the company's profit. Let us transform equation (8.8) in function of G and we obtain:

$$M P_0 + G = W_0 + K \tag{8.10}$$

In this last expression, K represents the monetary expense of the training, but it is necessary to bear in mind that it does not measure the extended or total cost of the training because it does not include the time that the person devotes to his training, time which he could have dedicated to something else. Therefore, the difference between those who could have produced in that time, $M P_0'$, and what is produced, $M P_0$, is the opportunity cost of the time dedicated to the training.

If we define C as the sum of the opportunity costs and the training expenses, equation (8.10) converts to:

$$M P_0 + G = W_0 + C$$

If we compare G and C, the difference measures the return for the company on providing training. This equilibrium condition not only takes into account the pecuniary aspects but also introduces all the important aspects at the moment when deciding on an investment in training the workforce. Becker points out: 'our treatment of on-the-job training produced some general results of wide applicability' (Becker 1964: 11).

These two specific examples show the method that Becker uses to expand economics to every problem that presupposes the allocation of scarce means among alternative ends. In the manual he wrote for his economics classes, he states: 'it includes the choice of a car, a marriage mate, and a religion; the allocation of resources within a family; and political discussion about how much to spend on education or on fighting a Vietnam War' (Becker 1971: 1). Economics is, in Becker's view, decision-making and an allocation of means and ends. In each decision, prices are the fundamental elements in deciding among the different ends. Becker states: 'in this process prices play a crucial role in the non-market sector where monetary prices do not exist, because economists have ingeniously discovered "shadow prices" that perform the same function' (Becker 1971: 3). In this way, we can have at our disposal the necessary tools to understand all human behaviour. If we start from situations of equilibrium, whether with market prices or shadow prices, the hypothesis of maximizing utility offers us a theoretical basis for analysing any human choice. So it is clear from the following statement: 'it is my belief that economic analysis is essential to understanding much of the behavior traditionally studied by sociologists, anthropologists and other social sciences. This is a true example of economic imperialism!' (Becker 1971: 2).[3]

Second stage: consolidation of the theoretical framework

Becker's maturity as a researcher is usually associated with the publication of *The Economic Approach to Human Behavior* (1976).[4] In this book, he explains with clarity and forcefulness the purpose of his research. In his own words: 'the combined assumptions of maximizing behavior, market equilibrium, and stable preferences, used relentlessly and unflinchingly, form the heart of the economic approach' (Becker 1976: 5). There is no doubt about the objective that Becker proposes:

> I do not want to soften the impact of what I am saying in the interest of increasing its acceptability in the short run. I am saying that the economic approach provides a valuable unified framework for understanding *all* human behavior.
> (Becker 1976: 14)

It is necessary to stop and consider the assumption of stable preferences in order to understand the proposed method. Furthermore, the key to Becker's method is based on the hypothesis of the stability of preferences in order to extend the utility function. What does Becker understand by stable preferences? This hypothesis of stable preferences has a first formulation, which corresponds to this second stage of his research. In this first version he eliminates all references to temporal preference. On the other hand, in the later works of his third period, he reformulates this hypothesis in order to admit temporal preference (Becker 1996: 4). In this section we are going to show the first formulation, and in the third section we will look at the final reformulation of this hypothesis.

In order to formulate the first version of the hypothesis of stable preferences, Becker recognizes that economic access to reality usually ends when it comes up against tastes. So: 'on the traditional view, an explanation of economic phenomena that reaches a difference in tastes between people or times is the terminus of the argument' (Becker 1995: 184). Against this traditional view, Becker offers an alternative opinion, in which 'the economist continues to search for differences in prices or incomes to explain any differences or changes in behavior' (Becker 1995: 185).

Becker poses the problem of the formation of preferences, utilizing the *extended* utility function. We can model the preferences at each moment as the commodities, Z_i, which enter the function as arguments. If we bear in mind equation (8.4), each Z_i represents an alternative or preference.

We prove that although they are related to the goods in the market, X_{ji}, their production depends entirely on the individual, since t_{ji} and S_j represent the time and the human capital that the person devotes to the attainment of that preference. Therefore, Becker argues, this formulation is an interpretation of the formation of the tastes of the persons. If we take into account that each good is associated with a shadow price, we obtain the necessary constraint to represent the formation of tastes *as if* the person maximized his utility. The problem is formulated in equation (8.6).

If we represent the conditions of a first-order solution to equation (8.6), we obtain:

$$\frac{\dfrac{\partial U}{Z_i}}{\dfrac{\partial U}{Z_j}} = \frac{UM_i}{UM_j} = \frac{\pi_i}{\pi_j}$$

which in its best-known form

$$\frac{UM_i}{\pi_i} = \frac{UM_j}{\pi_j}$$

proposes the equality of the marginal utilities weighted by shadow prices. Becker, with his *extended* utility function, manages to generalize the scope of application of the law of marginal utilities, weighted by price.

With the quantification of the non-monetary aspects which intervene in decisions, Becker interprets each act *as if* the person acted in the following way: let us suppose that we observe a decision made by a person at a certain moment, B. At this moment, we show that, for example, this person decides not to marry. Obviously, before B, this person does not know the decision that he is then going to take. Thus, our problem is to explain how from A one passes to making the decision at B. Our starting point is A and we have to determine the variables and the process why the decision is made. Let

$$U = U\left(Z_1, \ldots, Z_c, \ldots, Z_m\right) \tag{8.11}$$

be its *extended* utility function, where among other commodities is the 'commodity' to marry, Z_c. Obviously this 'commodity' has its own production function:

$$Z_c = f_c\left(X_{1c}, \ldots, X_{kc}; t_c; S_c\right) \tag{8.12}$$

where the X_{ic}, with $i = 1, \ldots, k$, are the goods necessary to form a family; t_c, the time devoted by this person to look for a mate, and S_c, the human capital which he deploys in the search for a partner. This 'commodity' has a shadow price:

$$\pi_c = \alpha_c(P) + \beta_c(t) + \gamma_c(S)$$

which depends on the prices of the goods and the valuation of the time, t_c, and human capital, S_c, necessary to marry.

At A he is in an equilibrium situation in which he still values marrying, that is to say:

$$\frac{UM_i}{\pi_i} = \frac{UM_c}{\pi_c}, \quad \text{for every } i = 1,\ldots,m$$

If he knew that at B, the shadow price of marrying has increased because with the passage of time it becomes more difficult to live with another person, that is to say, $\pi_c' > \pi_c$, the equilibrium which existed at A is broken at B.

The situation would be:

$$\frac{UM_i}{\pi_i} > \frac{UM_c}{\pi_c'}$$

Faced with this disequilibrium, the preference for the 'commodity' marrying decreases since its shadow price has been increased and, as the sign of inequality demonstrates, this person has a greater preference for other commodities. This means that his consumption of other commodities increases and, in consequence, its marginal utility decreases.

Therefore, the equilibrium which determines the decision not to marry implies a greater production of other substitutable commodities and thus the equality between marginal utilities weighted by shadow prices is re-established. The condition of equilibrium in B would be:

$$\frac{UM_i'}{\pi_i} = \frac{UM_c}{\pi_c'}$$

where it is observed that faced with the increase in the shadow price of marrying, π_c', he decides to remain single or to increase his consumption of other commodities, up to the level which equals both marginal utilities weighted by the shadow prices, that is to say, UM_i'.

The only assumption that we need in order to explain this process is the *stability of preferences* over time. Becker argues that we can consider that once the relevant variables that have intervened in the decision at B have been specified, this person would like to take at A the decision which he really takes at B. Thus, if this person at A knew that at B the shadow price of marrying was very high, then he would not get married. In short, if this person acted *as if* at A he knew the conditions that are in force at B, obviously, he would like to choose what he really chooses at B: not to get married. This hypothesis of stability is defined by Becker: '"the stability of preferences" supposes that the choices that an individual *would like* to make in the future, if he knew now what would happen in the interim, are exactly the same as the choices he *would actually make* then' (Becker 1996: 11).

In this first formulation of the hypothesis of stable preferences, the thesis says that tastes or preferences are stable over time *if we consider the extended utility function*. That is to say, if with this function we can propose any decision, even though the goods involved vary, we will always be able to model the change in tastes, by adding or eliminating these goods from the production functions of the commodities. As he recognizes: 'George Stigler and I in *De Gustibus* explicitly considered extended utility functions, not subutility functions' (Becker 1996: 6). If we take these functions, with the assumption of stability, we guarantee the stability of preferences because, when we talk about tastes, we are generally referring to changes in the goods that we consume and not to the commodities that we produce, which are basically the same for all of us: love, family, etc.; everything that is totally human.[5]

In this formulation the role of temporal preference is despised. He states:

> in spite of the importance frequently attached to time preference, we do not know of any significant behavior that has been illuminated by this supposition . . . [we] have partly translated 'unstable tastes' into variables in the household production functions for commodities.
>
> (Becker 1995: 204)

To advance in our understanding of Becker's work, it is necessary to differentiate two points. When Becker states, at this time, that tastes are unstable, he is referring to *the stability of the commodities of the extended utility function and not to the goods in the market, which enter as variables of the production functions of these commodities*. It is important to differentiate these two aspects because Becker himself did not differentiate them explicitly until years later in the publication 'De gustibus non est disputandum' (cf. for a new formulation Becker 1992). Let us summarize what we have explained so far, so that we are quite clear about the manifest differences that are offered by the two approaches being studied and to clarify the model that we are going to analyse critically in the following chapters:

1   For Becker, the economic problem consists in decision-making. Starting from a known situation, the researcher has to determine and explain the decision made by the person. Therefore, the first difference lies in the fact that for Becker, economics is the study of decisions in known situations, whereas for Mises the important thing is the process of the formation of ends and means in the action itself.

2   From the beginning Becker's approach is based on another foundation. He does not consider the verification of the hypothesis with the real object of study important. All his reasoning is based on the utilization of the hypothesis, *as if*

He does not consider it important to investigate the real determinants of the action: he recognizes that 'the economic approach does not even assume that humans consciously maximize' (Becker 1981: x). The objective of economics as a science is not to explain what a price is or what an exchange is. For Becker, his objective, starting from empirical evidence, is to explain economics with some hypotheses and to contrast his analysis with this evidence, independently of whether these hypotheses explain the reality, the object of the study. Bearing in mind this starting point, the study of the formation of the structure of ends and means is unimportant. Becker always starts off from ends and means that are known to the researcher. His *extended* utility function supposes an advance on the classical function because, in this latter case, only the equilibrium situation is taken into account, while in the first case the passing from one situation to the next situation is made dynamic. However, all the equilibrium points under study are known beforehand.

3   With this scheme, Becker's economic approach to human behaviour can be resumed in three hypotheses: *maximization of the extended utility function, market equilibrium and stable preferences over the time of the commodities that enter as arguments of the extended utility function.*

The example we have used to explain the hypothesis of the stability of preferences in its first version has been deliberately chosen because it is a particular case of the general formulation that Becker (1981) offers to make, as he says: 'an economic approach to the family, not in the sense of an emphasis on the material aspects of family life, but in the sense of a particular theoretical framework for analyzing many aspects of family life' (Becker 1981: ix). To demonstrate the pertinence of that example as a clear model of the Beckerian methodology, we are going to generalize his formulation so that it corresponds to any commodity produced in the family, and not only the fact of being single. That is to say, we are going to extend this particular utility function to obtain the household production function.

In our example, we start from equation (8.11), where Z_c was the 'commodity' to marry, whose production function was equation (8.12). We will now consider a commodity in general, Z_i and we obtain its production function as a generalization of the production function of the 'commodity' to marry. We will have:

$$Z_i = f_i\left(X_i, t_{hi}, E_i\right) \tag{8.13}$$

where x_i are the goods necessary to produce the i-th commodity, t_{hi} is the time employed in its production and E_i represents the domestic qualifications, which include the human capital, the social medium, the climate, etc. The shadow price of this commodity, π_i, will depend not only on the goods in the market but also on the time employed in the production of each unit of Z_i. That is to say:

$$\pi_i = p_i \frac{x_i}{Z_i} + w \frac{t_{hi}}{Z_i}$$

means that the shadow price is the average cost of the goods and times necessary to produce Z_i. If we substitute the value of π_i in equation (8.5) we have the following constraint of equation (8.13):

$$\sum p_i x_i + w \sum t_{h_i} \equiv S \qquad (8.14)$$

Maximizing (8.13) with respect to (8.14), we obtain the following set of equilibrium conditions:

$$\frac{\dfrac{\partial U}{Z_i}}{\dfrac{\partial U}{Z_k}} = \frac{UM_i}{UM_k} = \frac{\pi_i}{\pi_k}, \quad \text{for all } i, k$$

In short, *the united hypotheses of market equilibrium, stable preference in the extended utility function and the maximization of utility define, as a condition of equilibrium, the law of equality of the marginal utilities, weighted by the shadow prices.*[6]

Third stage: the latest technical developments

Becker's latest works constitute the synthesis of all the contributions he has made. This synthesis pursues two objectives: (1) to delimit the scope of application of his theory; and (2) to expound synthetically the essence of his method of approach to human action. As regards the first objective, his statements could not be clearer. He says: 'the rational choice model provides the most promising basis presently available for a unified approach to the analysis of the social world by scholars of different social sciences' (Becker 1995: 651). Besides the appreciation of the generality of his analysis he does not consider that there exists any alternative approach, as is revealed in the following words: 'I do not believe that any alternative approach – be it founded on "cultural", "biological" or "psychological" forces – comes close to providing comparable insights and explanatory powers' (Becker 1996: 4). This certainty in the scope of application of his method is based on the clear perception that Becker has of attaining the second objective that we have defined. In other words, he considers that his theory constitutes a unitary framework for the comprehension of all human behaviour.

Until his third stage, Becker did not focus on the modelling of the changes in the preferences for goods in the market. If, as we have pointed out in the second objective, Becker attempts a unitary theory of all human behaviour, then this theory has to serve to explain every preference and it is obvious that the preferences for the goods in the market vary. He has to confront the problem that in the first formulation of the hypothesis of stable preferences was eliminated: the temporal preference. Obviously, the first time he expounded his new orientation, this caused a surprise. He himself commented:

Some of you might be surprised to hear a co-author of the *de gustibus* point of view, with his emphasis on stable preferences, waxing enthusiastically about the formation of the preferences. But what *de gustibus* assumes is that *metapreferences* are stable.

(Becker 1995: 232)

Therefore, he differentiates between metapreferences to refer to the *extended* utility function and preferences to refer to the utility of goods in the market.

He wrote *Accounting for Tastes* in order to demonstrate that with the three hypotheses the preferences can be modelled. In this book, he proposes the following formulation of *extended* utility:

$$U = U\left(x_t, y_t, z_t, P_t, S_t\right)$$

where x, y, z are goods; P_t and S_t are personal capital and social capital respectively at the moment t. In this formulation the *extended* utility continues to be stable over time, but both the goods and the personal and social capital depend on past decisions. He needs, in some way, to introduce into his formulation the fact that every human decision about goods in the market depends on past and future decisions. The hypothesis of *forward-looking* behaviour fulfils this objective in the new formulation of the hypothesis of stable preferences. He offers the following definition of the hypothesis of *forward-looking* behaviour: 'this hypothesis implies only that individuals try as best they can to anticipate the future consequences of their present choices' (Becker 1996: 9).

This hypothesis tells us that the person is forward-looking, that is to say, that he undervalues future goods with respect to present ones.[7] To resolve this problem, Becker assumes that 'individuals choose their discount rates (temporal preference) within a framework in which the preferences are *consistent* over time' (Becker 1996: 11). In Becker's hands, temporal preference becomes the union of *forward-looking* behaviour with the hypothesis of stable preferences. Therefore, the hypothesis of stable preferences can be reformulated, stating that the person acts *as if* his behaviour were forward-looking and stable over time – Becker advances this hypothesis in Becker (1995: 634).

In order to have a clear understanding of this third hypothesis, we are going to finish specifying the elements of the *extended* utility function that Becker uses to model the preferences. It is necessary to obtain formulas for both personal capital and social capital. With respect to the former:

$$P_{t+1} = x_t + \left(1 - d_p\right)p_t$$

where P_{t+1} is the personal capital stock next period, x_t is the sum invested in personal capital in the present period, and d_p is a constant depreciation rate. With the hypothesis of the stability of preferences, this formula is interpreted in the following way: the person acts *as if* he invested in himself until he obtains the capital that he really obtains in the following period. In other words, he maximizes his personal capital taking into account his rate of temporal preference.

Regarding the social capital, we have:

$$S_{t+1}^i = X^i + (1 - d_s) S_t^i$$

where S_{t+1}^i is next period's social capital of person i; X^i is the consumption of social goods by all persons in i's network; and d_s is the depreciation rate on social capital. With the hypothesis of stable preferences, this formula is interpreted in the following manner: a person acts *as if* he invested in social capital until he obtains the same sum as he really obtains in the following period. With this new formulation, we can conclude that Becker's theoretical analysis is synthesized in his three hypotheses: (1) market equilibrium, (2) maximizing behaviour, and (3) stable preference.

This theoretical framework is used in Becker and Murphy (2000) to explain social interrelations. They state: 'the analytical approach relies on the assumptions of utility maximization and equilibrium in the behavior of groups' (Becker and Murphy 2000: 5). This approach considers that the social environment is stable and therefore it enters as an argument in the extended utility function. Consider the utility function:

$$u = (x, y; S) \tag{8.15}$$

where x and y are goods or services of all kinds, which we will refer to simply as goods. The variable S represents social influences on utility through stocks of social capital. And the fundamental assumption is that S and x are complements, so that an increase in S raises the marginal utility from x.

Let us consider that each person considers S exogenous to his own preferences, so $S = S_0$. Then a person would maximize the utility function in equation (8.15) subject to his budget constraint:

$$p_x x + y = I$$

where y is the numeraire and I is income.

With this formulation we can find how the social capital stock acts on x demand. If we calculate the first-order maximization conditions we obtain

$$\frac{dx}{dS} = \frac{p_x U_{yS} - U_{xS}}{D > 0} \text{ if } U_{xS} > p_x U_{yS} \tag{8.16}$$

Thus, the effect of the changes in social capital on x does not depend on whether an increment in S increases or decreases the utility of this person, U_s. For example, an adolescent will consume more drugs if his friends also do, independently of whether the consumption of drugs diminishes the individual's utility. In this way, Becker and Murphy point out a crucial problem: how do people choose friends or neighbours who allow them to increase the social capital which originates increments in their personal utility? That is to say, the level of social capital affects individual choices. Let us pose the question the other way round: can we use the individual to explain the formation of social capital stock? That is, although an isolated person does not alter the social capital stock significantly, can we aggregate individual behaviour to model the way in which the choices of the members of the same social determine their social capital?

Consider a group that is big enough for the variations in consumption of a good by any of the members to have an insignificant effect on the capital stock. In this way, S will be the average consumption of the members of the group:

$$S = X = \frac{1}{N}\sum x^j, \text{ where the sum is over } j \in G \qquad (8.17)$$

and N is big enough for the changes in x^j to hardly affect S. A typical person of the group G chooses the quantity x^j, which maximizes his utility, subject to his budget constraint and a determined value of S, according to equation (8.17).

Each j-th consumer maximizes his demand function:

$$x^j = d^j\left(e^j, p, S = X\right), \text{ where } j = 1, 2, \dots, N \qquad (8.18)$$

The variable e^j represents the inherent characteristics of the j-th person, such as his income level or his marital status; p is a variable that is common to all members of G, such as the price of x; and X is the level of social capital which the j-th person considers optimal. By summing over all the x^j, we solve for the equilibrium level of X:

$$X = \sum \frac{d^j\left(e^j, p, X\right)}{N} = \sum \frac{x^j}{N}, \text{ or } X = F\left(e^j, \dots, e^n, p\right) \qquad (8.19)$$

As we have assumed that S and x^j show great complementarity, a change e^j will not have a great effect on x^j. That is to say, a change in the income of the j-th individual will not have a big effect on his demand for the good x, since the social capital stock will not be affected. For example, an increase in income of the j-th individual will not affect to any great extent his demand for children or his probability of getting divorced if the income of the families of his social group has also not increased. Therefore, Becker and Murphy argue, correctly, that an isolated individual choice does not justify the variations in the social capital stock of the group G. But the sum of all the individual effects does have great importance since it is transmitted through the role that the social capital plays in the demand of all the individuals. In other words, the social capital diffuses the effect of the interactions among the individuals. If we take the derived total of equation (8.19) we obtain:

$$\frac{dS}{dp} = \frac{dX}{dp} = \frac{\sum dx^j}{N} = \frac{\sum \partial x^j}{N} + \frac{\sum \left(\frac{\partial x^j}{\partial S} \Big/ \frac{dS}{dp}\right)}{N} \qquad (8.20)$$

or simplified

$$\frac{dS}{dp} = \frac{\frac{1}{N}\sum\frac{\partial x^j}{\partial p}}{1-m}, \text{where } m = \frac{1}{N}\sum\frac{\partial x^j}{\partial S} > 0 \tag{8.21}$$

The numerator of equation (8.21) shows the average change in the individual demands due to the variations in p. For the interaction among the individuals, these small increments are being accumulated until they affect the social capital stock, as the denominator of this equation shows. The coefficient m is called the social multiplier by Becker and is determined by equation (8.16). However small it may be, this effect is positive, so that the denominator of equation (8.21) is less than one. So, a small change in individual demand is multiplied through the complementarity of the behaviour of the individuals in the group. Thus, for example, a change in a family's income has little effect on the number of children, but a generalized increment in the income of the group G varies substantially the number of children in these families. Becker and Murphy conclude: 'this could explain why declines in fertility over time caused by economic growth have generally been much greater than fertility differences between families at a moment in time' (Becker and Murphy 2000: 14). This analytical apparatus makes a great explanatory game possible, as is shown in the chapters of the book *Social Economics*, in which the formation of social capital is analysed. We can state that Becker's theoretical approach is fully developed and offers a fruitful basis for the analysis of social reality, which has been greatly developed over the last few years.

Becker's theoretical model

With the formulation of the three hypotheses that we have explained in the previous section, Becker states that he has a method which enables him to analyse all human behaviour, independently of the motivations of the person. As he points out: 'it is a *method* of analysis, not an assumption about particular motivations' (Becker 1995: 633). Therefore, it is not necessary to get involved in a classification of the different means and ends that a person may desire. The basic hypotheses that support his analysis are:

> to assume that individuals maximize welfare as *they conceive it*, whether they are selfish, altruistic, loyal, spiteful, or masochistic. Their behavior is forward-looking, and it is also assumed to be consistent over time. In particular, they try as best they can to anticipate the uncertain consequences of their actions.
> (Becker 1995: 634)

His method is built upon the hypothesis of stable preferences, as we have already explained. His fundamental contribution has been to introduce this hypothesis in order to extend the neoclassical theory of prices to areas which were considered to lie outside economics. But his extension supposes a view of the world and in particular of the reality of the person. It is true that he recognizes that he does not really state that people consciously maximize their utility, but that it is a very fruitful working hypothesis. What is more certain is that Becker does want to explain to us the real world of people, and this is why he has to introduce this hypothesis. He recognizes that this hypothesis 'is a thesis that does not permit of direct proof because it is an assertion about the world, not a proposition in logic' (Becker 1995: 185).

In the first part of the book we saw that all Misian analysis is based on the historicity of the person. On this basis, we saw the only way that persons have to overcome the passing of time is to make projections about themselves into the future, from a given set of conditions, and to exercise their creative capacity to generate possibilities of action and to structure them in means and ends. We differentiate in the project between the flow of time and the synoptic character of time, like the two aspects of human reality: *it is flowing because it is historical and it makes projections into the future because it is open to the future, because it has a creative capacity*. Becker's scheme takes a totally different starting point. He does not predicate that his hypotheses are declarations about human reality, but says they are assumptions that are necessary in order to proceed to statistical calculations. However, the way of proceeding implies a specific treatment of the reality of human beings which it is necessary to deal with. The historicity of the person and his entrepreneurship are two sides of the same coin. The view that is taken of the second aspect implies a vision of the first aspect. If, as Becker points out, persons have *forward-looking* behaviour, the view that he has of this behaviour determines the concept of the human capacity to make projections into the future. The stability of preferences, understood as the conjunction of forward-looking behaviour and stability over time, implies a view of the world, as Becker recognizes. Our objective is to show this representation of the world in this section.

Becker's forward-looking behaviour is a very special view of the historicity of the person. He begins by recognizing: 'this book assumes that *forward-looking* persons recognize that their present choices and experiences affect personal capital in the future, and that the future capital directly affects future utilities' (Becker 1996: 7). That is to say, he poses the causal relation cause–effect, seeking the antecedent to the action in the past. He states: 'forward-looking behavior, however, may still be rooted in the past, for the past can exert a long shadow on attitudes and values' (Becker 1995: 634). This scheme is radically different from that explained in the first part of this book. There we saw how for Mises, the antecedent of the causal relation is in the future, but it exercises its effect on the present. Becker, on the other hand, poses the causal relation from the past because he needs his forward-looking behaviour to be integrated in the hypothesis of stability over time. We are going to proceed slowly because this point is essential if the reader is to understand Becker's position. In Mises' work, once it is accepted that the causal antecedent is in the future, we have to admit that the person, when making projections into the future, goes outside what is statistically verifiable. Becker cannot take this position because he needs the statistical treatment of causality. That is why he inverts the antecedent–consequent relation.

He achieves this inversion with his hypothesis of stable preferences over time. If we start from the study of a past situation in which we already know the decision

that was taken, we can interpret it assuming that if that person knew the consequences of his decision, he would really choose what happened. That is, he acts *as
if* he maximized his preference over time. But curiously this time which Becker
introduces is detached from the fluidity of the person and it is not based on the
fact that there only exists the present of the action. What he introduces in its place
as an argument of the *extended* utility function is an *ex post* reconstruction of
the synoptic structure of the project. In this way each decision is the result of
maximizing utility.

Let us look at an example to clarify what we want to say (Becker 1995: 91–121).
Let us have a situation where a decision has been made, which we want to explain
as the result of the maximization of the following *extended* utility function:

$$U = U\left(Z_1, \ldots, Z_m\right)$$

where each Z_i has the following function of production:

$$Z_i = f_i\left(x_i, T_i\right)$$

where x_i is the vector of goods in the market utilized in the production of Z_i, T_i is
the vector of time utilized in the production of the *i*-th commodity. The problem
which we have to resolve is to find the equations that determine the constraint of
the function objective, that is to say, to define:

$$g\left(Z_i, \ldots, Z_m\right) = Z$$

The way Becker proposes for finding values for *g* and *Z* is 'to assume that the utility
function is maximized, subject to separate constraints on the expenditure of market
goods and time, and to the production functions of the commodities' (Becker 1995:
94). But these quantities of goods in the market and the time employed are known,
because we already know the decision that has been taken in that situation. Thus,
we suppose that this person acts *as if* he wanted to choose before the decision what
he really wanted to choose in the decision, and given that he is a person with
forward-looking behaviour, our problem is to weigh up the goods in the market
and the time utilized in the production of each commodity produced. In other
words, once the decision-making is known, Becker constructs *ex post* a hypothetical
model that fits the decision made. He starts from known situations of equilibrium
and describes a hypothetical process of passing from one situation of equilibrium
to another.

The necessary constraints will be constraint of goods in the market:

$$\sum_{1}^{m} p_i x_i = I = V + T_w \varpi \tag{8.22}$$

where p_i is the vector of market prices, T_w is the vector of the hours worked and ϖ
is a vector giving the earnings per unit of T_w. The constraint of time is:

$$\sum_{1}^{m} T_i = T_c = T - T_w \tag{8.23}$$

where T_c is the total time spent at consumption, and T, is the total time available. The functions of production can be written in the following manner:

$$T_i \equiv t_i Z_i \tag{8.24}$$
$$x_i \equiv b_i Z_i$$

where t_i is the vector of the time devoted to the production of the i-th commodity and b_i is the similar vector for the goods in the market.

In equations (8.23) and (8.24) it can be clearly seen how the *ex post* reconstruction of the process is made. Both the time and the commodities that enter both functions are known beforehand, since we start from the knowledge of the decision made. If we operate with them and we substitute T_i in equation (8.22), we have:

$$\sum p_i x_i + \sum T_i \varpi = V + T \varpi \tag{8.25}$$

If we substitute (8.24) in (8.25) we obtain:

$$\sum (p_i b_i + t_i \varpi) Z_i = V + T\varpi, \text{ where } \begin{array}{l} \pi_i = p_i b_i + t_i \varpi \\ S = V + T\varpi \end{array}$$

Therefore, the constraint necessary to maximize the *extended* utility function is:

$$\sum_{i=1}^{m} \pi_i Z_i = S$$

In short, the union of the hypotheses of optimizing behaviour and of the stability of preferences over time enables Becker to pose any human decision as the following problem of maximization, whose equilibrium conditions we have already explained in the previous section in equation (8.6).

The dynamization of the neoclassical model carried out by Becker is done without taking into account the historicity of the person. The person as a reality disappears and his place is occupied by *homo economicus*. As Professors R. Febrero and P. Schwartz indicate in their prologue: 'he [Becker] reduces his axioms to only one: that all actors in the social game are *homines economici* – economic persons, rational agents who maximize their advantages in different cost situations' (Becker 1995: xvii).

This *homo economicus* who makes decisions by means of the *extended* utility function is the element that Becker uses to explain the value of moral norms. The following example illustrates the way of integrating the moral norms within the social capital of *homo economicus* (Becker 1996: 225–30). Becker proposes an approach to studying the creation of norms. Suppose we have a society divided into two social classes. The superior class, R, has very big properties at its disposition, and is looking for a way of introducing respect for private property among the inferior class, M, with the aim of reducing the costs that the first class incurs in police, guards, etc. As Becker says, the solution to this problem means being aware that 'there is considerable evidence that church attendance is correlated with socially responsible behavior' (Becker 1996: 227). Therefore, the superior class benefits from such behaviour and will wish to subsidize the clergy and the buildings, and to pay the other expenses which help to promote such norms.

In order to formalize the analysis, let us consider the following utility function of a person of the inferior class:

$$U = U\left(X, N, Y\right) \tag{8.26}$$

where X are the commodities derived from the attendance at mass, N are the moral norms created and Y represents other commodities. We assume that

$$\frac{dU}{dN} < 0$$

to indicate that the norms that benefit the superior class prejudice the inferior class. Faced with this situation, Becker wonders, 'why will people attend church, if this behavior increases N and therefore diminishes their utility?' (Becker 1996: 227) The only answer is that the goods that they receive in exchange, that is to say, X, compensate for the loss of utility. Let us denote, with $S(N)$, the sum in euros that each person who attends church must receive, and with $C(N)$, the quantification of the loss of utility which this person must tolerate by assuming the moral norms. The equilibrium condition will be:

$$S(N) - C(N) \geq 0 \tag{8.27}$$

That is to say, a person of the inferior class will accept the norms regarding private property if the quantification of the good which he receives exceeds his loss of utility for accepting this norm.

If we consider that the superior class acts collectively to reduce $S(N)$ to the minimum necessary for the social norms to be adopted, then the condition is converted into an equality:

$$S(N) - C(N) = 0 \tag{8.28}$$

The superior class will be prepared to face this expense if its benefit $G(N)$ exceeds the total amount of $S(N)$ and the cost of the promotion and the creation of the norms, $K(N)$. We obtain as a general result:

$$G(N) \geq \left\{C(N) + K(N)\right\}L \tag{8.29}$$

L being the number of persons of the inferior class who attend mass. Becker reaches the following conclusion:

> This equation shows that the gain to the upper class from these norms must exceed the loss to other classes by enough to cover the cost of producing the norms, *K*. No one is harmed when the norms are created according with these equations, since they (the norms) add to the well-being of the upper class without making other classes worse off. Other classes agree to absorb harmful norms in their preferences because they receive enough for doing that.
>
> (Becker 1996: 227)

9 Critical analysis of Becker's definition of economic behaviour

Stability of preferences

In this chapter we are going to analyse Becker's proposed method for studying human behaviour. As we saw in the previous chapter, Becker's method of analysis is based on a precise characterization of economic behaviour, which can be summed up as 'assuming behavior is forward-looking and consistent over time' (Becker 1995: 635). In other words, with the theoretical basis constituted by the assumptions of maximizing behaviour, market equilibrium and the stability of preferences depending on the *extended* utility function, Becker proposes the study of every human act from the starting point of *homo economicus*. This theoretical scheme, and consequently Becker's method, are totally different from that of Mises. As we have shown in the first part of this book, Mises' theory is based on the study of the real individual; he never loses sight of this reference to reality in his study. On the other hand, Becker's work, as we are going to explain, constructs some assumptions whose only function is to serve as a protective shell for some supposedly scientific statistical corroboration. He constructs his hypotheses in such a way that all reference to the real object of study disappears on the altar of a supposedly scientific method, with a clearly positivist stamp.

Our criticism of Becker is aimed at the theoretical basis which sustains the pretension to universality of his approach to all economic behaviour. It is not a partial criticism of secondary aspects, but is directed at the very essence of his theory: *the essential insufficiency of* homo economicus *to explain human action.*

The criticism is developed on two levels:

1   In the first place, this insufficiency refers to the adequacy of his *homo economicus* for the explanation of all behaviour in general. In this chapter we will demonstrate that the hypothesis of the stability of preferences in the *extended* utility function, which Becker introduces to extend the neoclassical model to every type of human behaviour, supposes *the loss of the subjective aspect* of human action. The generalization of *homo economicus* as the basis for explaining every action eliminates the object of the study. The historicity of the person disappears in its double aspect: the flow of time and the possibility of making projections into the future as the origin of the structure of means and ends. In other words, in Becker's work the means–end relation, which constitutes the object of the study of economics, is dislocated from its real framework of reference: the human person.

2   In the second place, within the classical scope of application of *homo economicus*, that is to say, within the theory of market prices, the hypothesis of the stability of preferences is not necessary. With the hypotheses of maximizing behaviour and market equilibrium we can establish the law of equality of marginal utilities weighted by the prices as a condition of equilibrium. But as we shall see in the following chapter, *the conjunction of these two hypotheses continues representing the means and ends outside its framework of reference*. This does not mean we want to say that the incorporation of the hypothesis of the stability of preferences is an incorrect generalization of the neoclassical theory of utility. Our task is exactly the opposite. As we showed in the previous chapter, Becker develops the neo-classical model to its ultimate consequences, while maintaining its internal coherence. Therefore, the Beckerian approach to all human behaviour is insufficient not only for the hypothesis of stable preferences but also because of the insufficiency of the other two hypotheses as a basis for explaining prices. In other words, the weakness of this model is based not on an incorrect general-ization of the neoclassical model in its classical version, but in the deficiency of its three basic hypotheses.

Faced with this criticism, Becker would argue that it is irrelevant to contrast his theories by analysing the reality of his assumptions, and he would point out that the only ground for rejecting his theories is by statistical verification with reality In fact, the essence of our criticism is that on losing human subjectivity as the origin of the ends and the means of action, and by trying to convert them into data as used in physics, he eliminates the historicity of the person. This elimina-tion not only supposes the atemporality of the neoclassical model, but also eliminates the historicity of the person in its double aspect: the flow of time and the possibility of making projections into the future. In other words, Becker eliminates the subjective aspect of the action when seeking a supposed scientific 'objectivity'. In this situation it is pertinent to ask oneself, what is Becker really contrasting? If, as himself recognizes, he does not state that persons consciously maximize their behaviour; if people of flesh and blood are not his object of study; if the theoretical hypotheses do not make statements about people, then what reality does he want to explain us?

The relation between Becker and Friedman

To answer the questions posed at the end of the previous section, it is necessary to understand Becker's scientific position. It is true that Becker is a positivist, but saying that is not enough to understand his scientific pretensions. The best way to understand him is through his acknowledged master, Milton Friedman. Becker recognizes, in his first work, his '[gratitude to Milton Friedman] for training in economic analysis and for continually emphasizing that economic analysis can be used for the solution of important social problems' (Becker 1957: 4). In all his proposed scientific schemes, Becker takes Friedman's position to its ultimate consequences. His generalization of the *as if* clause to all human behaviour is the logical development of the role which the hypotheses play in scientific research, in the manner conceived by Friedman.

Although it was published a long time ago, Friedman's (1953) article 'The methodology of positive economics' is the point of reference for all positivist methodology in economics.[1] The effect that this article, the object of our criticism, had was really curious. It is a masterpiece of marketing. Never before had an article about methodology been so controversial. Even though it has often been criticized negatively, the fact is that the methodological prescriptions advanced in this essay have been accepted to a great extent. The analysis of the article is focused on the following points: (1) first, to try to clarify the methodology and the philosophical support for the object of the science which Friedman is defending. (2) As a consequence of his position *sui generis*, Friedman considers that scientific hypotheses do not have any relation to reality: they are *unreal*. (3) If the hypotheses are unreal, we only need to postulate that the person acts *as if* he will maximize his utility.

The philosophy of science defended by Friedman

One characteristic of Friedman's work is the lack of clarity in defining what he wants to demonstrate and in specifying his basic arguments, which leads his reader to commit constant errors of interpretation. For example, Friedman's acceptance of the reinterpretation of his article by Boland (1984) as *essentially correct* gave Boland a motive to reject all criticism that was not directed in the first place against instrumentalist epistemology. But the curious thing – and this is what we are going to demonstrate in this section – is that in this article Friedman does not base his clearly instrumentalist methodology on instrumentalist epistemology but on a mixture *sui generis* of positivism and conventionalism.

At the beginning of the article, he states that the differences between the natural and social sciences concerning the object of study are not fundamental ones: that is to say, that positive economics is or can be an objective science in precisely the same sense as physics (Friedman 1953: 4). This statement fits very well with the positivism of the Vienna Circle. He goes on to say that the object of science is the development of theories capable of providing 'valid and meaningful predictions about phenomena not yet observed' (Friedman 1953: 7). This statement, however, is not even accepted by the logical empiricists, who in the 1950s gave greater importance to explanation. In order to find a similar epistemology, it is necessary to go back to the nineteenth century, and the positivism of Comte, who denied that science had the possibility of explanation. Finally, he refers to conventionalism in the following statement: 'economics as a positive science is a body of tentatively accepted generalization about economic phenomena that can be used to predict the consequences of changes in the circumstances' (Friedman 1953: 39).

Given these three opposing views of the philosophy of knowledge, which do not clarify, in his opinion, whether or not the theoretical entities exist, he solves this problem by ignoring it. These contradictory versions about science denote a great intellectual tension in deciding in favour of one of them; he considers that only those that come from the natural sciences are relevant, and goes so far as to state:

> To suppose that hypotheses have not only 'implications', but also 'assumptions' and that the conformity of these 'assumptions' to 'reality' is a test of the validity of the hypotheses *different from* or *additional to* the test by implications [is a] widely held view [but] is fundamentally wrong and productive of much mischief.
>
> (Friedman 1953: 14)

With this statement he rejects all studies directed, first, to studying the possibility of a particular methodology for economics, and second, to asking questions about the irreducible principles of human action: thus he cannot be further away from Misian praxeology. Friedman's next step, perhaps being conscious of these problems, is to go on to state that 'truly important and significant hypotheses will be found to have "assumptions" that are widely inaccurate descriptive representations of reality, and, in general, the more significant the theory, the more unrealistic the assumptions' (Friedman 1953: 14).

This position has two important consequences: (1) as Popper (1963) points out, a theory that is neither true nor false can never be rejected, but only considered inadequate. On this level we begin to understand the problems that Becker's position is going to present. *If we cannot contrast the scientific hypotheses with reality, which is the object of the study, then the theory can neither verify not falsify.* (2) Second, his preoccupation with the power of prediction leads him to put statistical correlation before causal explanation, if the former gives better results. So the principle of causality is no longer necessary. Let us take the following example to clarify the spurious relations which can be established if causality is rejected: given that in spring, lambs are born and storks appear, we can predict the number of lambs from the number of storks.

Having reached this point, where we can see that Friedman does not define himself epistemologically and methodologically he accepts instrumentalism, let us see what he has really done in practice. In his first works he emphasized that it is the power of prediction that evaluates the theories, but in a later work of great importance, his Nobel Prize acceptance speech, he favours those theories with more realistic hypotheses. In this speech, Friedman reviews some of the changes in economic theory about the relation between inflation and unemployment. He sees these changes as 'the typical revision process in scientific hypotheses: as the scientific response to the rejection through experience, of an accepted hypothesis' (Friedman 1977: 453). He describes the different stages in the analysis of the relation between inflation and unemployment: the first stage consists of the acceptance of the Philips curve with a negative slope. In the second stage he introduced a long-term vertical Philips curve, together with a series of curves with negative slope, whose levels correspond to different levels of inflationary expectations. In the third stage he begins to explain the apparently positive relation between inflation and unemployment.

Friedman considers that these changes are produced by the failure of previous hypotheses to offer predictions that were consistent with the empirical evidence. Up to this point all this sounds very instrumentalist, but he goes on to indicate that the new theories are 'very rich and rationalize a broader range of experience'

(Friedman 1977: 470). Where are the prescriptions that he defended before? What view are we left with? Nobody knows his answer, but this continual contradiction seems to indicate that he uses all his instrumentalism to justify some a priori judgements which have nothing to do with Mises' praxeological categories. What Friedman thinks about experimental judgements is that economic events are repeated in accordance with the theory of frequency. If we know the past, future events will be repeated with the same frequency as in the past. Economic policy enables us to modulate the development of economic activity. In other words, Friedman is more interested in convincing us of the good effects of a certain economic policy rather than in the truthfulness of the arguments that he offers.

The concept of hypothesis in Friedman

Friedman considers that hypotheses are unreal, that is, they cannot be tested against reality. This position poses two problems. The first refers to the unreality of hypotheses in relation to their verification against the facts and the second refers to the importance of the postulated theoretical terms.

The first problem has already appeared in the previous section when dealing with the *unreality of hypotheses*. Let us use an example from physics to explain this concept: suppose that when Galileo investigated the movement of bodies falling from a short height or along inclined planes, he considered that the resistance of the air had very little effect. That is, he supposed it was irrelevant to that stage of his study. Therefore, we can say the objects move *as if* there were not any air resistance or *as if* there were a vacuum. In many passages Friedman accepts this concept. For example:

> A hypothesis is important if it 'explains' much by little, that is, if it abstracts the common and crucial elements from the mass of complex and detailed circumstances surrounding the phenomena to be explained and permits valid predictions on the basis of them alone. . . . It takes account of, and accounts for, none of the many other attendant circumstances, since its very success shows them to be irrelevant for the phenomena to be explained.
>
> (Friedman 1953: 14)

In fact, following our example, Galileo did not deny that air resistance existed, but considered that it was irrelevant in this case. It is here that Friedman interprets this hypothesis very badly, since he states that the more important the theory, the more unreal are its hypotheses: that is to say, they are descriptively false, or, in his own words:

> To be important, therefore, a hypothesis must be descriptively false in its suppositions. . . . To put this point less paradoxically, the relevant question to ask about the 'assumptions' of a theory is not whether they are descriptively 'realistic', for they never are.
>
> (Friedman 1953: 14)

This conception of hypothesis opens the door to the position defended by Becker, when stating that it is not necessary for people to maximize consciously: we only have to consider that they act *as if* they maximized. But if we do not have to affirm anything about the behaviour of any real person, why limit this hypothesis to the study of people? We can perfectly well make a biological study, by supposing that living organisms reacting to the *as if* stimuli will maximize their utility. It is not a preposterous idea, if we bear in mind that Becker states:

> The title [*A Treatise on the Family*] also moves beyond my earlier assertion that the economic approach is applicable to all human behavior, by not including the qualifier 'human'. This is intentional, for I have come to the conclusion that the economic approach is applicable to the biological world as well.
>
> (Becker 1981: x)

Confronted with this position it is pertinent to ask oneself, what role do hypotheses have in theories for Friedman? The hypotheses, whatever their acceptance, can be divided into two groups. The first is formed by those hypotheses that are fundamental and which we can call basic hypotheses. The second group contains the auxiliary hypotheses of the basic hypotheses. He states that it is evident that the theoretical terms of the basic hypotheses cannot possibly explain or predict real facts, unless a sufficient number of theoretical terms are coordinated with observable characteristics of things; that is to say, there must exist the second group of auxiliary terms, that are observational and not theoretical and show correspondence with the observable characteristics of the facts. In fact, these auxiliary terms cannot substitute the basic hypotheses; that is, they cannot be eliminated for any reason. Yet this is what Friedman does, which is to be expected because as an instrumentalist, he gives priority to the statistical relation among events over the causal explanation.

Let us see how Friedman does this with an example: when Friedman comments on the law of Galileo, which we have mentioned, he emphasizes that the law is postulated for falling bodies in a vacuum, but he declares that the law functions in a large number of cases but not in others. Therefore, he suggests that the law can be reformulated thus: 'under a wide range of circumstances, bodies that fall in the actual atmosphere behave *as if* they were falling in a vacuum' (Friedman 1953: 18). Furthermore, he thinks that the law can be reformulated without even mentioning the word *vacuum* in the following way: 'under a wide range of circumstances, the distance that a body falls in a specified time is given by the formula $S = \frac{1}{2}GT^2$' (Friedman 1953: 18).

He maintains that the circumstances in which the law functions must be specified as an essential part of the law, although this specification needs revision in the light of later experience. That is to say, in the last version proposed, he omits all mention of the theoretical term, vacuum. He supposes that the theoretical terms can be replaced in general by other non-theoretical ones, without altering the meaning and function of the theory. In other words, the facts should not be explained according to the theories, but rather the theories are constructed ad hoc in order to confirm empirical evidence. For the explanation of human behaviour, we only have to suppose that if people act *as if* they will maximize utility.

The as if *clause comes from Friedman's hypotheses*

Friedman explains the use of the *as if* clause by the example of the neoclassical rational maximization of expected returns. He describes the formula in the following way: 'under a wide range of circumstances individual firms behave *as if* they were seeking rationally to maximize their expected returns and had full knowledge of the data needed to succeed in this attempt' (Friedman 1953: 21). He admits that, as a rule, businessmen do not have such knowledge and they do not do the intricate calculations to obtain the maximum indicated. What is more, he states that the immediate determinants of entrepreneurial behaviour may be something else – for example, habit or luck. However, he proclaims that these facts do not affect the validity of his hypothesis. The relevant evidence, continues Friedman, is the complete set of facts in relation to the implications of the hypothesis, including the factor that the companies whose actions are markedly inconsistent with this hypothesis do not survive for very long.

Continuing, he offers another reformulation of the principle of maximization: 'whenever this determinant happens to lead to behavior consistent with rational and informed maximization of returns, the business will prosper and acquire resources with which to expand' (Friedman 1953: 22). What is the difference between these two? In the second case, the considerations mentioned under the *as if* clause of the first formulation are irrelevant to the contents of the hypothesis. In particular, in the second case it is not necessary to consider that the companies look for an objective, which is the impression given in the first formulation. The phrase the *maximum expected returns* simply represents a set of rules that economists use to calculate a magnitude.

The only premise, in this case, is a vague empirical generalization about the calculation of the magnitude of the profits, but there is not any specific determinant about the explanation of entrepreneurial behaviour. That is, the result is very poor. If, as Friedman states, we do not need to verify our theories against reality and the object of the study is to gauge its power of explanation, we can logically extend its scope of application to any phenomenon that needs explanation. This position gets worse if we bear in mind that Friedman substitutes theoretical terms for statistical corroboration in such a way that, faced with a fact, any hypothesis that we chose ad hoc makes it possible to explain the phenomenon.

Critical analysis of the theoretical approach of Becker to human behaviour

Introduction

Becker's work is the utilization of Friedman's methodology in order to extend the neoclassical model. In fact, Friedman and Becker have a very well-defined conception of scientific work. Without getting involved in a detailed study of the composition of scientific theories, which obviously is outside the scope of this study, we are going to mention a series of basic relations in order to analyse Becker's position in its exact sense and scope. We are not concerned, therefore, with considering the epistemology, but with presenting the necessary elements present in every theory. In every scientific theory, as an expression of objective knowledge, it is necessary to differentiate three elements that constitute knowledge. In the first place, there is the subject, the person who knows or investigates. In second place, there is the object of knowledge, that is to say, the real object of the study; and in third place there is the relation between the subject and the object, which constitutes knowledge itself.

Figure 9.1 Structure of knowledge

If we examine Figure 9.1, we will see the relation that exists between the three elements. The central part is occupied by knowledge, which is the relation that exists between the subject and the known object. Knowledge borders on three adjacent grounds: psychology, logic and ontology. If knowledge is the correlation of the subject-object, where thought intervenes, knowledge touches on psychology because psychology deals with the individual subject and with thought as the experience that the subject has lived. If knowledge is that correlation of the subject-object where thought intervenes, it also touches on logic, because logic deals with stated thoughts; not so much because they are lived experiences of the ego, but because they are lived experiences which state that they say something about an object. But ontology also borders on knowledge, because knowledge is a correlation between the real subject and the real object.

Bearing in mind this relation, we can modify Figure 9.1 slightly and obtain Figure 9.2. This simple scheme represents the three elements present in all knowledge which has pretensions to the truth: the scientist and his personal experiences; the theoretical proposal itself, that is to say, what is proposed, and what is proclaimed.[2] In other words, epistemology borders on psychology, logic and ontology. It is

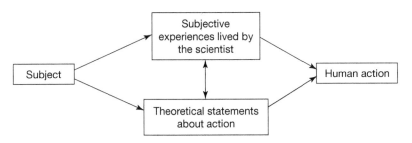

Figure 9.2 Structure of scientific knowledge

important to take into account these three adjoining elements, which are present in all knowledge. They have often been confused. As García Morente points out:

> One of the problems of modern philosophy is going to lie in the confusing of its adjacent elements; in confusing thought as an experience lived by the subject, with thought as a statement of the subject, that is, confusing psychology and logic.
>
> (García Morente 1996: 139)

So if one asks, what is the origin of the notion of a sphere? there are two ways of replying: (1) one can reply from the psychological area of knowledge, saying that the notion of a sphere comes from the innumerable times in our lives that we have perceived round stones, of pebbles rolling in the bottom of rivers. (2) Or we can reply from the area of logic, defining a sphere as a circumference that turns around its diameter.

This difference is important for understanding Becker's position. Those scientists who, like him, belong to the Anglo-Saxon positivist tradition have reduced knowledge to its psychological aspect of lived experiences and of experimental facts, ignoring or eliminating the logical components, that is to say, the necessity and universality of theoretical hypotheses; and there are as well the ontological components, that is, the real object of study.

The theoretical model of Becker

Our objective in this book is the comparison of the supposed universality of two generalizations about every human action from the point of view of economic theory. We can, therefore, consider that our scope of study is every human action. If we use the scheme of scientific knowledge that we have introduced, we will show that in all our exposition we are talking about the relation that exists between these three elements present in all knowledge. We are going to look at Figure 9.3 in great detail in order to represent Becker's approach to all human behaviour. In this section we are going to demonstrate that in Becker's theory, once the nexus between

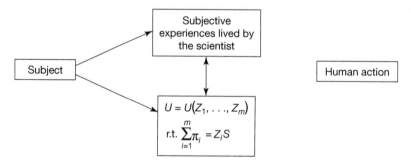

Figure 9.3 Structure of Becker's theory

the hypotheses and the object under study is broken, the situations are the same as in Friedman's work.

The loss of the subjective aspect of the action

Becker has based his explanation on the 'facts', that is to say, he has reduced his explanation to the psychological component, and with the introduction of the '*as if*' clause, he separates the theoretical statements from the reality under study. In this scheme of things reality is volatilized. It is not necessary to ask what human action is. The only important thing is that by virtue of customs, habits and experiences, Becker is convinced of a series of empirical 'facts'.

This positivist position reaches its maximum expression in Becker, but it had already been denounced by Parsons (1934), using the theory of action. Parsons' criticism of the incipient positivism of the Anglo-Saxon economics school has been highlighted by Kirzner as one of the critical pioneering works in the neoclassical interpretation of economics as a mechanical theory of choice (Kirzner 1992: 125). This process, which has culminated in the elimination of the ontological element in Becker's theory, is the consequence of trying to copy the methods of physics and attempting to work with objective 'data', which correspond to empirical 'facts'.[3] The process, which has reached its culmination in Becker, consists of denaturalizing the treatment of the means–end relation that is the core of economics.[4]

We must be quite clear about the reality that Becker is trying to convert into objective 'data': let us have another look at the demonstrations in the first part of this book. If we consider the ends as a desired unreality (cf. Chapter 7), then strictly speaking, *the ends are not given*. As Parsons says:

> In order to be sure what we are talking about we can say an 'end' can refer to a state of things, which can be observed by the person himself or by someone else, *after* it has materialized. But during the time when the action is initiated, that is, when the end is considered as a factor of the action, then this is not the case. *So the end is subjective for the person.*
>
> (Parsons 1934: 514, my italics)

If we consider the means of action (cf. Chapter 4) as the subjective perception that a person gives to a thing for the attainment of an end, then *the means are not given either*. The things are there, but the means are imagined through the properties of the things. Strictly speaking, the means are the possibilities that the person considers that he can undertake. The end, therefore, is a necessary and universal praxeological category for understanding the action of the individual. A means of action, like the end, is a praxeological category, which is to say, *it is a logical and necessary category*.

In conclusion, if economics deals with the means–end relation, *our reality, the object of study, is subjective*. In other words, economics is an objective science because it studies the subjectivity of the person.[5] If we eliminate the subjective point of view, we lose the real object under study.

To achieve his objective, Becker has to eliminate the subjective aspect. For this, he works with impressions of facts that have happened in space and time. In his analysis, he always starts from known facts. It may be that white workers in the marketplace in the USA have higher salaries than black workers, or that in higher-income families the number of children is smaller than in lower-income families. He establishes two situations: one prior to the decision and a second one when the decision is made and, between the two, he introduces his hypotheses that enable him to explain the decision that has been taken as the optimization of the means and the ends that are given.[6] Let us suppose that the problem that we want to analyse is the superiority of the salaries of whites over those received by blacks in the USA. Obviously, we all know this occurs and therefore nobody denies this situation. Thus, Becker argues, we can explain the fact by supposing that the whites act *as if* they maximized their university studies, whereas the blacks act *as if* they maximized their other activities, and in this way, the whites earn more money because they choose to maximize their performance in their work.

In this reasoning there is no logical need for these really to be the true motives. Becker's hypotheses are neither necessary nor universal. They are only *feasible, but what Becker ignores is that once the hypotheses are separated from reality, any hypothesis is valid.* We can give various alternative explanations. For example, the blacks earn less because they are dominated by the power of the whites; or as the whites are more sensitive to the sun, they prefer to be covered up and this is the reason for their good university results. With this we want to say that if the hypotheses are not rationally necessary for the understanding of the phenomenon under study, they can be multiplied infinitely.

The supposed statistical verification

This situation does not only make it possible to utilize any ad hoc hypothesis to maintain the supposed optimizer. Let us bear in mind that Becker introduces the assumption of stability to generalize the optimization of every action, but it is more important to establish that these hypotheses cannot be either verified or falsified. Münch (1987) has made a synthesis of the contributions made in the last few years on the basis of Parsons' argument. This synthesis of Parsonian stamp recognizes the following elements in every theory of action (Münch 1987: 156): (1) every action is directed towards an end and implies a temporality. (2) The means of action are constituted by the person in each situation with some resources. (3) There are the norms of valuation that the person uses to constitute the structure of means and ends. These three elements can easily be recognized in the dynamic structure of the action, which we developed in the first part of this book. On the contrary, Becker's theory does not contribute any of the three elements. In his scheme of things, the means–end relation is separated from its framework of reference, which makes his hypotheses neither universal nor necessary for the understanding of the action. Münch takes the work of Becker as an example of this dislocation of the hypotheses with respect to the object of study (Münch 1987: 232, note 13) and says about this: 'for economic theory, these assumptions *are ad hoc hypotheses outside their framework of reference*' (Münch 1987: 183, my italics). Becker starts from the decision that is already known, and constructs on his hypotheses a world that is supposedly theoretical that has nothing to do with reality. Münch defines the working method of this type of scientist in the following manner: 'this method of introducing new objectives is frequently used to armour-plate economics against falsification. This means that the theoretician usually constructs the situation until it has "economic sense" again' (Münch 1987: 179).

In other words, the preferences that enter as arguments in the *extended* utility function do not state anything about the real motives of the person. They are the objectives that the scientist introduces in the extended utility function, so that the decision taken has 'economic sense'. The elimination of the subjective aspect of the action makes it possible to introduce any explanatory hypothesis because the historicity of the person is eliminated. A change is produced in the explanatory basis from the real man to a hypothetical construction called *homo economicus*. This change is fundamental in Becker's work. The stability of preferences cannot be supposed for the real man but it can be supposed for *homo economicus*. About *homo economicus* a situation can be constructed whose resolution demands, as a condition of equilibrium, the law of the equality of marginal utilities weighted by shadow prices.

Let us consider, for example, Becker's analysis of social capital, explained in the previous chapter. The basic hypothesis assumes that individual demand, x, is complementary to social capital, S. Thus the first-order conditions expressed in equation (8.16) guarantee us a positive relation between the demand for the good and social capital. In conclusion, we can calculate in the social multiplier with equation (8.20). The question then arises, is this hypothesis of complementarity necessary and universal? Will it not be a hypothesis introduced ad hoc to give economic sense to the proposed model? There are thousands of real examples in which that hypothesis is not feasible. There are daily social interrelations in which the relation between the social environment and the individual is highly negative. That is to say, the social capital, S, generates a considerable rejection in the demand for x. An example of this situation in a family is the children's rejection of the religious beliefs which their parents practise and wish to transmit to their children. Another example is the increase in the number of civil marriages of the children of parents married in church. Therefore, this hypothesis of complementarity does not shine any light on people's real motives. It does not allow us to understand how each person rationalizes his sentiments and projects into the future his structure of means and ends. It is necessary simply to give an economic sense to an already known decision or social situation. But it does not explain the process generated. Becker and Murphy recognize:

> This approach is adequate for dealing with many kinds of behavior when the social environment is stable. However, it cannot analyze behavior that aims to change this environment, as when a family moves because it believes a different neighborhood would be better for its children. Moreover, it says little about how exogenous changes in the social environment alter behavior, and

nothing about how the aggregation of all behavior itself determines the social environment.

(Becker and Murphy 2000: 8)

As we have already mentioned, if these mathematical hypotheses are not predicated on reality, which is the object of study, it is not possible to either falsify or verify. So what role do they play in the theory? That is, if the *extended* utility function has to be concave so that the first and second maximizing conditions are complied with. What do these equilibrium conditions imply? Becker says:

> The required second-order conditions of our model are somewhat strong. . . . However, these restrictions are invoked for their analytical convenience, not for their economic plausibility. When second-order conditions fail, multiple optima can exist, and our comparative static results will be only local ones. If multiple optima exist, small changes in the incentives to accumulate time preference can produce large changes in time preference. The large preference changes are consistent with our conception of rationality even though they may, to many observers, appear to be evidence of 'multiple selves'.
>
> (Becker and Mulligan 1997: 754)

With this economic approach to human behaviour, each isolated fact may be considered to be the result of a maximization of utility. So each human act can be explained as if the person maximized utility. However, as the maximums of this process are local ones they cannot be extrapolated to other situations. That is to say, each decision is isolated from the other decisions. Therefore there is no guarantee that each isolated act is the result of the same conditions which explain and generate the other acts. So, as the authors have pointed out, each act may be considered to be the result of a distinct self and the multiplicity of local optimums may be considered to be the result of multiple selves. In short, this economic approach does not guarantee the unity of the self, while it is the subject who acts. In Figure 9.4 the mathematical hypotheses do not guarantee the existence of the reality which is the object of the study. But how can we explain human action without resorting to a subject who acts? Where do the acts we want to explain come from if there is no actor?

Conclusions of the critical analysis with respect to the theories

1   Mises starts from a theoretical structure of necessary and universal structures. His working method is to explain any act, however insignificant it may be, as the particular concretion of these categories. He maintains his position within the critical realism that the universality and necessity of the hypotheses demand. The axiom of action shows that the concept of person is pertinent and something that cannot be renounced in explaining human action.

2   Becker adds some ad hoc assumptions to his working method as a necessary
    theoretical support in order to start working on subjective empirical evidence.
    The only possible conclusion about the theory is offered by Professor Rubio
    de Urquía (1993). He considers that Becker's approach is not viable for two
    reasons:

    a   Becker considers that the neoclassical theory of the assignment of resources
        is the basic general theory of any assignable process. That is, he considers
        that the neoclassical functional theory of prices can explain any assignment
        of resources. As we have seen in the first part of this thesis, praxeology offers
        an explanation of this assignable process, subsuming the assigned element
        into the broadest framework of the process for the constitution of the
        structure of means and ends. Therefore, Misian praxeology offers a theory
        with a wider anthropological basis than the neoclassical assignable process
        based on the Beckerian assumptions.

    Let us consider Figure 9.4. Mises always bears in mind that if the objective of
    economics is to explain the means–end relation, 'the subjective aspect' is
    fundamental for the understanding of each act. It may be that the praxe-
    ological categories, as we have developed them in the dynamic structure of the
    action, are incomplete.[7] However, the only way to make theoretical progress
    is to advance in the knowledge of man, to advance in the understanding of the
    subjective aspect of the action.

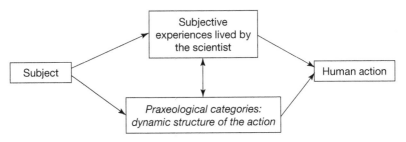

Figure 9.4 Structure of Mises' theory

    b   Becker proposes that all the projects or production processes of the human
        action, including those of the family, are reducible to the neoclassical model
        of assignation. It is the opposite process to that undertaken by Mises.
        Praxeological economics offers an acceptable basis for the study of every
        human action because it has extended its anthropological basis until it
        becomes a theory of action, with clear similarities to other theories of action,
        used principally in sociology. In praxeology, the difference between non-
        monetizable and monetizable scopes of action is very finely maintained and
        it is this fine difference that disappears in Becker's work. Our conclusion,
        on a theoretical level, is that the Beckerian scheme of things is defective
        because it loses the subjective point of view of the action. His assumptions

and the use of the *as if* clause describe some properties of the person which make him into a mere caricature of human reality, and convert his suppositions into mere ad hoc hypotheses.[8] If one really wants to copy physics, one must recognize that the role played by the categories of space, time, substance, causality and action and reaction are converted into praxeological categories in the social sciences and not into a literal translation of their role in physics. This is because economics does not deal with bodies, or substances; economists deal with means–end relations that constitute the world of what is really human.

Conclusions of the critical analysis regarding the method

We are now ready to respond to the questions that we posed at the end of the introduction to this chapter. What reality does Becker want to explain to us? This question is absolutely pertinent, because if Becker proposes a method, every method is by definition a route to somewhere; it is the way for us to approach something. Against Becker's statement about the impossibility of demonstrating his hypotheses because they are not logical propositions but rather undemonstrable affirmations about the world, we have explained that the basic hypotheses of a model are logical propositions that say something about the world. For example, Mises' axiom of action is a proposition that does not proceed from experience but is necessary for the explanation of the action.[9] These logical principles of every theory are affirmations or negations of reality. They are, in Kant's terminology, a priori synthetic judgements. It must not be forgotten that scientific theory borders on ontology.

The basic hypotheses of a model, that is, the a priori axioms or judgements, have two essential tasks: (1) first, all the a priori axioms precede the experience based on knowledge. To produce knowledge, it is necessary to apply these laws or structures. Their first function 'is to make knowledge possible through their implementation' (Rábade 1969: 89). (2) The second task of the a priori axioms consists of imposing some determined characteristics not derived from experience: universality and necessity. Rábade says in this respect:

> We have to base these characteristics of knowledge on basic structures, and dynamic structures of the subject, structures that seek to impose the character of universality and necessity, in certain conditions, on our knowledge. As these structures belong to the inherent constitution of man, they must be fulfilled in the knowledge of every man who finds himself in the same conditions.
>
> (Rábade 1969: 90)

We can conclude by stating that all experimental knowledge must be based on universality and necessity. Knowing something is not only based on what each individual wants to put into the process of knowledge: there also needs to be stronger evidence. Knowledge always has an intersubjective component of universality.

The characteristics of universality and necessity are basic to man and in consequence to all human knowledge.

This second task of scientific hypotheses shows us Becker's position very precisely. If Becker does not affirm the universality and the necessity of theoretical hypotheses about the object being studied, what then is he affirming? His positivist posture proposes the study of reality from a model of equilibrium which has reached its optimum state. With this scheme it is not necessary to state anything about the private behaviour of people, but to consider that we can interpret reality with this situation of perfect equilibrium. All his analysis is based on a fantastic state of perfection.

The consequences of this method are explained by Mises with great clarity:

> A new sophisticated version of the image of the perfect society has arisen lately out of a crass misinterpretation of the procedures of economics. In order to deal with the effects of changes in the market situation, the endeavors to adjust production to those changes, and the phenomena of profit and loss, the economist *constructs* the image of a hypothetical, although unattainable, state of affairs in which production is always fully adjusted to the realizable wishes of the consumers and no further changes whatever occur. In this imaginary world tomorrow does not differ from today, no maladjustments can arise, and no need for any entrepreneurial action emerges. The conduct of business does not require any initiative, it is a self-acting process unconsciously performed by automatons impelled by mysterious quasi-instincts. There is for the economists (and, for that matter, also for laymen discussing economic issues), no other way to conceive what is going on in the real, continually changing world than to contrast it in this way with a fictitious world of stability and absence of change.
>
> (Mises 1966: 365)

Becker's aim of convincing us of the goodness of the market without establishing himself on a solid theoretical base can be seen clearly in his treatment of moral norms. As we saw in the previous chapter, his analysis of private property is centred on two suppositions: (1) moral norms generally prejudice one social class, and (2) the value of these norms can be quantified and expressed in money. If we look again at the conclusions which we reached about the importance of private property in the first part of this book, we will be able to show that the differences between praxeology and Becker could not be more different. Our principal conclusion was to demonstrate that the work of Kirzner, Rothbard and Hoppe shows that the importance of private property is the social recognition of personal autonomy, and the exercise of each person's creative capacity and the right to enjoy the use of this private property.

This definition has three fundamental consequences:

1   The markets have an ethical basis. Every person bears in mind some moral norms when acting;[10] that is to say, man can be moral or immoral but never

amoral. Therefore, moral norms not only have useful value in the action, but are fundamental constituents of human action. This is the reason for a broader-based anthropological definition of property, revealed in this new light; private property is the right and the duty of every person when carrying out his actions. Therefore, it cannot be reduced to its monetary aspects, as in Becker's work.

2   If private property, as praxeology understands it, is the foundation of the market, this implies that in the market the reciprocal relations are relations between private properties. Thus each person may use his creative capacity and hope for the realization of the exchanges in an institutional framework. The fundamental characteristic of these exchanges based on private property is that both parties win out on the exchange.[11] As Mises points out:

> cooperation under the principle of the division of labor is favorable to all participants. It is an advantage for every man to cooperate with other men, even if these others are in every respect – mental and bodily capacities and skills, diligence, and moral worth – inferior.
>
> (Mises 1966: 40)

In praxeology, therefore, private property is the foundation of the market, which makes it possible for the exchanges to tend to be coordinated in this institutional framework, and for the profit to be mutual for both parties. Using an expression in current use, *the exchanges are a positive-sum game.* This is a totally different scheme from Becker's. The thing to consider is that the exchanges in his institutional framework are *zero sum*, which means the profit for one is a loss for the other. The most curious thing about this position is his idea that the losses come from the acceptance of moral norms.

3   Closely linked to the previous consideration, we can go on to pose the question, Why are moral norms accepted, then? Becker's answer is that they are accepted because the monetary compensation exceeds the loss of utility. But as always, this reply does not contain any necessity or universality. It is an ad hoc hypothesis, introduced to give 'economic sense' to a situation. Following Rothbard in his criticism of utilitarianism (Rothbard 1998: 206–15), we can give the following counter-example: starting from the situation described by Becker, there may exist a case in which the inferior class decides to maximize its utility, once property has been eliminated, and be compensated for its losses with other goods. So, for example, the prohibition on private property after a social revolution would be compensated by the survival of the superior class. This new situation, according to Becker, would also be in equilibrium since its members' remaining alive would compensate for the loss of the properties of the superior class. In this way, the inferior class will improve, while the superior will not get worse because it is compensated with its survival. Thus the hypotheses of the model allows an ad hoc rationalization of the fact that is to be explained. The whole analysis is defective from the beginning. It is surprising that Becker, being conscious of this situation, states:

However, the norms produced in our analysis are *biased* in favor of R since they are the only group that is assumed to be able to act collectively. Not *all* 'functional' norms are produced, since norms that hurt R and benefit M may not evolve as long as M cannot act effectively as a group.

(Becker and Murphy 2000: 147)

These paradoxical conclusions which are permitted by Becker's method are the result of his theoretical position. Without a study of the relation between the ethical and theoretical levels for the study of human action in general and market exchanges in particular, the conclusion about Becker's method of defending the free market and private property is best given by Hoppe:

These considerations [that is, Becker's] can only convince somebody of libertarianism who has already accepted *the* 'utilitarian' goal of general wealth maximization. For those who do not share this goal they have no compelling force at all. And thus, in the final analysis, libertarianism is based on nothing but an arbitrary act of faith (although popular).

(Hoppe 1993: 204)

We hope that this book is useful for demonstrating that within liberalism, not everybody defends the idea of having reached a final insuperable position and that private property only has a useful value. The methodological conclusion has to be that there is a liberalism that proposes a method, based on a theory built upon the real man, which allows for a more complete and real explanation of the things that happen to us.

10 Critical analysis of Becker's definition of economic behaviour
Maximizing behaviour and market equilibrium

According to the classification made by Mayer (1994), there are two types of theories that explain price formation. To meet their cognitive objectives and to deal with the appropriate instruments for the attainment of their objectives, there exist: (a) the genetic–causal theories, which, by explaining price formation, attempt to understand the correlations of prices through the knowledge of the laws of their genesis, and (b) the functional theories, which, by determining equilibrium conditions, seek to describe the relation of correspondence between already existing prices in a situation of equilibrium. The Misian theory of prices belongs to the first group. The praxeological explanation of prices starts from the formation of the structure of means and ends, beginning with people's subjective valuations. These types of theories owe their name to their scientific pretensions to explain prices from their genesis, by using as suitable instruments the categories that are necessary to understand individual action.

The second group of theories, the functional ones, are described perfectly by Mayer:

> Equilibrium theory seeks to provide *the structural or formal law* of the equilibrium situation by presenting the clear, reciprocal relations between price levels and supply, demand and output quantities, costs and so forth. All elements, which reciprocally maintain equilibrium in the state of rest, are taken to be simultaneously 'given' (i.e., existent), if not also simultaneously 'known' (in the mathematical sense). No element is given before any other: there is no one-way causal connection between them, but they all mutually determine one another; they relate to one another in *all-round, reversible dependence*, in 'general interdependence', as variable elements of a closed system, so that if one element changes in quantity all the others automatically place themselves in a relation of correspondence.
>
> (Mayer 1994: 59)

Becker belongs to this second group of theoreticians. His theory of prices takes as its starting point the hypothesis of market equilibrium, which proposes a *given* state of equilibrium that can be explained as the result of people's maximizing behaviour.

The two schemes could not be more different, especially bearing in mind that they are trying to explain the same phenomenon. It is not necessary to look for phenomena as complex as the family to compare the explanatory strength of the two theories. With such daily phenomena as market prices we can get a clear idea of the radical differences that exist between praxeology and *homo economicus*. Therefore, in this chapter we are going to focus on the explanation that each author offers for market prices. This analysis is the most appropriate for demonstrating the radical insufficiency of the Beckerian hypotheses to approach every type of human behaviour, including market exchanges. In the previous chapter we showed that the hypothesis of stable preferences of the *extended* utility function dislocates the theory of reality under study. We showed that this dislocation is not the result of a poor generalization of the neoclassical utility theory. Furthermore, the introduction of the hypothesis of stable preferences is the logical amplification that maintains the internal coherence of the model. The insufficiency is not the result of a defective amplification but is rooted in an essentially inadequate theoretical basis.

Therefore, the hypotheses which support the functional explanation of prices present the same radical inadequacy as the hypothesis of stability: (1) the hypothesis of optimizing behaviour proclaims the passive choice of an optant facing distinct known alternatives.[1] (2) This first hypothesis demands that the situation that is represented is in equilibrium to be able to determine the simultaneous relations among the different alternatives which make it possible to give 'economic sense' to the optimization. In short, if in more general fields the conjunction of the three hypotheses postulates as the condition of equilibrium the law of the equality of marginal utilities weighted by shadow prices, in the concrete case of market prices, the conjunction of the hypotheses of optimizing behaviour and market equilibrium postulates as a condition of equilibrium the law of the equality of the marginal utilities weighted by market prices. Whether they are shadow prices or market prices the scheme that supports the theory is the same: *the elimination of the subjective aspect of action.*

The Beckerian explanation of prices

The law of the equivalence of marginal utilities in equilibrium

As we demonstrated in Chapter eight, Becker poses every type of human behaviour as the following problem. The utility function

$$U = U\left(Z_1, \ldots, Z_m\right) \tag{10.1}$$

is maximized subject to the constraint:

$$\sum_{i=1}^{m} \pi_i Z_i = S \tag{10.2}$$

Let us characterize the *extended* utility function for the case in which all the commodities, Z_i, have a market price, that is, p_i. Obviously the commodities that enter as arguments in the *extended* utility function can be obtained in the market. We can characterize the general formulation of equations (10.1) and (10.2) for the market exchanges and we obtain:

$$U = U\left(Z_1, \ldots, Z_m\right) \tag{10.3}$$

$$\sum_{i=1}^{m} p_i Z_i = S \tag{10.4}$$

Equation (10.4) can be denoted by $\Theta(Z)=B$. Our objective in this section is to show how the hypothesis of optimizing behaviour and market equilibrium has as a logical consequence that these constraints impose the law of equality of marginal utilities weighted by prices, as a condition of equilibrium.[2]

According to the functional theory of prices, the reason why the equilibrium between supply and demand is produced is that the last units consumed of each good give the same satisfaction. Thus the marginal utilities of all the goods that enter in the utility function are equal. With this law, Becker can determine the *m* equations of the system $\Theta(Z)=B$. These will be the equations which show that once the equilibrium has been attained, it will not be abandoned. So:

$$\theta_i\left(Z_1, \ldots, Z_m\right) = \frac{\partial U}{\partial Z_i} = 0, \text{ for } i = 1, 2, \ldots, m$$

Starting from these initial conditions, when equilibrium is reached, the prices will indicate the relations between the quantities of commodities and the prices of the resources that re-establish the equilibrium.

The law of the equivalence of marginal equalities postulates the equality in the satisfaction produced by the last unit consumed of each good. In continuous terms the condition of equilibrium is:

$$\frac{\partial U}{\partial Z_1} = \frac{\partial U}{\partial Z_2} = \ldots = \frac{\partial U}{\partial Z_i} = \ldots = \frac{\partial U}{\partial Z_m}$$

What has been the genesis of this law? The first formulation of the law of the equivalence of marginal utilities is found in Jevons' (1965) price theory – in reality, the first formulation of this law can be found in the work of H. Gossen and it is know as Gossen's second law (Gossen 1983). The starting point for deriving price formation is the initial system of necessities and the positive or negative quantities of pleasure produced by the consumption or the efforts of work. Jevons' contribution consisted in constructing the economic theory on the concept of *final degree of utility* (Jevons 1965: 52). He defined this concept as 'the degree of utility of the last addition, or the next possible of a very small quantity to the existing' (Jevons 1965: 51). He expressed it in the following way: $\Delta U/\Delta Z$, where U is the level of additional utility obtained by employing a total quantity of the commodity Z. All economists accept this ratio. Both the economists who defend genetic–causal price theories and those who defend functional theories admit as completely evident that the satisfaction of a need depends on the amount consumed. No economist doubts the validity of the law of decreasing marginal utility, but, as Mayer points out: 'it is extremely interesting that from now on the ways diverge' (Mayer 1994: 74).

The interpretation of utility based on man was developed at the same time by Carl Menger (1981), the founder of the Austrian School, William Stanley Jevons (1965) and Léon Walras (1954). The fundamental difference lies in the distinct interpretations of this concept. For the Austrian School this concept is not a measure. This concept of subjective utility, as it is interpreted from praxeology, attempts to explain the process by which the means are fitted into the action. Mises defines its objective very precisely: 'action does not measure utility or value; it chooses between alternatives' (Mises 1996: 122). Therefore, with this law it is not licit, in the Misian theory, to go on to quantifications and measurements of utilities. In other words, in praxeological economics there does not exist any maximizing principle that can be mathematized. On the other hand, as Mayer points out, Jevons doubted the possibility of measurement at the beginning of his research, considering that utilities could only be compared. In the development of his research, he treated the utilities in the same way as Walras, i.e. as perfectly measurable quantities (Mayer 1994: 74). Mayer refers to the following paragraph: 'the intensity of present anticipated feeling must, to use a mathematical expression, be *some function of the future actual feeling and of the intervening time*' (Jevons 1965: 34).

This point is of prime importance because from the law of decreasing marginal utility, the paths of the genetic–causal theories and the functional theories start to diverge. Although the three authors have become known as the co-discoverers of the same starting point in the theory of value, the conceptual treatment of marginal utility is different for each of them, principally between Menger on the one hand and Walras and Jevons on the other. Therefore, the construction of their theories and thus the ulterior theoretical developments start from distinct concepts of the same subject (cf. Endres 1984, 1991; Jaffé 1976; Kauder 1965; Pribram 1983). If we bear in mind that in order to relate the quantities of the different goods and their prices, the law of decreasing marginal utility is not sufficient and the divergence between the genetic–causal theories (Menger, Böhm-Bawerk, Mises) and the functional theories (Jevons, Walras, Marshall, Becker) is more than remarkable. For the first group of authors, the way to make progress in their research was to investigate the relations between different persons with different valuations of different goods. The latter group thought that they had found what they needed in what later writers called the law of equality of marginal utilities.[3]

Jevons started on this divergent path when he considered that the ratio $\Delta U / \Delta Z$ was perfectly measurable. He defined it in the following terms:

The *limit* of this fraction $\Delta U / \Delta Z$, or, as it is commonly expressed, dU/dZ, is the degree of utility corresponding to the quantity of the commodity Z. *The*

> *degree of utility is,* in mathematical language, *the differential coefficient of U considered as a function of Z, and it will itself be another function of Z.*
>
> (Jevons 1965: 51)

To reach the formulation of the equality of marginal utilities, Jevons investigated the distribution of goods among alternative uses. He divided the quantity of a commodity Z into two quantities, Z_a and Z_b, which represent the quantities of the commodities Z dedicated to alternative uses a or b. Jevons considered that the effort to attain the highest total was made:

> when the person remains satisfied with the distribution he has made, it follows that no alteration would yield him more pleasure; which amounts to saying that an increment of commodity would yield exactly as much utility in one use as in another . . . we must, in other words, have the final degrees of utility in the two uses equal.
>
> (Jevons 1965: 59–60)

If we denote with ΔU_a, ΔU_b the increases in utility produced by the alternative consumptions of Z_a and Z_b, when the distribution is complete, according to Jevons, one has the equality:

$$\Delta U_a = \Delta U_b$$

If we apply the law of decreasing marginal utility, we can take infinitesimal increases of Z_a and Z_b:

$$\frac{dU_a}{dZ_a} = \frac{dU_b}{dZ_b} \tag{10.5}$$

In short, the final degrees of utility of the two uses are the same. The same reasoning is applicable between any two uses, and therefore, for all the uses simultaneously. Jevons says:

> The same reasoning which applies to uses of the same commodity will evidently apply to any two uses, and hence to all uses simultaneously, so that we obtain a series of equations less numerous by a unit than the number of ways of using the commodity. The general result is that that commodity, if consumed by a perfectly wise being, must be consumed with a maximum production of utility.
>
> (Jevons 1965: 60)

If, instead of a general commodity susceptible to different uses, that is to say, the commodity Z, with uses a, b, c; we consider different commodities in the utility function, i.e. $Z_1, Z_2, \ldots, Z_i, \ldots, Z_m$, we can generalize the equality (10.5), obtaining:

$$\frac{\partial U}{\partial Z_1} = \frac{\partial U}{\partial Z_2} = \ldots = \frac{\partial U}{\partial Z_i} = \ldots = \frac{\partial U}{\partial Z_m}$$

And thus we reach the restrictions necessary to formulate the theory of prices as a problem of maximization, subject to restrictions of simultaneous satisfaction of needs. In other words, we reach the law of the equality of marginal utilities weighted by price in the version of Becker. It is important to emphasize that if we accept this law, the calculation of the equations is an analytical problem. It is a purely mathematical problem based on the conditions that are supposedly given in reality. These conditions are given by the system of equations postulated by the law of the equality of marginal utilities. Mayer is totally correct when he points out: 'this group of equations is the only one whose content is a *synthetic judgement*, a claim about real processes' (Mayer 1994: 77). This is the essential point, because, as Mayer says, the hypotheses which sustain this law are, in spite of Becker's statements to the contrary, *an interpretation of the world subject to rational analysis.*

In short, to reach its formulation we have started from: (1) the market is in equilibrium. The consumer chooses between distinct alternative quantities of known goods, which gives him satisfaction. Becker's study starts from the hypothesis that the level of satisfaction that each and everyone of these commodities provides is known. In other words, *one knows simultaneously the levels of utility,* $\partial U / \partial Z_i$. (2) The consumer acts *as if* he maximized his utility. If we bear in mind that the market is in equilibrium, all the levels of satisfaction are known, therefore the consumer opts for the consumption that gives him the higher level of satisfaction. If we start from a known situation and if we can only choose between levels of satisfaction which some commodities provide, the only logical and rational choice is to choose the one with the highest level of satisfaction. In short, the conjunction of the two hypotheses establishes that the optimum choice is the comparison of the levels of satisfaction attributable to the different commodities.

Critical analysis of the Beckerian theory of prices

Criticism of the hypothesis of market equilibrium and maximizing behaviour

The best way to expound the criticism of both assumptions is to start with the arguments offered by Mayer and then to proceed along the lines indicated. Mayer based his criticism of the derivation of the law of the equality of marginal utilities on the two hypotheses that sustain it: (1) the continuous character of the utility curves of the economic subjects, and (2) if we start from the hypothesis of market equilibrium, the problem of maximization posed by each individual can only be resolved when this individual assigns any increase in income to guaranteeing the increase in utility of all the goods. In other words, the last euro spent should produce the same increase in utility whatever the good on which this last euro is spent.[4] In short, the consequence of these two assumptions is that any increase in income, however small it may be, will be divided among the resulting increases of all the goods consumed by the individual – and vice versa, any decrease in income, however small it may be, will represent a reduction in the consumption of *all* the goods. Mayer questions whether this is really the case and he replies: '[these hypotheses] are not true nor can they be true' (Mayer 1994: 79). Mayer presents his arguments in three steps in ascending order of importance.

The first step

Let's be realistic, says Mayer. If a person's income increases, for example by 10 per cent, we observe that this increase in income is not utilized to increase all the possibilities of consumption. The consumption of some goods remains constant; some other goods will show increases in consumption in different proportions; while others will show a reduction in consumption, and yet *others stop being consumed, being replaced by more sophisticated goods* (Mayer 1994: 79). This example, argues Mayer, demonstrates the real contradiction of the law of the equality of marginal utilities: *consumption varies when faced with increases in income in different proportions.* Let us add to Mayer's statement that this example is essential for understanding the reality of consumption and market prices because it points directly at the core of the question: *new goods may appear, or some of the present ones may disappear.* Without saying so explicitly he describes the real sequence of consumption. He is already aiming at the historicity and the flowing structure of the action. In this first step he does not question the essence of the action, but only describes what is empirically observable and concludes by saying: 'the derivation of the law of the equality of marginal utility from external experience must therefore be regarded as completely unsuccessful' (Mayer 1994: 80).

The second step

If the hypothesis of variations in consumption of all the goods when faced with variations in income is false, this will be due to the falsity of the assumptions which precede it in the process of reasoning. Therefore, Mayer in this second step analyses the assumptions of continuity and simultaneity in the satisfaction of necessities. Mayer criticizes both assumptions with the following argument: continuity in the satisfaction of needs supposes that all the needs have the same intensity of scarcity at the same time, in order for the final increases in goods to produce the same increase in satisfaction. *But this implies that all the needs are compared, one with another, and that they are simultaneously satisfied.* In Mayer's words:

> The interconnection between different wants is not at all one of general, mutual *dependence*, but largely involves a genetic and thus *unilateral* (causal) determination of the immediacy of particular wants by the process of the satisfaction of other wants. Thus, we learn from experience that wants of a particular kind (quality) are first triggered or raised from latency to reality, when wants of a different kind are already satisfied partially or totally.
>
> (Mayer 1994: 81)

This argument presents more elements of action than have appeared in the critical analysis of Misian praxeology: human historicity in its double aspect of flow and projection towards the future (see Chapter 7). In the project the means and the ends are not given, they are latent. As the execution of the project advances, the activities are carried out. In the activity in progress the needs are immediate, and the means and the ends of the project acquire a present character. Once an event has been carried out, the latent needs in the next activity appear clearly: they pass from latency to reality. Passing to reality implies that these needs press for their resolution here and now. The project is carried out over time. Therefore, the satisfaction of need is sequential. There is no real simultaneity of satisfactions.[5] Having reached this point, there are conclusive arguments against the hypotheses that confirm the supposed validity of the equality of the law of marginal utilities. But Mayer wants to clinch the argument:

> In order to make this result of our critical analysis more secure, but also positively to demonstrate the basic mental fact from which the connection of individual demands to various goods derives, we should return now to the ultimate foundations of economic theory, the structural laws of the system of wants.
>
> (Mayer 1994: 81)

The third step

Mayer considers that the functional theory of prices is inadequate to represent reality. He focuses on three aspects:

1   The use of mathematical apparatus makes it seem irrational to satisfy a need completely, otherwise all the other needs would be completely satisfied at the same time. However, as the total satisfaction of all the needs is not possible at the same time, the functional theory proposes that needs have to be partially satiated. This leads to the absurd conclusion that hunger or thirst has to be only partially satisfied.
2   In the equilibrium it is considered that degree of intensity caused by the last unit consumed must be the same for all the goods, but in this view, one loses sight of the fact that at certain levels of satisfaction:

> at a certain point of intensity some qualities of feeling turn into others of which other external goods are the correlate. . . . The desire for commodity A completely dies out after a certain amount has been consumed; in its place appears the desire for commodities B, C, D, etc., which was not there before.
>
> (Mayer 1994: 82)

This sentence points directly at the informative structure of the project that we have developed in our critical analysis of Misian praxeology (see Chapter

7, page 105). The information that is generated in the activity is integrated in complex systems, in such a way that new information feeds back to all the latent possibilities of action. This structure enables the realization of a project to generate an activation of other projects. The clearest example of this branching structure is the ordering of the ends depending on their intensities. Many projects have to be set aside because they do not have enough resources at the present time. This situation occurs in all projects, not only in economic ones. In economics a project has to be delayed until enough money has been obtained to carry it out – but it is also necessary to defer the satisfaction of reading a book in German until one knows the language.

3   The last aspect of the functional theory of prices to highlight is its inadequacy to represent the reality of the action. Mayer begins by indicating that all satisfaction is transitory: 'it becomes apparent that since each individual satisfaction or pleasure or enjoyment is transitory, it is possible to do this only in the form of a (periodically repeating) *sequence*, a succession of desired (mental) conditions' (Mayer 1994: 82). In this sentence he defines the structure of the project: it is a sequence, it is mental, it is not real; and he gathers together the desired conditions. Talking about the desired conditions, in which period do they operate? Mayer indicates two alternatives: (a) considering a period which is restricted to the minimum period given by the rhythm of life; and (b) considering a long period of life, which includes several of these sequences or what he calls *the welfare curve of the entire life*.

Mayer bases the explanation of the utility of needs on this second alternative, integrating them in the structure that '*organizes the sequence as a whole*' (Mayer 1994: 83). It is easy to identify the organizing structure which he mentions with the dynamic structure of the action, which we have developed, and to identify the integrated sequence with the reality which originates prices: the action of the man.[6] The following text supports this identification:

> This is why the usual system of curves and scales existing alongside one another for each individual kind of commodity is so inadequate, for reality always involves a *total sequence* and not isolated partial sequences for each species of good . . . the essence of things is a *sequence*.
>
> (Mayer 1994: 83)

Deepening the criticism of the functional theory of prices

The initial taste for expounding the conclusions in the abbreviated form of mathematical equations has substituted the problem of the origin of prices for the problem of determining simultaneously the quantities that are exchanged. As Böhm-Bawerk indicates: 'although it may be considered a perfectly unobjectionable procedure [the use of mathematical nomenclature], I still find its resulting unavoidable suppression of any personal and subjective point of view to be questionable and doubtful' (Böhm-Bawerk 1959b: 233). The problem of the functional theory of prices is not methodological. The essential and radical difference between the theories of Becker and Mises is theoretical. In the functional theory of prices a basic change is produced which annuls the subjective aspect of the action. One can follow the process, which, starting from the law of decreasing marginal utility, unbalances the needs and the satisfactions that Becker manages in his initial framework and creates the *homo economicus*.[7]

Both theories start from the idea that persons, when acting, have a representation in their mind of the needs they must satisfy in order to carry out the project. The person imagines all the necessary resources and their valuations in the synoptic structure of the project. The synoptic structure of the project is essential for the project to take shape. This structure is an atemporal representation of the management of the resources, which the human agent must carry out. The only means man has of overcoming the flow of time is to anticipate it – that is, by making projections for himself beyond the present towards the future. In fact, in the organizing synopsis of the project all the sequence of the action occurs *simultaneously*. *But this simultaneity is imagined; it does not have a real entity*.[8] Becker takes this simultaneous and unreal representation of the means and ends, which is an aspect of the action, and he separates it from the historicity of the person, who is the framework of reference in which it makes sense to talk of projects. In this scheme the historicity of the person disappears. There are only known situations; thus they are past situations. Mayer points out that the only way to provide stability for the law of the equality of marginal utilities is to construct a system of needs, which is false with regard to reality but which is consistent with what is proposed by the law. In short, the only way to make the law in question operative is to operate in an atemporal world of passive optants.

The only way to work with this scheme is to suppose that a known situation is the result of the simultaneous updating of all the activities included in the project. This position has a certain sense, if we bear in mind that every action is the result of a project that is carried out. But it cannot be deduced from that observation that the act and the project are simultaneous. In his scheme of things, Becker forgets that the project is not only a mental model to use, but a mental model to realize sequentially.[9] The project demands the capacity to project oneself into the future, outside present time, to go beyond what is immediately given and to realize the activities which are only latent in the project. Therefore, between the intended project and the reality there is an abyss that separates unreality from reality. The only way that persons have of avoiding this abyss is to act, to convert the latent unreality into present reality by executing the action. In conclusion, Becker reduces the individual to a mere optant of the present elements; when, in fact, persons are creative and active optants of realities through the project.

The Austrian explanation of prices

In this last section we are not going to give a detailed explanation of the Austrian theory of prices, a task that would greatly exceed the scope of this work. Our objective is to demonstrate that this theory of prices is the particular application of the praxeological categories. Unlike Becker's economic approach, which attempts to reduce all human behaviour to a generalization of the functional theory of prices, we will demonstrate an alternative theory that bases the explanation of prices on the subjective valuations of individuals. The praxeological categories provided by Mises are the basis for the explanation of *every* human action. To arrive at prices we have to apply the Misian methodology and to travel deductively along the following path:

1 Individual action: explanation of individual valuations with the law of decreasing marginal utility.
2 Action in the social framework: direct exchanges.
3 The introduction of money as a means of payment: indirect exchanges.
4 Market prices: the basic law of price determination.

Individual action: explanation of the variations with the law of decreasing marginal utility

All the criticism by Mayer which we have developed in the previous section has been focused on the falsehood of passing from the law of decreasing marginal utility to the law of the equality of marginal utilities weighted by price. But the law of decreasing marginal utility remains intact. As Mayer points out:

> The validity of 'Gossen's first law' remains unaffected; but since that law refers only to the isolated sequence of satisfaction in the consumption of each kind of commodity, it is by itself not sufficient to derive the structural law of the aggregated sequence of satisfaction.
>
> (Mayer 1994: 83)

We need to establish this law exactly, because it is going to constitute the starting point of the Misian genetic–causal theory of prices that we are going to expound. In order to explain prices, it is necessary to have the structural law that originates them. In the Misian theory, this role is played by the dynamic structure of the action, from which the aggregated sequence of satisfaction can be interpreted. Within this sequence, the law of decreasing marginal utility enables us to integrate the valuation of an isolated good. The explanation of this law is the first deductive link to integrate the theory of prices within the general framework of the theory of action. As Mises points out: 'thus the law of marginal utility is already implied in the category of action' (Mises 1996: 124).

Let us pose the problem by asking ourselves why goods so necessary for life, like air, do not have a price, whereas other goods that do not supply any urgent need, for example diamonds, are so highly valued. So there is the apparent paradox that air or water, whose utility for the development of life is not doubted by anyone, have no economic value, whereas diamonds, which do not have any objective utility for the development of life, have an extremely high economic value. In order to resolve this paradox it is necessary to differentiate between two ways of understanding the relation between the goods and the needs of people. In the first place, this relation can be understood as the capacity of the properties of the good to promote human welfare. Water is useful because, objectively, it has a physical-chemical composition that quenches thirst. This use of water is stated about each and every one of the precise measures of water that we will consider. As Böhm-Bawerk says: 'it is the possession of *the capacity for usefulness* that is particular to that species [in this case, water]' (Böhm-Bawerk 1959b: 133).

In the second place, we can understand this relation between the good and the welfare of man by the scarcity of the good in relation to the satisfaction of needs. In this way, we do not focus on the physical-chemical properties of water but on the relation that exists between the availability of water and the subjective needs of man in every situation. We do not focus on the good in general, but on the fact that the availability of the good becomes the condition for the satisfaction of needs. As Böhm-Bawerk points out: 'the gaining or the losing of the good must be the condition on which a gratification stands or falls' (Böhm-Bawerk 1959b: 127). The difference between the two concepts is fundamental for the resolution of the paradox that is posed, because, as Böhm-Bawerk states:

> All goods have usefulness, but not all goods have value. In order that there be value, usefulness must be paired with *scarcity*. This does not mean absolute scarcity, but relative scarcity in comparison with demand for the goods of the kind in question.
>
> (Böhm-Bawerk 1959b: 129)

For the determination of the place of any good in the scale of the person's values, utility is obviously decisive, but it is not a general objective utility derived from the vital character of the good. The economic value is determined by its subjective utility; it is determined by the relation between the relative quantities of the good (its scarcity) in relation to a person's needs. Mises adds in this respect: 'for praxeology the term utility is tantamount to importance attached to a thing on account of the belief that it can remove uneasiness' (Mises 1996: 120). That is to say, the utility is not derived only from the real properties of the good. The utility that determines the value of the good is a specific utility, resulting from the consideration of the thing as a means of action. For the carrying out of a project we need a certain quantity of the goods, which are considered to be means.

However, the greater the quantity of the good available, the less will be the pleasure produced by each additional unit and the lower will the good be placed on the person's scale of values. This occurs because by increasing the satisfaction of a need, the utility of each dose is diminished. If there is a loss of a unit, the person only has to renounce the minimum utility in each case. Therefore, the utility of any unit cannot be greater than that last unit. In other words, the utility of the last unit, i.e. the minimum utility, determines the utility of any other unit and thus that of the totality of the existing units. For example, the place of water in our scale of values is not determined by the infinitely great utility of a glass of water which would save us from dying of thirst if we only had that unique glass of water, but rather it is determined by the utility of the last dose of water which we use to have a bath or to water the flowers.[10] We call this utility of the last unit *marginal utility*.

With these considerations the following theses, which are known by the name of the law of decreasing marginal utility, can be formulated:

1   Marginal utility diminishes as the stocks increase, that is, on augmenting the possibility of satisfying the need.
2   However, marginal utility determines the utility that the person attributes to all the other units.
3   On increasing the quantity, the place occupied by the good in the person's scale of values descends, an assumption that does not change the scale of needs.
4   The utility of all the goods increases when the quantity increases, but by decreasing degrees, since the marginal utility, considered absolutely, decreases.

With these theses we can resolve the paradox of value. Diamonds, whose objective utility is minimal, are valued because they are scarce in regard to the subjective needs of the persons. On the other hand, water or air, which have an immense objective utility, are superabundant in relation to the person's subjective needs and therefore have a very low economic value. The key idea to be understood is scarcity in relation to the use which one wants to give to the good.

Böhm-Bawerk's example here is quite clear (Böhm-Bawerk 1959b: 132): let us suppose there is a colony of farmers who are supplied with firewood from a wood and our problem is to determine the value of an isolated tree. We can follow two theoretical lines: (1) if we followed the line proposed by Jevons, we would count the number of trees, we would then give a utility to this number as the provider of firewood and we would calculate the variation of this utility before the disappearance of an individual tree. We would obtain $\partial U / \partial Z_i$, that is to say, the measurement of any tree based on its capacity to provide firewood in any situation. In other words, we would obtain a univocal measurement of the tree, independently of the particular situations. That is to say, the relative scarcity disappears with regards to the subjective needs. (2) If we start from the concept of relative scarcity, there is no way to obtain a univocal measurement. We will obtain different valuations according to the particular conditions which determine the use that will be given to the tree. For example, if the person's objective is make a bonfire to get warm, then cutting down a tree does not suppose a great loss with respect to the total trees available for firewood. Therefore, an isolated tree will have little value. However, if the objective is to cut down the whole wood to grow cereals, the value of the tree will be extremely high because each tree represents the only means of warming oneself.

Let us borrow another example from Böhm-Bawerk (1959b: 131): suppose that a miller makes two requests. In the first one, he requests permission to fill a bucket with water from the current that works the mill. In the second one, he requests permission to divert the course of this current. If we followed Jevons and Becker, we would calculate one unique value for the good 'water' and we would fall into two grave errors: (1) if we give the water a high valuation and we decide that it is very valuable, the miller would refuse to let anyone fill a bucket of water. This refusal is totally absurd, if we bear in mind that this bucket full of water taken from the current does not affect the working of the mill in the least. (2) On the other hand, if the measurement of the value is low and it is decided that the water has no value, the miller will divert the course of the current, leaving his business without any source of power. As these two examples show the problem of working with what Böhm-Bawerk calls 'abstract categorical value' (Böhm-Bawerk 1959b: 133), i.e. quantifications of the levels of utility for each good, then this means the root and branch elimination of the subjective aspect of valuation. With respect to this quantification he says: 'there simply does not exist such a thing, *when the value is understood as the real meaning of the goods for man*' (Böhm-Bawerk 1959b: 133, my italics).[11]

Action in the social framework: direct exchanges

The basic study of the Austrian School concerning the conditions of direct exchange is that made by Böhm-Bawerk. It is necessary to start from a situation in which money does not exist. In this primitive situation, he considers that there will be exchanges, provided that they are advantageous to both parties. What does he understand by an advantageous exchange? For Böhm-Bawerk, an advantageous exchange means that 'the goods [a person] receives have greater subjective value than those with which he parts' (Böhm-Bawerk 1959b: 215). It can clearly be seen that the starting point is the law of decreasing marginal utility as we have established it in the previous section. For example, in ancient times, if a person had a horse, this person would be prepared to exchange it for ten barrels of wine, if he valued the wine more highly than the horse. And vice versa, the person who had the wine would be prepared to make the exchange if he valued the horse more highly than the wine he possessed. Both persons, with different valuations of the goods, do well out of the exchange. In Böhm-Bawerk's words: 'an exchange is economically possible only between persons whose valuations of the good and the medium of exchange differ and, indeed, differ in opposite directions' (Böhm-Bawerk 1959b: 216).

There are two distinct possibilities in the advantageous exchange. The person who we have taken as an example was willing to exchange the horse for 10 barrels of wine. There may have been a second person willing to exchange his horse for 20 barrels of wine. It is clear that the first person had a greater margin to make the exchange for a number of barrels that the second person would not accept. The first one would be willing to make the exchange. Böhm-Bawerk says that the first person had a greater capacity to make the exchange than the second person. That is to say, with a lower valuation of the good than he had initially, in comparison with the goods that this person wanted to acquire, he has greater capacity for making the exchange. The first person would accept fewer barrels than the second person. He has more possibilities of closing the deal. In Böhm-Bawerk's words: 'that candidate for the exchange has the greater capacity for exchange who places the lowest valuation on his own goods in comparison with the goods of others which he wishes to acquire' (Böhm-Bawerk 1959b: 216). Thus we already have the two basic rules which permit the exchange: (1) the exchange is produced if there are different valuations. The valuations totally differ in the contrary sense. (2) The greater the capacity of exchange, the greater are the possibilities of making it.

The introduction of money as a means of payment: indirect exchanges

To explain the emergence of money, we are going to follow the explanation offered by Menger in its historical genesis. Suppose there is an armourer of the Homeric epoch who wants to sell the two suits of armour that he has made (Menger 1981: 257–86). This person goes to the market looking for someone who wants the armour. From the previous section, it is clear that in order for the exchange to take place, the armourer must find another person who values his suits of armour and will offer him a quantity of bronze and food that the armourer values more highly than his suits of armour. The possibilities of exchange in these conditions are very small. He would have to waste a lot of time or renounce the exchange, if he was determined to receive the commodities he wanted and he would not accept in exchange for the suits of armour another commodity, which besides having the characteristics of a commodity also had a greater *selling power* capacity than his suits of armour. With this term, Menger refers to the fact that if the armourer accepts cattle for his suits of armour, the possibility of meeting people who want the cattle are greater than the possibilities of meeting a person who wants the suits of armour. In this sense, the cattle have more selling power than the suits of armour. The armourer can accept the exchange of his suits of armour for a number of head of cattle, and once he has acquired these commodities, which are easily sold, he will enter into contact with those people in the market who can offer him copper, fuel and food.

This process depends entirely on the capacity of the persons to discover the advantages of cattle as a medium of exchange. In praxeological terms, through entrepreneurial alertness the persons discover that the utilization of the cattle as a medium makes the exchanges possible. That is, the discovery of money creates the possibility of greater exchanges. Menger says:

> With economic progress, therefore, we can everywhere observe the phe-
> nomenon of a certain number of goods, especially those that are most easily
> saleable at a given time and place, becoming, under the powerful influence
> of *custom*, acceptable to everyone in trade and thus capable of being given
> in exchange for any other commodity. These goods were called *Geld* by our
> ancestors, a term derived from *gelten*, which means compensate or pay. Hence
> the term *Geld* in our language designates the means of payment as such.
>
> (Menger 1981: 260)

This example demonstrates that the origin of money is spontaneous. It arises from the existing economic relations without needing state measures. The success of a commodity in establishing itself as money comes from the expansion of the know-ledge of the great benefits achieved by skilled individuals, thanks to their decision to accept commodities with high selling power in exchange for all the other commodities over a long period of time.

Different goods have achieved the category of money at different times and in different places. It is important to demonstrate that the consideration of a good as money is very closely connected to the real possibilities of each people in each epoch. In the nomadic and agricultural peoples, cattle became the money. They transported themselves in an epoch when there were no roads. They were easy to maintain, if there was an abundance of pasture, and they were stored in the open air. In Greece, payments, commodity prices and punishments were calculated in head of cattle. It was not until the time of Solon that these were substituted for payment in money at the rate of one drachma for a sheep and five drachmas for an ox. The continuing progress of culture with the division of labour and the foundation of cities and with a population basically dedicated to industry had the inevitable result of making the selling power of cattle disappear, as the selling power of other commodities, and especially that of metals, was increasing. The maintenance of animals in the city became difficult and expensive. As Menger points out:

> With the progress of civilization, therefore, cattle lost to a great extent the broad range of marketability they had previously had with respect to the number of persons to whom, and with respect to the time period within which, they could be sold economically.
>
> (Menger 1981: 236)

All the peoples with an advanced culture who had used cattle as money in the past, stopped doing this as they passed from nomadism to a sedentary agricultural culture and later on to an industrial culture, substituting metals for the cattle, especially metals which were easy to obtain and melt down and could be worked by men: those were copper, silver and gold. In Mexico, when the conquistadors arrived, there were various commodities that had the function and the situation of money: there were little packets which contained between 8 and 24 grains of cocoa, certain small pieces of cotton cloth, quills of goose feathers filled with gold and valued according to size, as well as strips of copper. The Hudson's Bay Company used the beaver skin as a unit of measurement: so three pine martens equalled one beaver, a silver fox equalled two beavers, a black fox or a bear were equal to four beavers, a shotgun cost fifteen beaver skins. All cultures have money; it is a standard of cultural development. In the upper Amazon, wax honeycombs were used as money, in Iceland and Newfoundland it was cod, in Maryland and Virginia it was tobacco and in the English West Indies, sugar. They used dates in the oasis of Siwa, tea-bricks in central Asia and Siberia, glass beads in Nubia and Sennar, and millet in the country of Ahir (Africa) (Menger 1981: 271).

Market prices: the basic law of price determination

The origin of money enabled people to generalize about exchanges. Money becomes the measure of price. The price is not a valuation, since it is subjective.

The price is the *expression of the relation of the exchange*. A price indicates that in such and such a place and on such and such a date an exchange took place. If we consider an isolated exchange, that is to say, one buyer and one seller, the valuation of the exchange is not univocal; both parties consider that they won out in the exchange. In other words, one cannot conclude that the value of the good that is exchanged is the price. Colloquially, on observing that a litre of milk is exchanged for 1 euro, one says that the litre of milk is worth 1 euro. But this way of speaking induces an error when suggesting that the valuation is determined by the quantities exchanged. This is false; one cannot talk about one unique, intrinsic valuation of butter and money. In reality, there are two valuations: the power of exchange between butter and the money of the buyer and the power of exchange of the seller. Both have to be different and to be in the opposite sense in order for the exchange to be produced. The explanation of price formation was masterfully developed by Böhm-Bawerk. This explanation is developed on four levels:

- First level: the determination of the price in an isolated exchange. This deals with the simplest case of a buyer and a seller, who with different valuations of the goods to be exchanged, start to negotiate to determine the price.
- Second level: the determination of the price in the case of unilateral competition among buyers. In this case, competition among various buyers with different valuations of the goods to be exchanged is introduced into the negotiation. This competition among the buyers tends to increase the price, depending on the valuations of the buyers.
- Third level: the determination of the price in the case of unilateral competition among sellers. In this situation, the competition among the sellers tends to lower the prices.
- Fourth level: determination of the price in bilateral competition. This is the general case in which a large number of buyers and sellers interact to determine a price, in accordance with the various valuations that each person has for the goods to be exchanged. Here one can observe the process of social interaction, which determines the price, based on the person's subjective valuations.

First level: the determination of the price in an isolated exchange

We will consider an indivisible good – for example, a horse for agricultural use – and we will express the power of exchange in thousands of euros. If instead of an indivisible good, a divisible one were used, as for example a kilo of sugar, the reasoning would not alter. Using the horse enables one to focus on the essence of price formation without getting lost in the details.

We have a farmer A who needs a horse and who associates the possession of the horse with a value of up to 300. He goes to see his neighbour B, who has a horse for sale which he associates with a value of 100. In this situation there exist the conditions for an exchange, and in the opposite sense. The problem that arises is to determine the price. This must be less than 300, since that is the top limit that A is willing to pay, and be greater than the 100 which is the minimum at which B is willing to sell. Given that both of them are willing to exchange provided that they can obtain a profit, however small this might be, the reply is 101, which is as good as 299.

If the price were 101, A would benefit more than B, but B also wins out, although minimally. Vice versa, if the price were 299, B would benefit more than A, but then A would have a minimum profit. As Böhm-Bawerk indicates: 'at what point between 100 and 300 the price will be fixed cannot be predicted with certainty. Every price between these two limits is economically possible' (Böhm-Bawerk 1959b: 217). The determination of the price will depend on the negotiating ability of the two parties. In the determination of the price from this simple case, there are no probabilities, but rather there are possibilities and human abilities in play. In this case, the conclusion is that in an isolated exchange between two persons who wish to make the exchange, the price will be determined within the interval which has an upper limit in the buyer's subjective valuation of the good, and a lower limit in the seller's valuation of the good.

Second level: the determination of the price in the case of unilateral competition among buyers

Let us introduce a new bidder. Besides A, there is another farmer Aa interested in buying the horse from B. The new bidder values the horse at 220. There is only one horse, so the two buyers will have to compete between themselves. The way to obtain the horse is to offer the higher price. While the offers are lower than 220, Aa will make bids, but as soon as A raises his offer to more than 220, Aa will be out of the bidding. It is true that neither A nor Aa knows the value that the other gives to the horse. Bearing in mind that both of them are seeking the most advantageous deal, they will begin by making low bids, which they will then slowly raise. In this case the price would be determined at between 300 and 220.

If two new buyers Ab and Ac appear, with valuations of 250 and 280 respectively, the bidding will continue until the buyer with the greatest power of exchange expels the rest. In order for A to expel Ab and Ac, he has to raise his bid higher than 280. The margin of the determination of the price is reduced; now the upper limit is 300 and the lower limit is 280.

The results of this example can be generalized with the following rule: when unilateral competition exists among different buyers, the competitor with the greater power of exchange is the one who will be the buyer. The price will be within the margins in which the upper limit is the buyer's valuation and the lower limit is the valuation of the last competitor who is expelled. That is to say, of the competitors expelled, it is the one who has the greatest power of exchange. It is thus independent of the seller's valuation limit, which then becomes irrelevant.

Third level: determination of the price in the case of unilateral competition among sellers

In this case, the result is the opposite of that on the second level. Now farmer A is the only buyer, facing five potential sellers, Ba, Bb, Bc, Bd, Be. The horses which they offer are of the same quality and their respective valuations are Ba 100, Bb 120, Bc 150, Bd 200 and Be 250. The sellers will compete among themselves, thus lowering the price. However, no seller will make an offer below his valuation. The first one to be expelled will be Be, who is the one with the least power of exchange. In other words, he is the seller who most values his horse compared to the money. The order of expulsions will be: Bd, Bc and Bb, the last being the one with the greatest power of exchange. The price will be determined between 100 and 120. Summing up, when unilateral competition exists among the sellers, it is the competitor with the greatest power of exchange who will carry out the exchange. The competitor is the one who values his product lowest in relation to the money. The price will be determined with margins whose lower limit is the valuation of the seller and whose upper limit is the valuation of the potential seller, with the greatest power of exchange among the expelled competitors.

Fourth level: determination of the price in bilateral competition

We now have the following situation. There exist ten potential buyers and eight sellers with different valuations of the possession of a horse in the case of the buyers and different valuations of their horse in the case of the sellers (see Table 10.1). The buyer Aa has the greatest power of exchange and would be willing to accept prices over 290, but if he begins bidding so high, he loses the opportunity of obtaining a greater profit in the exchange. The most logical behaviour is for him to begin with the same bids as the buyers with less buying power. For his part the seller Ba would be willing to sell for 100, but with this behaviour he loses the possibility of obtaining a greater profit, so he will demand the same price as the seller with little power of exchange. The situation at the start will be very restrained; the buyers on the one

Table 10.1 Potential buyers and sellers valuations

Potential buyer	Valuation of a horse	Potential seller	Valuation of his horse
Aa	300	Ba	100
Ab	280	Bb	110
Ac	260	Bc	150
Ad	240	Bd	170
Ae	220	Be	200
Af	210	Bf	215
Ag	200	Bg	250
Ah	180	Bh	260
Aj	170		
Ak	150		

hand will offer very low prices while the sellers, on the other hand, will demand very high prices. If, for example, the starting price is 130, the ten buyers will value the horse above this quantity and only Ba and Bb would be willing to sell. The sellers would act clumsily if they did not exploit the competition among the buyers to raise the prices. Both Ba and Bb have an interest in retarding the sale so that the prices rise.

If the price increases to 150 the ten buyers start bidding, but there are only three sellers. So the sellers will be willing to demand higher prices. If the prices go on rising, Ak abandons at 150, Aj at 170, Ah at 180 and Ag at 200. This price increase incorporates Bd and Be in the competition. In this situation, there is a demand for six horses and an offer of only five horses. If the buyers perceive the excess of demand, they can still force up the prices; in fact, they have incentives to do so. Up to where? If they increase up to 210, Af would retire. After the expulsion of Af, the supply and the demand would be equal, but the sellers do not know up to what point they can raise prices without expelling another buyer or adding another seller. If they force up the price to 215, Bf will enter the contest, and now more supply than demand exists. The excess of supply makes the buyers bid lower. The agreement will be produced within the range 210–215. There are five pairs who exchange and the excluded competitors cannot alter the result.

The upper limit is determined by the valuation of the last buyer who reached an agreement, Ae, and the valuation of the excluded potential seller who had the greatest power of exchange, Bf. The lower limit is determined by the valuation of the last seller of those who reached an agreement, Be, and the valuation of that excluded potential buyer who has the greater power of exchange, Af.

The pairs Ae–Bf and Be–Af are called *marginal pairs*. The competitors who enter in the last place and the person they expel form them. So the upper marginal pair Ae–Bf forms the limit 220–215 and the pair Be–Af forms the lower limit 200–210. Thus, the last buyer does not pay more than 215 so that the sixth competitor for the supply is excluded and the last seller asks more than 210 in order to expel the sixth competitor for the demand. To put it another way, of all the competitors it is those with less power of exchange who determine the price which balances the supply and the demand, so that all the exchanges are accomplished with the maximum profit. In short, the market price is established at a point between a margin that is limited and determined by the valuations given by the two marginal pairs. So, for example, Aa was willing to pay up to 300 and only paid between 210 and 215, with which he has a maximum profit of between 90 and 85. Ab makes between 60 and 55, Ac between 50 and 45, Ad between 30 and 25 and Ae between 10 and 5. On the side of the sellers Ba was willing to sell at 100 and sells at between 210 and 215, making a maximum profit of 110–115, Bb between 100 and 105, Bc between 60 and 65, Bd between 40 and 45 and finally, Be between 10 and 15.

We can take the subjective valuations of the profits associated with the measurement of the prices and we organize them from greater to lesser in Table 10.2. The table shows that the equality between the supply and the demand at a more or less uniform price is the result of the reciprocal impact of the subjective valuations that the persons give to the goods and to their means of exchange. To

Table 10.2 Profits of real buyers and sellers

Buyer	Seller
90–85	110–115
60–55	100–105
50–45	60–65
30–25	40–45
10–5	10–15

understand the importance of the price by only considering that a horse costs between 210 and 215 euros means to lose sight of the ten persons who have performed an economic activity, as a consequence of the different valuations associated with the possession or sale of the horse. In other words, to only consider the quantities exchanged, without making any reference to the persons, is to lose sight of the subjective aspect of the action. These ten persons give different meanings to the relation of exchange, 210–215 euros per horse.

Thus the price is not given in the data of the problem, but is discovered through a process in which profit opportunities are created and exploited. With this theory of Böhm-Bawerk, prices acquire their full importance in human action. Mises says: 'by means of its subjectivism the modern theory becomes objective science' (Mises 1981a: 180). And we can conclude with Böhm-Bawerk: '*price is, from beginning to end, the product of subjective valuations*' (Böhm-Bawek 1959b: 225, my italics). In other words, the price is only explicable with reference to the subject who acts.[12]

11 Conclusions

The critical analysis we have carried out compares the two economic approaches regarding human reality. In order to have a global view of what we have expounded, we are going to present our conclusions in the following order: first, a summary of the theoretical differences between the approaches, and second, a summary of the methodological differences, developing these in the particular case of the explanation of prices.

Theoretical differences

The theoretical differences are listed in Table 11.1, as are the different points of comparison that we have dealt with.

The concept of the economic point of view

The extreme divergence presented by the two authors from the beginning strikes us forcefully. From the first, each author builds his theoretical bases in such a way that no convergence is possible. Mises moves within the broader field. He starts from human action, understood as the process of change from unsatisfactory situations to other more satisfactory ones: this is the axiom of action.

Becker for his part is focused on a partial aspect of every action and for him the primordial character is the assignation. He focuses on a partial aspect of the whole plural process which constitutes the action. When an end is activated the other possibilities of action are suspended; they remain in a state of latency, but they continue to be feasible alternatives. Any information received may feed back to the whole structure of the action and alter it entirely. Therefore, Becker does not move in a dynamic process: he moves in isolated points of decisions that are already known. His approach to behaviour can be reduced strictly to an explanation of known decisions. As Kirzner states in this respect: 'he is going to identify (the real problem) with the movement of one known equilibrium position to another, with the "innovations" and with the dynamic changes but not with the dynamics of the same process' (Kirzner 1973: 27).

Table 11.1 Theoretical differences

Point of comparison	L. von Mises	G. Becker
1. Concept of the economic point of view	Theory of human action understood as a dynamic process: *praxeology*	Decision theory based on maximization with restrictions
2. Protagonist of the social process	The real man	*Homo economicus*
3. Key theoretical concept	Entrepreneurship understood as a creative capacity	First hypothesis: maximizing behaviour
4. Definition of the means–end relation	Discovery of means and creation of possibilities	The means and ends are 'given'
5. Dynamism of the key concept	The person constructs his structure of means and ends in the exercise of entrepreneurship; it is a dynamic structure	Static and atemporal analysis of choice when facing given alternatives
6. Scope of application of the key concept	All human reality. The relation between society–culture–person appears	All behaviour is reduced to maximizing behaviour
7. Division between areas of study	Essential difference between: (a) non-monetizable social interrelations; (b) monetizable market exchanges	There is no difference between areas. Every decision is quantifiable by means of market prices or shadow prices
8. Concept of society	Tendency to the coordination of social interrelations: solution to the 'problem of knowledge A'	The social framework is exogenous to the model. In the extended utility function there appears social capital, which includes the social elements
9. Concept of culture	Cultural transmission of the possibilities of action. Expansion of the same: Process of the *Social Big Bang*. Solution of the 'problem of knowledge B'	The cultural framework is exogenous to the model. In the *extended* utility function, there appears the social capital, which includes the cultural elements
10. Concept of competition	Dynamic process of discovery	Second hypothesis: model of market equilibrium
11. Levels of the study of social reality	It is divided into theoretical, historical and ethics	There is no such separation

Table 11.1 continued

Point of comparison	L. von Mises	G. Becker
12. Relation between ethics and the market	Ethical foundation of the market: anthropological definition of private property	Moral norms only have a useful and quantifiable value
13. Causality	The human agent determines the cause in the action	Causality is reduced to statistical inference
14. Structure of the means–end relation	It is based on the historicity of the person in its two aspects: flow and projection. Full importance of the subjective aspect	The means and the ends are 'data' outside the framework of reference: the subjective aspect disappears
15. The project	The end is projected going beyond the statistically given: the future is *something to be done*	Third hypothesis: stability of preferences over time. The future is a repetition of the past
16. Time	The flow consists of the fact that the person's present is made up of the past and the future. The future exercises its effects on the present through the project	Time is quantified without any reference to the historicity of man. It is reduced to analogical time of a clock
17. The information	It is subjective, practical, private and dispersed; it is transmissible	The information is given and *made objective* in the restriction of the extended utility function
18. Error	Possibility of *ex-post* error. The profit is as feasible as the loss	There is no possibility of error
19. Structure of the model	Praxeological categories, universal and necessary. Dynamic structure of the action	The three hypotheses determine, as a condition of equilibrium, the equality of marginal utilities weighted by prices

The protagonist of the social process

If, following Becker, we start from isolated points, forgetting about the process itself which generates the dynamism, there is no need to study man: that is, the subjective aspect of the action. It is enough for us to define a series of coherent hypotheses, which define a being called *homo economicus* who must be the agent of the changes in the model. In fact, this economic agent is not active; he is not a person of flesh and blood. To move within the study of the person as he really is, it is necessary to follow the Misian praxeology and focus on human beings and investigate the origin of the changes.

Key theoretical concept

Using praxeology and starting from Mises' work, Kirzner has established the lines along which to develop the concept the key concept of entrepreneurship. This function is not the exclusive patrimony of any group, but is exercised by everyone who acts. Kirzner indicates the two pillars on which the function rests: discovery and creative capacity. So by pure entrepreneurship, we can understand the deployment of the creative capacity of the person on the reality that surrounds him. The understanding of this definition is basic, because the establishment of the structure of means and ends depends on it. Pure entrepreneurship cannot be reduced either to a factor of production or to a mere piece of information. It cannot be reduced to the prime element, because the essence of entrepreneurship, alertness, is not one of the ingredients deployed in production, but it is the perception that this production can be profitable. Nor is it information that can be obtained in the market. More than objective information, entrepreneurship is the subjective capacity of managing objective information. With this scheme, Misian praxeology is directed towards the person, to the study of the subjective aspect of the action.

Becker reduces economic behaviour to operating with elements that *homo economicus* can manage. His principal hypothesis and the basis of his work are to assume maximizing behaviour. It is clear that this behaviour does not have the minimum connotation of the inherent creativity of the human being. This *homo economicus* maximizes when faced with the alternatives that are offered and which are determined by the decision that is being studied. In other words, *homo economicus* is *a mere passive optant*.

Definition of the means–end relation

The proper object of economic science, the means–end relation, is treated very differently by the two authors. For praxeology the means–end relation is dynamic. Each person in the exercise of entrepreneurship discovers means and ends and creates possibilities of action. He discovers new possibilities of action in the physical-chemical properties of things. Things may be there as resources, but until someone discovers a possibility of action in them, they cannot be considered as a means. To advance in the understanding of each individual action, it is necessary to investigate the motives of the subject of the action. The person, the subject of the action, is made the object of praxeological study. Obviously we are not discussing given means and ends. In praxeology, not only the ends but also the means are only comprehensible in relation to the person. For his part, Becker attempts to make the means–end relation 'objective', so that he can work with the 'data'. He begins the process of separating this relation from its framework of reference: human action.

Dynamism of the key concept

Entrepreneurship, as we have mentioned, cannot be reduced to a factor of production or to objective knowledge. Its exercise becomes real in the structuring of the means and the ends in projects, but it is of fundamental importance to make it clear that the creative capacity of the person is dynamic. Entrepreneurship is dynamic not because it is developed in time, but because it goes beyond what is immediately given. This dynamism which entrepreneurship develops is the transformation of the action and this is the basic concept that we must understand: that the end is an imagined reality and that the means must be constituted. The explanation of an economic phenomenon exceeds and encompasses the assignable aspects that it contains. Praxeology emphasizes the process, not the isolated acts which shape the action as a process. Therefore, if we pay attention to the dynamic structure, the key element that enables us to understand the assignable acts is the inherent dynamism of the process.

The economic behaviour explained by Becker can only be static; it is about isolated acts, which taken out of their framework of reference are presented as isolated decisions. Dynamism is not possible in this model. Everything is reduced to a static and atemporal analysis, which is incapable of integrating the dynamism of the person. In reality, Becker's definition of economic behaviour leaves out the essence of economics: the man of action.

The scope of application of the key concept

With the definition of entrepreneurship to hand, we are able to demonstrate that its scope of application is all ordinary reality. This universality enables us to study the relations that exist between society, culture and the individual. It is not a question of making a complete study of each element separately, since the reality that we observe is individual action. Our objective has been to show how every action is developed within the sociocultural framework, making it possible to start the study of the action from the most general context, that is, from the social interaction. Praxeology has a clear interdisciplinary vocation. The study of market phenomena with the stamp of praxeology offers a suitable basis for other fields, while *maintaining the autonomy of each area of study*. The objective is to search for a common basis to the social sciences. In Becker's work the study of society and culture does not permit such interdisciplinary study. He recognizes that the only unitary framework for the study of any behaviour is his own, going so far as to state that his method is a clear example of economic imperialism.

Division between areas of study

The interdisciplinary vocation is patent in the Misian division of 'economics in the broad sense' and 'economics in the narrow sense'. Within the common theoretical base there exists a clear difference between the non-monetizable social interrelations and the monetizable market exchanges. In the first of these, we can cite the family, marriage, etc. Everything that is essentially human is included. Therefore, praxeology has never proposed the monetization of all human action, as Becker does with the generalization of *homo economicus*.

The concept of society

Every action, whether it is social interaction or a market exchange, is carried out within some social institutions. As 'knowledge problem A' proposes, every action is developed in an institutional framework. The institutions make it possible for the expectations of the persons to concur and for the mutual benefit of the relations to be guaranteed. That is to say, the process of social institutionalization guarantees the coordinating tendency of the expectations. In Becker's work, all reference to the social institutions and to the social interrelations is reduced to arguments that appear in the variable social capital of the extended utility function. All their complexities are reduced to mere external data.

The concept of culture

The social institutions constitute the framework that sustains the social 'edifice'. But the possibilities of action are transmitted in society through culture. Tradition is the treasure that is transmitted from generation to generation; it is the set of possibilities of action that are handed down to future generations. In other words, each generation offers the next generation a solution to the 'knowledge problem A', but these possibilities which are transmitted have to be accepted by the recipients. These received possibilities must guarantee to the present generation the development of their creative capacity. The social institutions have their own dynamism, which depends on the opportunities that enable their members to exercise their entrepreneurship. Every social institution has to guarantee the person's development of entrepreneurship; that is to say, it has to resolve 'knowledge problem B'. In the case of work, for example, the decision to specialize (problem of knowledge B) is based on the fact that the division of labour is the behavioural norm (knowledge problem A). With these remarks we can conclude that we need the culture and society to understand the importance of pure entrepreneurship, since persons discover the means of action in society through culture.

With the praxeological categories social evolution is explained as the cultural transmission of the possibilities of action. Professor J. Huerta de Soto talks about a '*Social Big Bang*', referring to the process of expansion of the possibilities of action which exist in a society. Through individual actions the elements that are received are culturally altered, thus expanding the field of social interactions and market exchanges. So we can explain why the medieval world had fewer possibilities of action than our own. In Becker's work, all reference to culture, like society, is reduced to arguments that appear within the variable social capital of the *extended* utility function.

The concept of competition

In praxeology, competition is a dynamic process of discovery: the discovery of the means and ends in the whole scope of application of entrepreneurship which, in other words, is the human world. This process of competition has no negative connotations because the social interrelations and the market exchanges tend to coordinate the expectations, provided that the person complies with the moral norms. Using the expression used in game theory, we can say that the interrelations and the market exchanges are *positive sum*. The term '*Social Big Bang*' is well adapted to this explanation. The expansion of the possibilities of action, of disposing of greater means, is the consequence of the fact that competition is a positive-sum game. Becker introduces his second hypothesis of market equilibrium. Once he totally eliminates the dynamism from his scheme, Becker works with systems of simultaneous equations that represent atemporally all the elements that enter the means–end relation.

Levels of study of reality

In praxeology, social reality is studied on three levels:

- First level: interpretation of the results of the evolution. It understands the historical studies.
- Second level: formal theory of the social process. It understands the development of the praxeological categories.
- Third level: formal ethical theory. It understands the study of the ethical systems and is concerned with the study of the formation of individual value judgements taking the moral systems in force in society as its starting point.

This separation does not exist in Becker's work. But it is going to be of great use to us in explaining Becker's study of moral norms.

Relation between ethics and the market

The later developments of Kirzner, Rothbard and Hoppe have gone beyond Mises' utilitarianism and advanced the lines of research into the relation between ethics and the market. The arguments of these authors aim to demonstrate formally that private property is the basis of the market economy. Put like that, it does not seem to be a great novelty, but the important thing is the new definition of private property which this research makes it possible to develop. Thus a new definition of property, going beyond the monetary aspects, enlarges its anthropological basis using the praxeological categories: private property is the social recognition of personal autonomy, and of each person's exercise of his creative capacity and the usufruct of the results.

Causality

Mises deals with causality from the point of view of praxeology. He does not try to make a study of the philosophical problems that are posed by the bases of causality. His starting point is to recognize that the means–end relation presupposes the cause–effect relation. In other words, the axiom of action presupposes causality. The central problem for praxeology is not, therefore, the foundations of causality. Its objective is to determine the constitution of the causes of the action. In Mises' work it is the person who determines the causes and who values the relative importance of the events in the process of action. Motivated and guided by the end, each person interprets the elements that enter into the process.

Becker proceeds from physics and rejects all teleological conceptions of the action. He reduces the whole problem of causality to statistical inferences and moves in the plane of statistical relations where the future is a repetition of the past. He reduces the possibilities of action to a mere calculation of probabilities, ignoring that probability is based on repeatable and controllable phenomena and that human action is not only a future time, but a thing to be done in the future.

Structure of the means–end relation

The antecedent–consequent causal relation is very closely linked to the temporal before–after relation. Our conclusion in the previous point was that in the action the person determines the causes, but these causes do not temporally precede the action, because the cause which motivates the person to act, that is to say, the desired end, is a future unreality that exercises its effects on the present. Therefore, unlike in mechanics, where the causes temporally precede the consequences, in praxeology the causes act from the future.[1] This means the means–end relation depends entirely on the human time, on *the historicity of the person*. The core of the subjective aspect of the action is reached in this slow theoretical process: this is how from the inexorable flow of time the person makes projections into the future.

Becker's work breaks the nexus of the union between the means–end relation and the historicity of the person. The means and ends he manages are the 'data' outside its framework of reference. The subjective aspect of the action disappears from his study.

The project

The historicity of the person has two aspects: the temporal flow and the project. From the inevitable flow of time, the person imagines more desirable situations and tries to make them possible. This attempt to organize the means to try to attain the desired end is the activity of pure entrepreneurship. Therefore, a project is the creative integration of the means to attain the end. In other words, human reality is fluid because it is historical and it is projective because it is open to the future.[2] This projection into the future is formed in the *synoptic structure* of the project, consisting of the mental representation that the person forms of the different stages leading to the end.

Becker's position on this point is new with respect to other authors. Aware of the problem that time poses for generalizing the neoclassical model for all human behaviour, he introduces the hypothesis of the stability of preferences over time of the *extended* utility function. This hypothesis is simply the logical consequence of the two previous ones. If we consider that the future is a repetition of the past, this third hypothesis postulates that the choices that *homo economicus* would like to make in the future, if he knew what would happen in the meantime, are exactly the same choices that he would then really make. This hypothesis constitutes what he defines as the *anticipatory* behaviour of the person.

Time

Praxeology studies time starting from the historicity of the person. It is evident that time is duration: duration in a very precise order – past, present and future. In fact, the key concept for praxeology is the flow of time. Of this ordering of time into past, present and future, there only exists one of these parts, the present. That means the importance of the ordering is that each one of the parts stops being the next part. In other words, man does not live in time; it is not something external to his reality. His historicity means that the present is made up of the past and the future. The flow of time is irreversible: it flows from the past to the future. The only way that man has to overcome this flow is to make a mental representation of the successive steps to take in order to achieve his ends. This *synoptic structure* of the project works again on the present of the action. This influence of the future over the present is the material which entrepreneurship manages.

For his part, Becker focuses on the ordering of time, ignoring its very particular essence: the flow of time. He concentrates on the ordering for a very simple reason: all ordering admits of a metric. This metric, the analogical measure of time, is what Becker needs to record the time that passes from the passage of situation A to situation B, both of which are known. This view, which reduces time to a mere measurement, forgetting that this measurement originates in the person who relies on it from his historicity, supposes that time is something external to the human action. Time is something that occurs to *homo economicus*, it is something that comes from outside the situation. This 'externality' prevents *homo economicus* from being able to represent the historicity of the person in his full reality: the ability of making projections into the future.

The information

Praxeology considers that the information has the following characteristics: (1) it is a practical type of subjective information; it is not scientific. (2) It is private and dispersed knowledge. This information is a precipitate available to each person. (3) It is tacit knowledge. Any knowledge, however scientific it may be, is always the result of intuition or an act of creation. (4) It is transmissible. In close connection with 'The concept of society' and 'The concept of culture' (p. 182), in which we have expounded the conclusions concerning 'knowledge problems A and B', the analysis of the informative structure poses these problems again from the point of view of the information, recognizing that this accumulation of information which is culturally transmitted is practical information. That is because the problem of information is really only one: the social coordination of the individuals who act with practical, private, tacit and communicable information.

The information in Becker's approach is given and 'made objective' in the restriction of the extended utility function. Knowledge for Becker is one more factor of production, with a cost that can be calculated.

The error

In praxeology the error is as possible as success and profit. The praxeological categories are necessary for the explanation of the action, but they do not determine any result in the process. The entrepreneurial appreciation of the suitability of the means to the ends may be correct or erroneous. The result of this action is not known until it is executed. The error is the a posteriori corroboration of the bad projection of the action. In Becker's model there is no room for error. The *homo economicus* cannot verify its existence because the only possible error in this model is to make a mistake in the resolution of the simultaneous equations that define the problem. In fact, the only question that remains to be asked is, what has this problem to do with the reality under study?

Structure of the model

The general conclusion can be explained in three points:

1   Regarding Becker's work, the hypothesis and the use of the *as if* clause state some properties of the economic agent which convert him into a mere caricature of human reality, converting his suppositions into mere ad hoc hypotheses:

 a   The definition of the economic agent continues to present grave deficiencies. His *homo economicus is a passive optant when facing given alternatives.*
 b   The means of the operations in which *homo economicus* carries out his activity is external to the model. The Beckerian economic agent does not have any active role in society and culture.
 c   The means–end relation is dislocated from its framework of reference. On eliminating all reference to the subjective aspect of the action, the alternatives that are presented to the economic agent are already given.

2   Concerning the work of Mises: if really one wants to copy physics, it is necessary to recognize that the role that is played in physics by the categories of space, time, substance, causality, action and reaction is converted into praxeological categories in the social sciences and not into a literal translation of these physical categories. In economics, we do not deal with bodies, nor

with substances. We economists deal with means–ends relations, which constitute the genuinely human world:

a   The praxeological categories define the person as a *creative and active optant of realities through the project*.
b   The sociocultural framework, formed by the social and cultural institutions, constitutes the means of operations. The role of the person is active in the formation and maintenance of the institutions and in the transmission of the culture.
c   The means–end relation is based on the historicity of the person. The project is the dynamic constitution of the structure of the ends and means. Economics becomes an objective science when focusing on the individual subject.

3   The principal corollary of this book is to try to demonstrate that making advances in the study of man as a fundamental element for economics means basing economics on philosophical anthropology. It is not a question of making a general systemization of what man is. Rather it is the other way round. It is about utilizing the parts of the anthropological studies that have to do with directly with human action. If we take an overview of the principal themes in economics – the theory of value, theories of capital and interest, growth, economic cycles, etc. – we find that they all revolve around a key concept, which is the high point: *human action*. Therefore, the anthropological definition which we give to the economic agent becomes the principal problem. The smaller the anthropological base, as in the case of the Beckerian *homo economicus*, then correspondingly the means of operations in which *homo economicus* is involved, and the means–ends relations that we can study, are infinitely more reduced as compared with the reasons given by praxeology. So, the superiority of complexity that praxeology reaches in the analysis of human action with respect to the Beckerian scheme is clear.

Methodological differences

Two radically distinct working methods are based on the theoretical differences. Becker always stresses that his work must be considered as a method of approaching human reality. However, if we pay attention to the etymology of the word, then method is the path that leads us to something. It is, strictly speaking, the way for us to approach a problem. In this section, first, we are going to deal with the methodological differences in general, and then second, we shall give examples of these differences and compare them with the theories of prices developed in the last chapter.

In this section we are going to follow the same method as we did previously. Table 11.2 shows the fundamental methodological differences between the two authors.

Table 11.2 Methodological differences

Point of comparison	L. von Mises	G. Becker
1. Separation between areas of study	Clear distinction between: (a) non-monetizable social interrelations; (b) monetizable market exchanges	There is no such difference. All decisions are expressed in money
2. Type of reasoning	Deductive method: individual action in the social framework: the interrelations–appearance of indirect exchange–market prices	Determination of the extended utility function and its restrictions. Calculation of shadow prices
3. Formulizing	Formal reasoning for integrating human creativity and historicity	Mathematical formulation of the problem
4. Predictions	The theoretical objective is the explanation. The predictions are qualitative about the consequences of interventionism	The declared objective is quantitative prediction
5. Predictor	Each person anticipates future situations in the project	Social engineering

Separation between areas of study

It is necessary to begin these conclusions by starting from the seventh point of the theoretical differences, 'Division between areas of study' (p. 181). In Mises' work the difference between 'economics in the broad sense' and 'economics in the narrow sense', which correspond to social interrelations in general and to market exchanges in particular, aim not to use market prices outside the context in which they are fully valid. Therefore, Mises' method is clear: in order to explain the social interrelations, they should not be reduced to monetary expressions; rather one should use the praxeological categories. Unlike Mises', Becker's objective is precisely to reduce every human decision to monetary terms.

Type of reasoning

The Misian method of reasoning is deductive; bearing in mind the radical difference that exists in praxeology between the areas of study. It is always necessary to start from more general situations and then to introduce the elements necessary for the explanation of particular situations. Therefore, to arrive at the explanation of prices using the praxeological categories one must follow this process: (1) the explanation of the individual action; (2) action in the social framework: the social interrelations; (3) from these interrelations, one must focus on the exchanges, and within these on one group in particular: the commodity–money–commodity: indirect exchanges; (4) the explanation of market prices starting from the valuations of the persons who intervene in the exchange.

Becker's way of reasoning is totally distinct. In order to reduce all action to maximizing behaviour, he defines a system of simultaneous equations that establish not only the variables that enter as arguments in the *extended* utility function, but also the relations that connect these variables together in order to formulate the restrictions.

Formulism

The only way of integrating human historicity and creativity is to express them formally in words (verbal logic). It is a question not of trying to reject the use of mathematics on principle, but of recognizing that at the present time the mathematical elements necessary for describing the richness of the person do not exist. On the other hand, the very reduced anthropological assumptions on which *homo economicus* is based generate very simple models that are suitable for use in calculating conditioned maximums and minimums. Once Becker has reduced all that is genuinely human to a useful value, it is easy to assign a mathematical variable to this human reality. All the reasoning in Becker's work is mathematical.

Predictions

Praxeology does not deny the importance of prediction. In fact, if we bear in mind that prediction has to be based on rational explanation, that is to say, on causal explanation, together with the information pertinent to the phenomenon, it is not possible to make a quantitative prediction because the persons create the relevant information in the dynamism of the action. The necessary information does not exist a priori. In order to understand a past action we have to weigh up qualitatively the importance that the human agent gave to each element that entered into the action. Given that the core of praxeology is creativity and the project, the predictions that are made are against the effects which interventionist measures have on the expansion of the possibilities of action (*Social Big Bang*) and which limit the field of action of people.

Becker's declared objective is prediction and empirical verification. He gives very little importance to theoretical hypotheses, and the only gauge of his method that he admits is the empirical falsification of his results. What Becker does not consider is that the use of the *as if* clause is aimed at the construction of a situation which has 'economic sense' consistent with the initial hypotheses. In other words, he really does not predict the optimizing behaviour of the person of flesh and blood. Becker does not contrast his results with reality, which is the object of the study, but with his initial hypotheses. In other words, his models are protected against any falsification by the object of the study, which is reality.

The predictor

Praxeology tries to be an explanatory theory of reality and therefore each person makes predictions when he makes projections for the future. We all try to gauge the relative importance of each event in future actions. For Becker, the object of his method is the organization of society through the departments of economic analysis of the ministries: it is the *sweet modulation* of economic activity (social engineering).

An example of the two methods: comparison of the theory of prices

We finished Chapter ten with the comparison of the two theories of prices in order to provide an example of their working methods. For Mises prices are, from beginning to end, the result of persons' subjective valuations. His explanation follows a rigorous deductive method:

1   The individual valuations are based on the subjective aspect of the action. These valuations can be explained with the law of marginal utility.
2   The direct exchanges are based on the subjective valuations of the persons. These individual valuations are explained by means of the law of decreasing marginal utility. The exchange relations are generated by taking this law as a starting point.
3   The indirect exchanges are based on the generalized acceptance of a commodity as a means of payment. The explanation of money from the direct exchanges lies in the discovery of the utilization of the possibilities.
4   The basic law of price determination. The market price is established at a point between a margin which is limited and determined by the valuations given by the marginal pairs.

The Beckerian explanation starts from the existence of prices and his objective is to determine the formal laws of the situation of market equilibrium, presenting the reciprocal relations between the level of prices and the supply, demand and the quantities produced. In his explanation there is no room for the historicity of the person in its two aspects of the flow of time and the project, and it is reduced to the atemporal and simultaneous determination of the alternatives presented to *homo economicus*.

Notes

1 Two economic approaches to human behaviour in liberalism

1 Both the monetizable actions and the non-monetizable actions are social. As we will see in Chapter four, the market is a social institution. I am indebted to Professor José Juan Franch for the suggestion of emphasizing the social character of the market in the Austrian proposal.

2 For Becker the *homo economicus* is not reduced to choosing material ends with monetary prices. He enlarges the scope of its application, and its behaviour is characterized by the maximizing behaviour, market equilibrium and stable preferences.

3 A. Millán-Puelles (1974) establishes that the basis of economics cannot be anything other than a philosophical anthropology that serves as a basis for the understanding what man is as a living being.

4 As Huerta de Soto points out: 'However the accusation of imperialism is not justified when it refers exclusively to the scope of the application of economic science, and not to the use of the neoclassical approach: from the Austrian point of view as well, since economics is considered a general theory of human behaviour, it is applicable to all the fields in which human beings act. Only when the conception based on the strictly rational *homo economicus* is applied is the accusation of imperialism clearly justified, not with regard to the scope of application of the economic point of view correctly understood but in respect of the neoclassical attempt to apply the strictly rationalist approach to all human fields' (Huerta de Soto 1998: 103).

5 I. Kirzner declares that the neoclassical approach [Becker] explains the movement from one known position of equilibrium to the other one by means of the changes produced, rather than by the dynamics of the same process (Kirzner 1973: 27).

2 The definition of economic behaviour in the work of Mises

1 Obviously Mises does not equate praxeology with logic. Praxeology, as is indicated by Professor Huerta de Soto, is logical reasoning about the principles that explain the creativity of human action. Therefore, we have praxeology = logic + praxeological categories + creativity of the particular action.

3 The structure of the general theory of action of Mises

1 Etymologically, assign comes from the Latin *ad signare*, which means fix or mark what corresponds to a person or a thing. Therefore, strictly speaking, the assignment is produced when the end has been decided on.

2 This attempt at explanation is comparable to the student of medicine who explains the existence of the illness by the fever. The fever is the confirmation of the fact of the illness; it is the external empirical confirmation of its existence, but it explains neither

how it originated nor how to cure it, which is of fundamental importance not only for the doctor, but also for the patient.

3 I. Kirzner (1976) has developed the economic point of view of the Austrian School and, following him, J. Huerta de Soto (1998) defines the economic point of view as the theory of human action, understood as a dynamic process.

4 Maurice Blondel initiated this trend in 1893 in his book *L'Action*. In the first lines, he makes clear the importance of undertaking such a study: 'yes or no? Does human life have any sense and does man have a destiny? . . . The problem is inevitable. Man inevitably resolves it, and that solution, true or false, but voluntary and at the same time necessary, each one carries in his own actions. This is the reason why is it necessary to study *the action*' (Blondel 1973: vii). In the original: 'oui ou non, la vie humaine a-t-elle un sens, et l'homme a-t-il une destinée? . . . Le problème est inévitable; l'homme le résout inévitablement; et cette solution, juste ou fausse, mais volontaire en même temps que nécessaire, chacun la porte dans ses actions. Voilà pourquoi il faut étudier *l'action*.'

5 The original phrase was *pantón métron ánthropos*. The work of Protagoras, whose title is *On Truth*, has come down to use through Plato (Plato, *Teeto*, 15, 1e–52a).

6 Irrationality may also be understood in its metaphysical sense; that is, to conceive the existence of objects that could be real yet are absolutely unthinkable for human understanding.

7 At the end of Chapter 7 we will expound the praxeological treatment of error.

8 Another aspect which we do not go into is whether the copy of the physical model was correct. For an analysis of this subject see P. Mirowsky, *More Heat than Light*, a book in which the author offers some substantial arguments to demonstrate that the authors of this copy copied the physical model very badly (Mirowsky 1981).

9 Cf. Chapter 10, this volume, 'The law of the equivalence of marginal utilities in equilibrium', in order to contrast the theoretical differences in the treatment of marginal utility. The essential difference lies in the fact that, unlike the neoclassical school, for Mises this concept is not reducible to a mathematizable, optimizing principle.

10 There is no need to derive the maximization of the distinction between ends and means. As a demonstration, it is sufficient to revise the study of human action in Greek philosophy. In the Aristotelian *organum* 'the good' for the person is not the maximum, but the virtue of the golden mean, *mesotes*. For Aristotle the action must tend towards the golden mean and satisfy needs in a limited way.

In the medieval world, no direct attack against the Aristotelian concept was proposed. It was with the beginning of the modern world and the creation of the new science that the Aristotelian concept of human actions was questioned. It was Leibniz who introduced the maximizing principle. It is necessary here to pause briefly and consider the work of Leibniz to re-examine the extent of his proposals.

His philosophical programme introduced the infinitesimal calculus into philosophy to explain the creation of the world as the best of all possible worlds. His famous phrase *Dum Deus calculat fit mundus* (God made the world calculating) posed the question: what does God calculate? To which Leibniz replied that God calculates the possibilities, how many of these possibilities can exist at a given time. It is a question of considering that, within the infinite number of present possible worlds facing the divine mind, there is only a large, but finite, number of worlds that are compatible at the same time. This existing world is the world that has the greatest number of possibilities and although God could have surely made many poorer worlds, he could not have made any richer in essence.

If we carefully analyse this proposal we will see that it is untenable. Zubiri (1995) presents two lines of counter-argument:

1 Leibniz makes divine reason calculate with possibilities in the way that a person who knew the exhaustive infinite analysis of the mechanical forces of the universe would

calculate. In the words of Zubiri, 'According to Leibniz, God calculates with possibilities as a poor mathematician on Earth can calculate the solution to a problem with the data that is given' (Zubiri 1995: 175). *This paragraph is of enormous importance to our study, because to introduce maximization in the principle of action supposes that all the possibilities are given before they are produced.* To admit the maximizing principle implies that all the means and all the ends are given. The door is open to reduce man to a mere optant: his projective capacity and his capacity to plan the future disappear. The action is reduced to Becker's proposition. Man becomes a passive optimizer of known alternative situations.

2 This vision of God is anthropomorphism on a big scale. Not only does it suppose that divine intelligence functions like human intelligence, but also it introduces the principle of the best possibility as the regulatory principle of human intelligence. According to this, will is decided on the basis of what is known as the best possibility. This idea is totally false. *Man does not decide which is the best possibility, but human will consists in declaring that the best possibility is really the one that he desires.*

The perception of the system of means and ends does not imply that all the means and ends at the disposal of the human agent are known. The sensation of dissatisfaction, which the human agent perceives, activates the subjective and conscious formation of means and ends to alter his present situation. The important information for the generation of the system of means and ends is not known beforehand; it is not given, at the disposition of the human agent like the data of a mathematical problem. The reality is very different. The end that is pursued is in the future. It is an imagined reality one aspires to achieve. From the very moment of the concept of the end, this has the desired effect on the present (see Rubio de Urquía 1991). The person strives to discover the means necessary to make his imagined reality come true. To sum up, *the end is an imagined reality and the means must be constituted; they are not given.* The only thing given in the action is the past. When we say that the person considers the best possibility, that which he wants, we are referring to the fact that he generates the means and the ends voluntarily and consciously (cf. Wojtyła 1979).

Israel Kirzner says:

> Human action is a far broader concept than that of economizing; while the allocation of scarce means among multiple competing ends may be an *example* of human action, human action need not be allocative at all. 'Human action is purposeful behavior' (Mises 1966: 11). What acting man seeks to do is 'to substitute a more satisfactory state of affairs for a less satisfactory' (Mises 1966: 13). Nothing in these formulations confines them to the calculative allocation of scarce means with respect to competing goals.
>
> (Kirzner 1992: 130)

4 The discovery of means and the creation of possibilities

1 Hayek says: 'The problem is thus not merely a problem of how to allocate "given" resources – if "given" is taken to mean give to a single mind which deliberately solves the problem set by these "data". It is rather a problem of how to secure the best use of resources known to any members of society, for ends whose relative importance only these individuals know' (Hayek 1976a: 77–8).

2 As Kirzner says: 'In developing this aspect of entrepreneurship I was led to emphasize the capture of pure entrepreneurship profit as reducible essentially to the exploitation of arbitrage opportunities' (Kirzner 1985: 43).

3 As Kirzner says: 'but whereas in the case of entrepreneurship in the single-period market (that is the case of the entrepreneur as arbitrageur) entrepreneurial alertness meant alertness to present facts, in the case of [a] multiperiod [market] entrepreneurship must mean alertness to the future' (Kirzner 1985: 63).

4 For different types of entrepreneurship activity see I. Kirzner (1985: 84ff, 116).
5 See for this critic Chapters 9 and 10. Kirzner says on this reductive application of the entrepreneurship concept: 'the entrepreneurship discovery by an individual of new goals to pursue and new availability of resources cannot be subsumed under the allocative, maximizing model of individual decision making' (Kirzner 1985: 163).
6 Professor Huerta de Soto often used to resort to this example to explain the importance of entrepreneurship.
7 This constant innovation demonstrates the importance of inventiveness in the constitution of the social system. The typification of a custom is the result of generalizing an invention. First, a new instrument is created. Second, its use is generalized. Third, its use becomes customary. It is a transmissible custom and, as such, it is handed down in tradition to future generations.
8 Huerta de Soto makes the same criticism of Kirzner's position. See the prologue to the Spanish version of *Discovery, Capitalism, and Distributive Justice* (Huerta de Soto 1995).
9 Kirzner himself is conscious of the relation that exists between both problems. He states: 'the substitution of an inferior institution for another superior one requires more than a solution of the problem A: it requires the solution of problem B' (Kirzner 1992: 173).
10 As E. Husserl affirmed: 'To be human at all is essentially to be a human being in a socially and generatively united civilization' (Husserl 1954: 16).
11 In the original: '[bei dieser Ordnung] handelt es sich um die regelmässigen Formen des Zusammenlebens der Individuen. Sie werden als Institutionen bezeichnet'.
12 In the original: 'wenn die einzelnen Insitutionen nicht ausschliesslich den einzelnen Bedürfnissen zugeordnet werden können, dann muss das Bestehen solcher Institutionen offenbar noch auf anderen Ursachen beruhen'.
13 In the original: 'A beobachtet das Verhalten von B. Er schreibt B's Handlungen Motivationen zu und *typisiert*, angesichts der Wiederholungen dieser Handlungen, die Motive als wiederkehrend. . . . Dasselbe geschieht mit A in Beziehung auf B. . . . Das heisst, A und B beginnen Rollen zu spielen im Verhältnis zueinander'.
14 In the original: 'diese Grundbedürfnisse veranlassen, dass die Habitualisierung von Handlungen sofort in arbeitsteilige Kooperation zum Ziel der Befriedigung solcher Bedürfnisse übergeht'.
15 Kirzner points out: 'Hayek has emphasized the significance of the knowledge problem for the evolution of social and cultural norms and institutions. The intricate web of mutually sustaining expectations required for the emergence of our most valuable social institutions, Hayek argues, could never conceivably have been deliberately simulated by one centralized organization. What has nurtured the spontaneous emergence of such benign cultural norms and institutions, Hayek maintains, is the circumstance that social processes of spontaneous co-ordination have been able to evolve' (Kirzner 1992: 165).
16 Kirzner says: 'the latter crystallization of shared moral institutions consists, at each moment in history, of sets of explicit or tacit ethical convictions nourishing people's evaluation of and expectations concerning the acts of others. No understanding of the market can afford to ignore the fundamental insight that its institutional foundations are to be sought directly, not in economic considerations but in ethical ones' (Kirzner 2000: 84).
17 In the original: 'offenbar um solche, die es mit der Gegenseitigkeit menschlichen Verhaltens in konkreten, wiederkehrenden Lebenssituationen oder in kontinuierlich fortdauernden Beziehungen zu tunhaben'.
18 In the original: 'die spezifisch menschliche Form des gemeinsamen Lebens wird ihrerseits schon konstituiert durch das Konzept einer gemeinsamen Welt, die wir Kultur nennen'.
19 In the original: 'die Interpretation des Kulturbegriffs darf auch nicht davon absehen, dass Kultur immer in der Ordnung der gesellschaftlichen Wirklichkeit Gestalt gewinnt'.

20 In philosophy, the term for creation *ex nihilo* is reserved for God. It is the only reality that can be created from absolutely nothing. On the other hand, man never finds absolutely nothing. The most successful term for man is quasi-creation. On this subject X. Zubiri says: 'human beings produce the possibility of reality before producing the reality. Precisely this resembles divine Creation. Therefore I have written from time to time that human life is quasi-creation. It is a quasi-creation because it consists, rather than of producing reality, precisely of producing the possibility that is going to be actualized in the actions of its reality' (Zubiri 2003: 157).

21 In the original: 'überwiegend dient die schöpferische Tätigkeit des Menschen der Erfassung und Darstellung von Sachverhalten, die erst in diesem Medium erfassbar und darstellbar werden, aber doch ihre Realität nicht einer Willkür menschlichen Schaffens verdanken. Was in Prozess kultureller Überlieferung akkumuliert wird, das ist der Schatz der Erschliessung von Wirklichkeit, und nur was fernerhin den Umgang mit erfahrbarer Wirlichkeit zu erweitern und zu vertiefen verspricht, wird in der Überlieferung bewahrt'.

22 In honour of the truth, one must recognize that Kirzner is conscious of this situation. He states that in order to survive, the institutions have to solve not only the problem of knowledge 'A' but also 'B'. Although he does not provide any explanation and concludes: 'the explanation of such tendencies (the co-ordinating role of the institutions), if it exists, must be sought in another place' (Kirzner 1992: 179).

23 For this reason, Zubiri defines man as a quasi-creative optant. Quasi because it is not creation *ex nihilo*. Creation because, with the received resources, he generates new possibilities that were not within the grasp of his ancestors.

24 Macintyre offers, as an example, the astonishment of Captain Cook and his men on observing the contrast that existed between the sexual freedom shown by the Polynesians and the strict separation of the sexes when eating. It was taboo to eat together. When asked about the origin of this taboo, the Polynesians were incapable of giving a reasonable explanation. This prohibition, which regulated the behaviour of the Polynesians, had lost all the sense that it once had. It is not surprising that there were no social consequences when Kamemeha II abolished the taboos (Macintyre 1981: 105).

J. A. Marina offers an explanation of this situation. He has the impression that 'many regulations are a forceful summary of rules for solving problems that have now been forgotten. These are solutions that can be explained, but whose effectiveness is increased, if they are imposed by a process of moral obligation' (Marina 1995: 49).

5 The evaluative system

1 In this scheme is usual to resort to assumptions of this type: let us suppose we have a spaceship in which the passengers reach another world where there is only one scarce productive resource, Manna. Warned of the dangers of unleashing a struggle for its control, the passengers begin to debate the question of its initial distribution and conclude that the appropriate morally model of doing is by the rule of simple equality. This is an example of B. Ackerman quoted by Kirzner (1989: 147).

2 As Rothbard points out, Mises himself concedes, in one passage, that a government can propose certain programmes for demagogic reasons (Rothbard 1998: 285).

3 We can show the dispute between utilitarianism and objective ethics in this work, emphasizing the real problems which arise in the solely utilitarianist scheme of norms. However, it is also necessary to point out that resorting to natural law as a support for ethics poses problems which are made manifest in the utilitarianist position. See, in this respect, Yeager (2001). For a solution from the point of view of objective ethics based on natural law, see Hoppe (1993).

4 In the original: 'sondern durch den der Zugehörigkeit zur Gemeinschaft und durch den jeweiligen besonderen Beitrag zu ihr, der dann Verhältnisse gegenseitiger Anerkennung im Inneren und der Solidarität nach aussen begründet'.

5 In the original: 'ein Verzicht auf das Moment der Exklusivität im Eigentumsbegriff, der aus dem Eigentum ein bloßes Zugangs- und Teilhaberecht machen würde, liefe auf die Beseitigung des Eigentums selber hinaus'.
6 In the original: 'Arbeit beschafft die Mittel zum Leben nicht nur für den Augenblick, sondern vorausblickend auf die Zukunft und damit, ansatzweise, auf das Ganze des Lebens'.
7 Reciprocity does not mean that in the exchange the things that are exchanged have to have the same value. It is not the continuation of the Aristotelian idea of the justice of the exchange as being the equality in value of what is exchanged. The idea that I want to emphasize is that in the relation between private individuals, each one is seeking his interest in subjectively valued terms.
8 In Chapter 10 we will present the Austrian explanation of the conditions in which the exchange is produced.

6 Causality as a praxeological category

1 I am grateful to Antonio Ferraz, professor of philosophy and co-director of the X. Zubiri seminar given by the Fundación Zubiri, for his comments about the pertinence of the use of Zubiri's work for the objectives of this chapter.
2 See the section under the heading 'The Misian methodology' in Chapter three.
3 In the efficient Aristotelian causality, it is necessary to distinguish between the principles of intrinsic and extrinsic transformation. In this example of the jewel, the efficient principle is extrinsic to the bronze, since it is the artist who shapes it. On the other hand, the intrinsic efficient causality depends on the substance. I am grateful to Professor Dr Antonio Ferraz Fayoz for this detail.
4 I am grateful for the very accurate criticism made by this person and I hope that the arguments that are explained here will permit me to clarify my point of view on this subject.
5 Maurice Blondel also defends a concept of causality that is applied to human action and that is not reducible to the four classical causes. He asks the question: 'how can the different parts of an organic system cooperate in such a way that they become the means and the end, because an efficient cause finds in the other cause – the final cause – a spontaneous complicity with its own, which depends on the same ruling idea?' (Blondel 1973: 223) In the original: 'Comment diverses parties d'un même système organique peuvent-elles opérer de manière à devenir mutuellement moyen et fin, sinon parce que l'une, cause efficiente, trouve dans l'autre, cause finale, une spontanéité complice de la sienne sous la dépendance d'une même idée directrice?'
  He offers us the following solution to this question: 'the causal link is at the same time a subjective disposition and an empirical association. Its originality consists in being at the same time analytical a *priori* and synthetic *a posteriori*, because each one of the subjects which contributes to the effect produced is a principal agent' (Blondel 1973: 223). In the original: 'ainsi le lien causal résulte à la fois d'une disposition subjective et d'une association empirique. Son originalité, c'est d'être à la fois analytique a *priori* et synthétique *a posteriori*, car dans l'effet produit, chacun des sujets qui y contribuent est un agent principal'.
  We also find this expression in the work of Karol Wojtyła. In his book *Acting Person* he states: 'it is man's actions, his conscious acting, that make of him *what* and *who* he actually is. This form of the human becoming thus presupposes the efficacy or causation proper to man' (Wojtyła 1979: 118). 'The personal causation is contained in having the experience of efficacy of the concrete ego – but only when man is acting' (p. 98).
6 As Huerta de Soto points out, for praxeology, the human agent looks to the future with the eyes of a historian (Huerta de Soto 1992: 51).
7 On the characteristics of this knowledge consult the subsection 'The characteristics of the information' in Chapter 7.

7 The project

1 J. A. Marina quotes as an example the enthusiasm of Valle-Inclán, the famous Spanish writer, to unite words that had not been joined before (Marina 1993: 152).

2 A clear example is that offered by Marina about Einstein: 'Einstein himself, reflecting on his work, said that during all these years, he had a sense of direction, that of going in a straight line towards something concrete. It is very difficult to describe this sentiment, but I have experienced it as a type of overflying, in a certain visual sense' (Marina 1993: 135).

3 This same idea was masterfully expressed by Professor Julián Marías in the following words: 'my life is not a thing, but rather a doing, a reality projected into the future, that is argumentative and dramatic, and that is not exactly *being* but happening' (Marías 1996: 126).

4 In the original: 'le temps est ce qui empêche que tout soit donné tout d'un coup. Il retarde, ou plutôt il est retardement. Il doit donc être elaboration. Ne serait-il pas alors véhicule de création et de choix? L'existence du temps ne prouverait-elle pas qu'il y a de l'indétermination dans les choses? Le temps ne serait-il pas cette indétermination même?'

5 The fundamental role of time was highlighted by Menger (1981, Chapter 1). On this subject see the article by Endres (1984). He states: 'historical time reigns supreme in the Gründsätze' (Endres 1984: 900). Also, Max Alter points out: 'the process of change, being the causal process, is only thinkable as a temporal process' (Alter 1982: 153).

6 This same idea of the present is found in H. Bergson. He says: 'the present is arbitrarily defined as *what is*, when the present is simply *what is done*' (Bergson 1963: 1963). In the original: 'Vous définissez arbitrairement le présent *ce qui est*, alors que le présent est simplement *ce qui se fait.*'

7 Professor J. Huerta de Soto defines the plan as 'the mental representation of a certain type of projection that the actor makes of the different stages, elements and possible circumstances that may be related to the action' (Huerta de Soto 1992: 45).

8 Heidegger says in this respect: 'the decisive thing about *counting* time, from the ontological-existential point of view, should not be seen either, therefore, in the quantification of time, but it must be conceived more originally or starting from the temporality of the "being there" which counts on time' (Heidegger 1977, § 80: 412). In the original: 'Das existenzial-ontologisch Entscheidende Zeit*rechnung* darf daher auch nicht in der Quantifizierung der Zeit gesehen, sondern muss ursprünglicher aus der Zeitlichkeit des mit der Zeit rechnenden Daseins begriffen werden.'

9 Though it is true that Hayek is recognized for the first complete formulation of the problem, the importance of the information is implicit in the work of Menger. If we pay attention to the requisites that define the economic good (cf. the subsection 'Interpretation of Carl Menger's definition of economic resource', later in this chapter), the third of these postulates is the existence of the knowledge of causal relation by the person. That is to say, a thing becomes an economic resource if the human agent knows how to utilize it in order to satisfy his needs. As Endres points out: 'in the *Principles* [Menger] economic progress was underpinned by a growth in knowledge that connects economic goods with the satisfaction of human needs' (Endres 1991: 287).

10 In the first article by Hayek (1937), the reference to Mises' paternity of the scheme is in a footnote in German. In the second article, Hayek (1945), the reference is more explicit: it appears in the main body of the text and in English. He recognizes that 'the thesis that without the price system, we could not preserve a society based on such extensive division of labour as ours was greeted with a howl of derision when it was first advanced by Von Mises twenty-five years ago' (Hayek 1976a: 50, 89 respectively).

11 Hayek posed the problem in the following terms: 'the peculiar character of the problem of a rational economic order is determined precisely by the fact that the knowledge of the circumstances of which we must make use never exists in concentrated or

integrated form but solely as the dispersed bits of incomplete and frequently contra-dictory knowledge which all the separate individuals possess' (Hayek 1976a: 77).

12 The scheme which I use for analysing is based on Huerta de Soto (1992, Chapter 2).

13 Gerald O'Driscoll and Mario Rizzo are the Austrian authors who give most importance to the formation of the plans of action. See O'Driscoll and Rizzo (1985).

14 On this particular subject Huerta de Soto adds: 'this same idea was expounded quite a few years ago by Gregorio Marañón: he told of a private conversation he had with Bergson, a short time before his death, when the French thinker confessed the following: "I am sure that the great discoveries of Cajal were no more than objective verifications of the facts that he had foreseen in his brain, as true realities"' (Huerta de Soto 1992: 59, note 26).

15 Marina tells the story that once he met a friend, who was a builder, and he asked him if he had constructed a block of flats in Málaga that he was planning. The friend replied that he had but it was an office block in Barcelona. Marina comments: 'the reply was incoherent, as he should have denied that he had carried out the original project. However, my friend, who lived through the drifting of his first idea, considered it as one project that he had modified' (Marina 1993: 201).

16 Zubiri points out: 'the constitution of the resource from the event is somewhat fundamental . . . the resources are in great measure inherited from previous situations and formally consist, as resources of our own substantivity, of being possibility in the order of actions we are going to perform, and which, once performed through empowerment and appropriation, leave the "I" in a situation of being a resource upon which to mount its ulterior vital moments' (Zubiri 2003: 158).

17 This is the scheme that Professor J. J. Franch has followed in his magnificent book *Fundamentos del Valor Económico*. In order to define economic value, he starts from the requisites proclaimed by Menger and bases his study of economic value with reference to human action. He defines economic value as the real relation of the ultimate, complementary, concrete, future suitability of the valued object for human ends (Franch 1990: 21).

18 Franch expresses this idea in the following way: 'the different elements that make up the universe are not based on isolated pieces, but rather, among themselves, they form a complicated network of very different interrelations: some are similar to others, some are the effect of others, some depend on others, some are better coordinated among themselves than others, etc. The more they are coordinated with human objectives, the greater value they have; *the more possibilities of coordination, the greater the relation they will have*' (Franch 1990: 30).

19 On Menger's Christian education, and especially his Catholic education, consult Johnston (1972).

20 See Max Alter (1982: 153). On the philosophical basis of the Austrian School consult B. Smith (1990).

21 Menger's objective was to found the theory of value on the broadest possible anthropological base. As Raimondo Cubeddu states: 'after 1889, Menger forgot about methodological themes (or rather he developed schemes for a new "philosophical anthropology")' (Cubeddu 1993: 55).

22 Kirzner points out: 'ignorance consists not in lack of available information but in inexplicably failing to see facts staring one in the face, it represents genuine error' (Kirzner 1979: 131).

8 The definition of economic behaviour in the work of Becker

1 Since all the articles which we are going to work with in this chapter are collected in Becker (1995), for the comfort of the reader we are going to take quotes only from this book.

2 Becker uses the word commodity to signify all the useful things that the person

produces for his satisfaction. In such a wide definition, he includes 'children, prestige and esteem, health, altruism, envy and pleasures of the senses' (Becker 1981: 8).

3 The author who as far as I know first used the expression 'economic imperialism' was Ralph William Souter. We read in his book: 'the salvation of Economic Science in the twentieth century lies in an enlightened and democratic "economic imperialism", which invades the territories of its neighbours, not to enslave them or to swallow them up, but to aid and enrich them and promote their autonomous growth in the very process of aiding and enriching itself' (Souter 1933: 94, note 91).

4 The Nobel Prize winner for economics R. Coase recognizes that 'that the economic approach may be successfully applied in other social sciences is demonstrated in Becker's own work' (Coase 1988: 2). And in a footnote he cites Becker's most important work as *The Economic Approach to Human Behavior*.

5 This digression is important because the criticisms of Becker based on the fact that he does not pick up on the changes in the consumption of goods are irrelevant. As we have shown in the *extended* utility function, non-monetary commodities, such as marriage, discrimination, etc., are also introduced. As we shall see in the following chapter, the direct criticism aimed at the core of Becker's model is against the hypothesis of the stability of preferences and the hypothesis of maximization of utility. Obviously, if these two fail, the hypothesis of market equilibrium is also not accepted.

6 In Becker's own words: 'if the utility function of commodities is maximized subject to this full-income constraint, one set of equilibrium conditions equates the ratio of the marginal utilities of different commodities to the ratio of their shadow prices' (Becker 1981: 8).

7 Becker models temporal preference in Becker and Mulligan (1997). The temporal preference is explained in terms of the time spent, the effort and the goods necessary to create the personal capital that is necessary to create the future more accurately. With this model Becker considers that strongly addictive behaviour, such as smoking or drinking, presents forward-looking behaviour with consistent preferences over time. This apparently self-destructive behaviour is explained by the changes that the person makes in his social capital stock and this implies a change in the temporal preference.

9 Critical analysis of Becker's definition of economic behaviour: stability of preferences

1 Becker recognizes the pioneering role of this article (Becker 1976: 7, note 11). On the analytical tradition of the Chicago School see Reder (1982).

2 The concept of knowledge as the relation between subject and object is found in all knowledge that has pretensions to be true, *independently of the method of scientific research that is proposed*. As Martin Heidegger points out: 'the characterisation of truth as "concordance", *adaequatio, ομοιωσις*, is without doubt, very general and vacuous. *But there is some truth in this, when he maintains, without prejudice to the most heterodox exegeses of knowledge, what it is that this relevant predicate shows*' (Heidegger 1977, § 44: 215, my italics). In the original: 'Die Charakteristik der Wahrheit als "Übereinstimmung", adaequatio, *ομοιωσις* ist zwar sehr allgemein und leer. Sie wird aber doch irgendein Recht haben, wenn sie, unbeschadet der verschiedenartigsten Interpretationen der Erkenntnis, die doch dieses auszeichnenden Prädikat trägt sich durchhält.'

3 From this perspective, Becker's work is the culmination of the methodical application of Robbins' definition of economics: the assignment of scarce means among alternative ends (Robbins 1969: 16).

4 Parsons calls this position initiated by Robbins and reaching its culmination in Becker, 'radical rationalistic positivism' (Parsons 1934: 513).

5 Huerta de Soto says with respect to this: 'we must continue to emphasize that it is precisely the essentially subjective character of the elements of human action (ends,

means and costs), which, in an only apparently paradoxical way, confers full *objectivity* on economics, in the sense that this is a theoretical science, whose conclusions are applicable to every type of action' (Huerta de Soto 1992: 49, note 15).

6 Bergson criticizes the positivist presumptions of reducing human action to a mere piece of data. We find this interesting comment: '[the positivist proposition] may not be constructed unless it is situated with the hypothesis of a deliberation that is finished and of a resolution that is taken. . . . *This figure does not show me the action being carried out, but rather the action that has been carried out*' (Bergson 1963: 118, my italics). In the original: 'ne pourra être construite que si l'on se place dans l'hypothèse d'une délibération achevée et d'une résolution prise . . . cette figure ne me montre pas l'action s'accomplissant, mais l'action accomplie'.

7 If we apply Gödel's theorem to the praxeological categories, there is sure to be something that cannot be explained, because this theorem is interpreted in such a way that reality always surpasses theory. In this respect see Hayek (1976b, sections 8.66–8.86).

8 Professor Rubio points out that such an attempt to reduce all human behaviour to *homo economicus* 'is like wanting to base and constitute a theory of the growth of the human body on classical analytical mechanics, supposing to this end that the human body may resemble a small number of material particles of constant mass, attracted by force fields. Such an objective would not precisely constitute a progressive attempt at scientific biology, under the principle of the scientism of analytical mechanics and the presumption of its universal explanatory validity. It would be an absurdity' (Rubio de Urquía 1993: 565).

It is curious that he has used the word absurdity (disparity), because there is no more appropriate word for judging Becker's theory. 'The formal or theoretical absurdity or nonsense is *no more than a theoretical declaration without equal in reality*' (Zubiri 1997b: 285, my italics).

9 As Zubiri points out: 'upon knowing things in this way we know the necessity for their being as they are and consequently why they are not another way. We have not only defined the thing, but have demonstrated in it its necessity' (Zubiri 1981: 39).

10 Pannenberg uses the following text by J. Ritter to express the same idea: 'Im Unterschied zu anderen Lebewesen gelangt der Mensch nicht von Natur, sondern ethisch zur Verwirklichung seiner Natur' (Man differs from other living beings in that he does not fulfil himself naturally, but ethically) (Pannenberg 1983: 431).

11 For a more detailed exposition of the mutual advantages of market exchanges, consult Chapter 10, the section entitled 'The Austrian explanation of prices'.

10 Critical analysis of Becker's definition of economic behaviour: maximizing behaviour and market equilibrium

1 This passive conception of man has some consequences that are not usually taken into account. Karol Wojtyła has developed, in fine detail, the idea of the radical insufficiency that it means to reduce man to mere passiveness; to 'something happens in man'. To understand any human fact, it is essential to start from human activity, of the man who acts (Wojtyła 1979, Ch. 2).

2 The law of the equality of marginal utilities in equilibrium is found as the basis of all the functional theories of prices. Mayer points out: ' the law of the level of marginal utility, as the basic ratio essential to further derivations, can be found without exception in all mathematicians operating with the subjective factor – whether in the elementary form developed by Jevons, or, as in Walras and Pareto, in the form of the equality of the weighted (that is, divided by price) utilities of the last-acquired units of goods, the *weighted ophelimities*, as Pareto calls them' (Mayer 1994: 75).

3 If we consider how today it is commonly accepted among economists that the essence of the marginalist revolution consists of the calculation of the maximum values of

conditioned functions, then the divergence between Menger on the one hand and Jevons and Walras on the other is so great that we can say that Menger's contribution to this revolution has been nil. One should highlight the importance of J. A. Schumpeter's work in the formation of this view of the marginalist revolution. There are two particularly important moments:

First, Schumpeter (1908) presents his positivist vision of the unity of the method of science to economics and it is symptomatic that he should send Walras a copy of the book as the homage of a pupil to a master. In the letter which he sent, one can read: 'un nouvelle époque pour l'économie scientifique est marquée par vos beaux mémoires, qui, pour la première fois, ont traité la théorie économique dans une manière vraiment scientifique. Moi, je m'efforcerai toujours de travailler sur les bases indiquées par vous, de continuer votre œuvre' (Jaffé 1965: 378, vol. III). In English: 'his splendid works mark a new epoch in scientific economics; in them, economic theory is treated, for the first time, in a truly scientific manner. *I will always endeavour to work on the basis that you have indicated, for continuing your work.*'

Obviously, this posture of Schumpeter did not go unnoticed by his Viennese colleagues, followers of Menger. F. von Wieser commented critically on Schumpeter's attempt to reduce all economics to equilibrium models (Wieser 1994).

Second, the enormous repercussions of Schumpeter's great book *The History of Economic Analysis* (1954) had supposed the coronation of the equilibrium model as the paradigm of economic scientific method.

4 The best explanation of this second condition is the representation of the economy made by I. Fisher. It represents a pool, which contains a liquid. The pool is divided into compartments communicating through tubes. Each tube represents needs and the state of the liquid, and by changing the volume of liquid or the pressure, there is a continuous and homogeneous increase or decrease in the water level in all the compartments (see Fisher 1965).

5 Bergson makes the pertinent observation in his critique of positivism: '[to admit this proposition] is to admit the possibility of adequately representing time by space and *a succession by a simultaneity*' (Bergson 1963: 119). In the original: 'c'est admettre la possibilité de représenter adéquatement le temps par de l'espace, et une succession par une simultanéité'.

6 As Julián Marías points out: 'that is why, the *present* world, I want to say, that world that is constituted as such in my life, is *successive*, not in the sense that it "passes" or "elapses", but in the sense that it is composed of changing situations, whose elements "enter" and "exit"' (Marías 1995: 96).

7 These theoretical differences are present in the correspondence between Menger and Walras. In the brief correspondence they exchanged, the letter sent by Menger in February 1884 is very important. In this he clearly explains to Walras his reasons for rejecting the use of mathematics in theoretical research: 'wir müssen zurückgehen auf die Bedürfnisse der Menschen . . . auf die subjective Bedeutung (den subjectiven Wert), welche concrete güterquantitäten für die einzelnen wirtschaftenden Subjecte haben' (we must go back to human needs . . . to the subjective meaning [the subjective value] that a specific quantity of a good has for each economic individual) (Jaffé 1965: 4, vol. II).

The origin of *homo economicus* is found in Walras and Jevons, but not in the work of Menger. As Max Alter points out: 'the economic theory, which is taught in lectures on microeconomics, does not go back to Menger, Jevons and Walras. It goes back to Jevons and Walras, but not to Menger' (Alter 1982: 151).

8 Professor Polo says in this respect: 'we can only transform temporal events, because there is something atemporal in ourselves; we are *fabri* because we are *sapiens*' (Polo 1996: 184).

9 The following example by Hans Mayer enables us to highlight the differences between Becker and the Austrian School: let us consider a musical melody. Becker says we can

appreciate it *simultaneously* by knowing all of the notes in it, whereas Mayer says that we can only appreciate it by listening to the music cadence *sequentially*. In his own words: '[Becker's bet] is as if one were to express the experience of aesthetic value of hearing a melody – an experience determined by successive experiences of individual notes – in terms of aesthetic value of the simultaneous harmonization of all notes making up the melody' (Mayer 1994: 83).

10 Mises gives the next explication: 'if the supply available increases from $n-1$ units to n units, the increment can be employed only for the removal of a want which is less urgent or less painful than the least urgent or least painful among all those wants which could be removed by means of the supply $n-1$' (Mises 1996: 124).

11 Böhm-Bawerk cites the following example from daily life as a corroboration of the law of marginal utility as an explanation of the real value of goods for men. He presents us with a lawyer who has to make a valuation of material losses in a trial. The process is the following: first of all, he considers the lowest degree of satisfaction that the possession of the good gave to the victim, among the group of goods that he possessed. Second, he values the victim's group of goods after the loss. Obviously, the difference between these two is the valuation of the lowest level of satisfaction in the valuation scale which the good gave to the victim. It is easy to recognize that this value is the marginal utility of the lost good (Böhm-Bawerk 1959b: 146).

12 As Professor S. Rábade says: 'the subject is the place of the objectivization of the *other* in regard to the *other*' (Rábade 1969: 179). In this sentence the *other* refers to any object of knowledge different from the person's own reality. In this case, by substituting the *other* by the price, we can reinterpret the Professor Rábade's sentence by saying the person is the place of the objectivization of the price, in regard to price.

11 Conclusions

1 This concept is important for understanding that for Mises and the Austrians, it is future prices estimated entrepreneurially that determine present costs. This is the opposite idea to Becker's, which considers that present costs determine present prices.

2 Obviously, in every project there exists the difficulty of the management of the productive factors. These technical difficulties, in spite of being fundamental, are outside the scope of our study. If we focus on the dynamism of pure entrepreneurship, these technical difficulties are faced because *previously* possible future gain is perceived.

Bibliography

Alter, M. (1982) 'Carl Menger and homo oeconomicus: some thoughts on Austrian theory and methodology', *Journal of Economic Issues* 16(1): 149–60.

Antonelli, E. (1953) 'Léon Walras et Carl Menger à travers leur correspondance', *Économie Appliquée* 6: 269–87.

Aranguren, J. L. (1.997) *Ética*, Madrid: Editorial Biblioteca Nueva.

Arrow, K. J. (1974) 'Limited knowledge and economic analysis', *American Economic Review* 64: 1–10.

Bartley, W. III (1984) *The Retreat of Commitment*, La Salle, IL: Open Court Publishing Company.

Becker, G. (1957) *The Economics of Discrimination*, Chicago, IL: University of Chicago Press.

—— (1964) *Human Capital: A Theoretical and Empirical Analysis, with Special Reference to Education*, New York: National Bureau of Economic Research.

—— (1965) 'A theory of the allocation of time', *Economic Journal* 75: 493–508; reprinted in R. Febrero and P. Schwartz (eds) *The Essence of Becker* (1995) Stanford, CA: Hoover Institution Press.

—— (1971) *Economic Theory*, New York: A. Knopf.

—— (1976) *The Economic Approach to Human Behavior*, Chicago, IL: University of Chicago Press.

—— (1981) *A Treatise on the Family*, Cambridge, MA: Harvard University Press.

—— (1992) 'Habits, addictions, and traditions', *Kyklos* 45(3): 327–46; reprinted in R. Febrero and P. Schwartz (eds) *The Essence of Becker* (1995), Stanford, CA: Hoover Institution Press.

—— (1993) 'The economic way of looking at behavior', *Journal of Political Economy* 101(3): 633–59; reprinted in R. Febrero and P. Schwartz (eds) *The Essence of Becker* (1995), Stanford, CA: Hoover Institution Press.

—— (1995) *The Essence of Becker*, R. Febrero and P. Schwartz (eds), Stanford, CA: Hoover Institution Press.

—— (1996) *Accounting for Tastes*, Cambridge, MA: Harvard University Press.

Becker, G. and Mulligan, C. B. (1997) 'The endogenous determination of time preference', *Quarterly Journal of Economics* 112(3): 729–58.

Becker, G. and Murphy, K. M. (2000) *Social Economics: Market Behavior in a Social Environment*, Cambridge, MA: Belknap Press.

Berger, P. and Luckmann, T. (1966) *The Social Construction of Reality*, New York: Doubleday.

Bergson, H. (1896) *Matière et Mémoire;* reprinted in H. Bergson (1963) *Oeuvres*, 2nd edn, Paris: Presses Universitaires de France.

—— (1889) *Essai su les Données Immédiates de la Conscience;* reprinted in H. Bergson (1963) *Oeuvres*, 2nd edn, Paris: Presses Universitaires de France.

—— (1934) *La Pensée et le Mouvant*, reprinted in H. Bergson (1963) *Oeuvres*, 2nd edn, Paris: Presses Universitaires de France.

—— (1963) *Oeuvres*, 2nd edn, Paris: Presses Universitaires de France.

Blanschard, B. (1973) *Reason and Analysis*, La Salle, IL: Open Court Publishing Company.

Blaug, M. (1992) *The Methodology of Economics: Or How Economists Explain*, 2nd edn, Cambridge: Cambridge Univesity Press.

Blondel, M. (1973) *L'Action*, 3rd edn, Paris: Presses Universitaires de France.

Boettke, P. J. (1994) *The Elgar Companion to Austrian Economics*, Northampton, MA and London: Edward Elgar.

Böhm-Bawerk, E. (1962) 'Control or economic law?', in *Shorter Classics of Eugen von Böhm-Bawerk*, vol. 1, South Holland, IL: Libertarian Press.

—— (1959a) *Capital and Interest*, vol. 1, *History and Critique of Interest Theories*, South Holland, IL: Libertarian Press.

—— (1959b) *Capital and Interest*, vol. 2, *Positive Theory of Capital*, South Holland, IL: Libertarian Press.

—— (1959c) *Capital and Interest*, vol. 3, *Further Essays on Capital and Interest*, South Holland, IL: Libertarian Press.

Boland, L. (1984) 'A critique of Friedman's critics', in B. Cadwell (ed.) *Appraisal and Criticism in Economics*, New York: Allen and Unwin.

Buchanan, J. M. (1964) 'What should economists do?', *Southern Economic Journal* 30: 213–22.

Buchanan, J. M. and Viktor, J. (1991) 'The market as a creative process', *Economic Philosophy* 7(2): 167–86.

Cadwell, B. (1982) *Beyond Positivism: Economic Methodology in the Twentieth Century*, New York: Allen and Unwin.

—— (ed.) (1984) *Appraisal and Criticism in Economics*, New York: Allen and Unwin.

—— (1990) *Carl Menger and his Legacy in Economics*, annual supplement to vol. 22, *History of Political Economy*, Durham, NC and London: Duke University Press.

Care, S. and Landesman, C. (1968) *Readings in the Theory of Action*, Bloomington, IN: Indiana University Press, 1968.

Coase, R. (1988) *The Firm, the Market and the Law*, Chicago, IL: University of Chicago Press.

Csikzentmihalyi, M. (1996) *Creativity: Flow and the Psychology of Discovery and Invention*, New York: HarperCollins.

Cubeddu, R. (1993) *The Philosophy of the Austrian School*, London: Routledge.

Endres, A. M. (1984) 'Institutional elements in Carl Mengers's theory of demand: a comment', *Journal of Economic Issues* 18(3): 897–903.

—— (1991) 'Menger, Wieser, Böhm-Bawerk and the analysis of economic behaviour', *History of Political Economy* 23(2): 275–95.

Fisher, I. (1965) *Investigations in the Theory of Value and Price*, New Haven, CT: Yale University Press.

Franch, J. J. (1990) *Fundamentos del Valor Económico*, Madrid: Unión Editorial.

Friedman, M. (1953) *Essays in Positive Economics*, Chicago, IL: University of Chicago Press.

—— (1977) 'Nobel lecture: inflation and unemployment', *Journal of Political Economy* 85(3): 451–72.

García Morente, M. (1996) *Obras Completas*, J. M. Palacios and R. Rovira (eds), vol. 1, Madrid: Fundación Caja de Madrid.

Gehlen, A. (1977) *Urmensch und Spätkultur: philosophische Ergenisse und Aufsagen*, Frankfurt: Athenaion Verlag.

—— (1988) *Man: His Nature and Place in the World*, New York: Columbia University Press.

Goldman, S. (1970) *A Theory of Human Action*, Princeton, NJ: Princeton University Press.

Gossen, H. H. (1983) *The Laws of Human Relations and the Rules of Human Action Derived Therefrom*, Cambridge, MA: MIT Press.

Hamlyn, D. W. (1968) *Aristotle's 'De Anima'*, Oxford: Clarendon Press.

Hayek, F. A. (1937) 'Economics and Knowledge', *Economica*, new series, 4: 33–54; reprinted in *Individualism and Economic Order* (1976), London: Routledge and Kegan Paul.

—— (1944) *Road to Serfdom*, Chicago, IL: University of Chicago Press.

—— (1945) 'The Use of Knowledge in Society', *American Economic Review* 35(4): 519–30; reprinted in *Individualism and Economic Order* (1976), London: Routledge and Kegan Paul.

—— (1952) *The Counter-Revolution of Science*, Glencoe, IL: Free Press.

—— (1959) *The Constitution of Liberty*, Chicago, IL: University of Chicago Press.

—— (1967) *Studies in Philosophy, Politics and Economics*, London: Routledge and Kegan Paul.

—— (1973) *Law, Legislation and Liberty*, vol. 1, *Rules and Order*, Chicago, IL: University of Chicago Press.

—— (1976a) *Individualism and Economic Order*, London: Routledge and Kegan Paul.

—— (1976b) *The Sensory Order*, Chicago, IL: University of Chicago Press.

—— (1976c) *Law, Legislation and Liberty*, vol. 2, *The Mirage of Social Justice*, Chicago, IL: University of Chicago Press.

—— (1978) *New Studies in Philosophy, Politics, Economics and the History of Ideas*, London: Routledge and Kegan Paul.

—— (1979) *Law, Legislation and Liberty*, vol. 3, *The Political Order of a Free People*, Chicago, IL: University of Chicago Press.

—— (1988) *The Fatal Conceit*, Chicago, IL: University of Chicago Press.

Hazlitt, H. (1967) *The Failure of the New Economics: An Analysis of the Keynesian Fallacies*, Princeton, NJ: Van Nostrand.

—— (1998) *The Foundations of Morality*, New York: Foundation for Economic Education.

Heidegger, M. (1977) *Sein und Zeit*, Frankfurt: Vittorio Klostermann Verlag.

Hollis, M. and Nell, E. J. (1975) *The Rational Economic Man*, Cambridge, MA: Cambridge University Press.

Hoppe, H. H. (1988) *A Theory of Socialism and Capitalism*, Boston, MA: Kluwer Academic.

—— (1993) *The Economics and Ethics of Private Property*, Boston, MA: Kluwer Academic.

Huerta de Soto, J. (1987) *Lecturas de Economía Política*, 3 vols, Madrid: Unión Editorial, Madrid.

—— (1992) *Socialismo, Cálculo Económico y Función Empresarial*, Madrid: Unión Editorial.

—— (1994) *Estudios de Economía Política*, Madrid: Unión Editorial.

—— (1995) 'Prólogo', in I. Kirzner, *Creatividad, Capitalismo y Justicia Distributiva*, Madrid: Unión Edtorial.

—— (1998) 'The ongoing *Methodenstreit* of the Austrian School', *Journal des Économistes et des Études Humaines* 8(1): 75–113.

—— (2004) 'La teoría de la eficiencia dinámica', *Procesos de Mercado* 1(1): 11–73.

Husserl, E. (1954) *Die Krisis der europäischen Wissenschaften und die transzendentale Phänomenologie*, The Hague: Martinus Nijhoff Publishers.

Jaffé, W. (ed.) (1965) *Correspondence of León Walras and related Papers*, 3 vols, Amsterdam: North-Holland.

—— (1976) 'Menger, Jevons and Walras de-homogenized', *Economic Inquiry* 14(4): 511–24.

Jevons, W. S. (1965) *The Theory of Political Economy*, 5th edn, New York: Augustus M. Kelley.

Johnston, W. M. (1972) *The Austrian Mind: An Intellectual and Social History, 1848–1938*, Berkeley, CA: University of California Press.

Kant, I. (1930) *Kritik der reinen Vernunft*, Hamburg: Felix Meiner Verlag.

Kauder, E. (1965) *A History of Marginal Utility Theory*, Princeton, NJ: Princeton University Press.

Kirzner, I. (1963) *Market Theory and the Price System*, Princeton, NJ: Van Nostrand.

—— (1966) *An Essay on Capital*, New York: Augustus M. Kelley.

—— (1973) *Competition and Entrepeneurship*, Chicago, IL: University of Chicago Press.

—— (1976) *The Economic Point of View*, 2nd edn, Kansas City, KS: Universal Press.

—— (1979) *Perception, Opportunity and Profit*, Chicago, IL: University of Chicago Press.

—— (ed.) (1982) *Method, Process, and Austrian Economics. Essays in Honor of Ludwig von Mises*, Lexington, MA: Lexington Books.

—— (1985) *Discovery and the Capitalist Process*, Chicago, IL: University of Chicago Press.

—— (ed.) (1986) *Subjectivism, Intelligibility and Economic Understanding*, London: Macmillan.

—— (1989) *Discovery, Capitalism and Distributive Justice*, Oxford: Basil Blackwell.

—— (1992) *The Meaning of Market Process*, London: Routledge.

—— (1997) 'Entrepreneurial discovery and the competitive market process. An Austrian approach', *Journal of Economic Literature* 36: 60–85.

—— (2000) *The Driving Force of the Market*, London: Routledge.

Koopmans, T. C. (1957) *Three Essays on the State of Economic Science*, New York: McGraw-Hill.

Koslowski, P. (1982) *Ethik des Kapitalismus*, Tübingen: J. C. B. Mohr (Paul Siebeck) Verlag.

—— (1985) *Economics and Philosophy*, Tübingen: J. C. B. Mohr (Paul Siebeck) Verlag.

Kotarbinski, T. (1965) *Praxeology. An Introduction to the Sciences of Efficient Action*, Warsaw: Polish Scientific Publishers.

Kroeber, A. and Kluckhohn, C. (1952) *Culture. A Critical Review of Concepts and Definitions*, Cambridge, MA: Harvard University Peabody Museum of American Archeology and Ethnology Papers no. 47.

Lachmann, L. M. (1976) 'From Mises to Shackle. An essay on Austrian economics and the kaleidic society', *Journal of Economic Literature* 14(10): 54–62.

—— (1977) *Capital, Expectations and the Market Process. Essays on the Theory of the Market Economy*, Kansas City, KS: Sheed, Andrews and McMeel.

—— (1986) *The Market as an Economic Process*, Oxford: Basil Blackwell.

Lledó, E. (1995) 'Introducción a las éticas', in *Ética Nicomáquea–Ética Eudemia*, Madrid: Biblioteca Clásica Gredos.

Macintyre, A. (1981) *After Virtue*, London: Duckworth.

Malinowski, B. (1944) *Theory of Culture and Other Essays*, New York: Carolina Press.

Marchi, N. and Blaug, M. (1991) *Appraising Economic Theories. Studies in the Methodology of Research Programs*, Aldershot, England: Edward Elgar.

Marías, J. (1967) *History of Philosophy*, trans. Stanley Appebaum and Clarence C. Strowbridge, New York: Dover.

—— (1995) *Antropología Metafísica*, Madrid: Alianza Editorial.

—— (1996) *Persona*, Madrid: Alianza Editorial.

Marina, J. A. (1992) *Elogio y Refutación del Ingenio*, Barcelona: Editorial Anagrama.

—— (1993) *Teoría de la Inteligencia Creadora*, Barcelona: Editorial Anagrama.

—— (1995) *Ética para Náufragos*, Barcelona: Editorial Anagrama.

Mayer, H. (1994) 'The cognitive value of functional theories of price', in I. Kirzner (ed.) *Classics in Austrian Economics*, vol. 2, London: William Pickering.

Menger, C. (1981) *Principles of Economics*, New York: New York University Press.

—— (1985) *Investigations into the Method of the Social Sciences with Special Reference to Economics*, New York: New York University Press.

Millán-Puelles, A. (1974) *Economía y Libertad*, Madrid: Confederación Española de Cajas de Ahorro.

Mirowsky, P. (1981) *More Heat than Light*, Cambridge, MA: Cambridge University Press.

Mises, L. (1920) 'Die Wirtschaftsrechnung im sozialistischen Gemeinwesen', *Archiv für Sozialwissenschaft und Sozialpolitik* 47: 86–121; trans. S. Adler (1975) 'Economic calculation in the socialist commonwealth', in F. A. Hayek (ed.) *Collectivist Economic Planning*, Clifton, NJ: Augustus M. Kelley.

—— (1966) *Theory and History*, 2nd edn, New Rochelle, NY: Arlington House.

—— (1976) *A Critique of Interventionism*, New Rochelle, NY: Arlington House.

—— (1978a) *The Ultimate Foundation of Economic Science*, 2nd edn, Kansas City, KS: Sheed Andrews and McMeel.

—— (1978b) *Notes and Recollections*, South Holland, IL: Libertarian Press.

—— (1980) *The Theory of Money and Credit*, Indianapolis, IN: Liberty Press.

—— (1981a) *Epistemological Problems of Economics*, New York: New York University Press.

—— (1981b) *Socialism. An Economic and Sociological Analysis*, Indianapolis, IN: Liberty Press.

—— (1983) *Nation, State and Economy*, New York: New York University Press.

—— (1985) *Liberalism*, San Francisco, CA: Cobden Press.

—— (1996) *Human Action: A Treatise on Economics*, B. B. Greaves (ed.), 4th edn (revised), New York: Foundation for Economic Education.

Münch, P. (1987) *The Theory of Action: Towards a New Synthesis Going beyond Parsons*, London: Routledge and Kegan Paul.

Neurath, O. (1939) *International Encyclopedia of Unified Science*, Chicago, IL: University of Chicago Press.

O'Driscoll, J. R. and Rizzo, M. J. (1985) *The Economics of Time and Ignorance*, Oxford: Basil Blackwell.

Ortega y Gasset, J. (1946–83) *Obras Completas*, 12 vols, Madrid: Revista de Occidente.

Pannenberg, W. (1983) *Anthropologie in theologischer Perspektive*, Göttingen: Vandenhoeck und Ruprecht.

Parsons, T. (1934) 'Some reflections on the nature and significance of economics', *Quarterly Journal of Economics* 48: 511–45.

Parsons, T. and Shills, E. (1962) *Towards a General Theory of Action*, New York: Harper and Row.

Plessner, H. (1941) *Lachen und Weinen*, Berne: A. Francke Verlag.

Polo, L. (1993) *Quién es el Hombre*, Madrid: Rialp.

—— (1996) *Ética: hacia una versión moderna de los temas clásicos*, Madrid: Unión Editorial.

Popper, K. R. (1950) *The Open Society and its Enemies*, 2 vols, Princeton, NJ: Princeton University Press.

—— (1959) *The Logic of Scientific Discovery*, London: Hutchinson.

—— (1963) *Conjectures and Refutations: The Growth of Scientific Knowledge*, London: Routledge and Kegan Paul.

—— (1972) *Objective Knowledge: An Evolutionary Approach*, Oxford: Clarendon Press, Oxford.

—— (1982) *Postscript to the Logic of Scientific Discovery*, W. W. Bartley III (ed.), 3 vols, London: Hutchinson.

Pribram, K. (1983) *A History of Economic Reasoning*, Baltimore, MD: The Johns Hopkins University Press.

Rábade, S. (1965) *Verdad, Conocimiento y Ser*, Madrid: Editorial Gredos.

—— (1969) *Estructura del Conocer Humano*, Madrid: Del Toro.

Reder, M. W. (1982) 'Chicago economics: permanence and change', *Journal of Economic Literature* 20: 1–38.

—— (1999) *Economics. The Culture of a Controversial Science*, Chicago, IL: University of Chicago Press.

Robbins, L. (1963) *Politics and Economics*, London: Macmillan.
—— (1969) *An Essay on the Nature and Significance of Economic Science*, 2nd edn, London: Macmillan.
—— (1976) *Political Economy, Past and Present*, New York: Columbia University Press.
Roepke, W. (1942) *Die Gesellschaftskrisis der Gegenwart*, Zürich: Eugen Rentsch Verlag.
—— (1949) *Civitas Humana. Grundfragen der Gesellschafts und Wirschaftsreform*, Zürich: Eugen Rentsch Verlag.
—— (1950) *Mass und Mitte*, Zürich: Rentsch Verlag.
—— (1959) *Internationale Ordnung-Heute*, Zürich: Eugen Rentsch Verlag.
—— (1968) *Die Lehre von Wirtschaft*, 11th edn, Vienna: Julius Springer Verlag.
Ross, W. D. (1975) *Aristotle's Metaphysics*, 6th edn, Oxford: Clarendon Press.
Rothbard, M. N. (1970) *Man, Economy and State*, Los Angeles, CA: Nash Publishing.
—— (1998) *The Ethics of Liberty*, 2nd edn, New York: New York University Press.
Rubio de Urquía, R. (1991) 'Ética y procesos de asignación de recursos', *Información Económica Española* 691: 7–15.
—— (1993) 'Los procesos de producción de la acción humana, la teoría neoclásica de los procesos de asignación de recursos y la economía de la familia', *Revista Española de Pedagogía* 196: 551–71.
Scheler, M. (1961) *Man's Place in Nature*, New York: Noonday.
—— (1973) *Formalism in Ethics and Non-Formal Ethics of Values*, Evanston, IL: Northwestern University Press.
Schumpeter, J. A. (1908) *Das Wesen und der Haupinhalt der theoretischen Nationalökonomie*, Leipzig: Duncker und Humboldt Verlag.
—— (1950) *Capitalism, Socialism and Democracy*, London: George Allen and Unwin.
—— (1954) *History of Economic Analysis*, New York: Oxford.
—— (1961) *The Theory of Economic Development*, New York: Oxford.
Shackle, G. L. (1970) *Decision, Order and Time in Human Affairs*, Cambridge: Cambridge University Press.
—— (1972) *Epistemics and Economics*, Cambridge: Cambridge University Press.
Smith, B. (1990) 'Aristotle, Menger, Mises: an essay in the metaphysics of economics', in B. J. Cadwell (ed.) *Carl Menger and his Legacy in Economics*, annual supplement to vol. 22, *History of Political Economy*, Durham, NC and London: Duke University Press.
Souter, R. W. (1933) *Prolegomena to Relativity Economics*, New York: Columbia University Press.
Sowell, T. (1980) *Knowledge and Decisions*, New York: Basic Books.
Stigler, G. and Becker, G. (1977) 'De gustibus non est disputandum', *American Economic Review* 67: 76–90; reprinted in G. Becker (1995) R. Febrero and P. Schwartz (eds) *The Essence of Becker*, Stanford, CA: Hoover Institution Press.
Taylor, R. (1980) *Action and Purpose*, Atlantic Highlands, NJ: Humanities Press.
Thomsen, E. (1992) *Price and Knowledge*, London: Routledge.
Valverde, C. (1995) *Antropología Filosófica*, Madrid: Editorial EDICEP.
Walras, L. (1954) *Elements of Pure Economics*, London: George Allen and Unwin.
Weber, M. (1978) *Economy and Society*, Berkeley, CA: University of California Press.
—— (1964) *The Theory of Social and Economic Organization*, New York: The Free Press.
Wicksteed, P. H. (1933) *The Common Sense of Political Economy*, 2nd edn, London: Routledge.
Wieser, F. (1967) *Social Economics*, New York: Augustus M. Kelley.
—— (1971) *Natural Value*, New York: Augustus M. Kelley.
—— (1994) 'The nature and substance of theoretical economics', in I. Kirzner (ed.) *Classics in Austrian Economic*, vol. 1, London: William Pickering.
Wojtyła, K. (1979) *Acting Person*, Dordrecht: Reidel Publishing Company.

Yeager, L. B. (2001) *Ethics as Social Science: The Moral Philosophy of Social Cooperation*, Northampton, MA: Edward Elgar.

Zubiri, X. (1974) 'La dimensión histórica del ser humano', *Realitas*, vol. 1, Madrid: Sociedad de Estudios y Publicaciones.

—— (1981) *Nature, History, God*, trans. T. B. Fowler, Washington, DC: Xabier Zubiri Foundation of North America.

—— (1982) *On Essence*, trans. A. R. Caponigri, Washington, DC: Xavier Zubiri Foundation of North America.

—— (1995) *Los problemas fundamentales de la metafísica occidental*, Madrid: Alizanza Editorial.

—— (1997a) *Sentient Intelligence: Intelligence and Reality*, trans. T. B. Fowler, Washington, DC: Xavier Zubiri Foundation of North America.

—— (1997b) *Intelligence and Logos*, trans. T. B. Fowler, Washington, DC: Xavier Zubiri Foundation of North America.

—— (1997c) *Intelligence and Reason*, trans. T. B. Fowler, Washington, DC: Xavier Zubiri Foundation of North America.

—— (2003) *Dynamic Structure of Reality*, trans. N. R. Orringer, Chicago, IL: University of Illinois Press.

Index

Printed in the United States
by Baker & Taylor Publisher Services